RED FABER

RED FABER

A Biography of the
Hall of Fame Spitball Pitcher

Brian E. Cooper

*To Jerry Clark, a
great fan of a
great game.
Best wishes!
Brian Cooper
8/18/07*

McFarland & Company, Inc., Publishers
Jefferson, North Carolina, and London

LIBRARY OF CONGRESS CATALOGUING-IN-PUBLICATION DATA

Cooper, Brian E., 1954–
    Red Faber : a biography of the hall of fame spitball pitcher /
Brian E. Cooper.
    p.   cm.
    Includes bibliographical references and index.

    ISBN-13: 978-0-7864-2721-5
    (softcover : 50# alkaline paper) ∞

    1. Faber, Red, 1888–1976.   2. Baseball players — United States —
    Biography.   3. Chicago White Sox (Baseball team).   I. Title.
GV865.F23C66   2007
796.357092 — dc22   2006031273

British Library cataloguing data are available

Cover design by Brian Davis. Images courtesy of the Tri-County
Historical Society, Cascade, Iowa.

Manufactured in the United States of America

McFarland & Company, Inc., Publishers
    Box 611, Jefferson, North Carolina 28640
    www.mcfarlandpub.com

To my wife, Ann.
Her support for my project —
and especially her patience during the countless hours
I spent at the computer instead of with her —
made this book possible.

Acknowledgments

So many individuals and organizations assisted me that I fear that I have omitted some here. If so, please accept my apologies.

First, my thanks to the following individuals: Robert Byrne, Ann Cooper, Brian Davis, James E. Elfers, Dr. Alfred Faber, Urban C. Faber II, Connie Gibbs, Michael Gibson, Mark Hirsch, John Hooper, Mary Lee Hostert, Robert Kurt, Linda Mathewson, Bill Nowlin, Jessica Reilly, Lee Simon, John Skipper, Mary Ione Theisen, Bill Thompson, Stew Thornley, and Paul Zingg.

I also thank the Carnegie-Stout Public Library, Dubuque, Iowa; the Cascade (Iowa) Public Library; the *Cedar Rapids* (Iowa) *Gazette*; the Center for Dubuque History, Loras College, Dubuque, Iowa; the Chicago Historical Society; the Chicago Public Library; the Drake University Library, Des Moines, Iowa; the Grayslake (Ill.) Municipal Historical Museum; the Historical Society of Iowa Library, Des Moines and Iowa City; the Midwest Jesuit Archives, St. Louis, Missouri; the National Baseball Hall of Fame, Cooperstown, New York; Saint Louis University, Pius XII Library; the Society for American Baseball Research; the Tri-County Historical Society, Cascade, Iowa; and the *Waterloo/Cedar Falls* (Iowa) *Courier*.

Contents

Introduction

The soft-spoken son of an Iowa hotelier, Urban Clarence Faber pitched 20 major-league seasons. All were with the Chicago White Sox, who ranked among the best, worst and most crooked teams in baseball. Pitching in 669 regular-season games and playing decades before pitch counts and relief specialists infiltrated the game, Faber posted complete games in 56 percent of his 483 starts. A fiery competitor, he was the second-to-last spitballer still throwing the pitch (legally), and he did so long after it was otherwise outlawed. In 1917, he made World Series history with three victories over John McGraw's New York Giants. He was physically unable to play in the 1919 World Series, which eight teammates "threw" to Cincinnati in a gambling scandal. Had he been healthy, we might never have heard of the Black Sox scandal.

He was the American League's best pitcher in the early 1920s, which coincided with the opening of the Lively Ball Era. A decade later he was, at age 45, the oldest player in the majors. Red Faber is not mentioned in the same breath as Babe Ruth, Ty Cobb or Walter Johnson, and many baseball histories overlook him, but he more than held his own against the greats of his day — as affirmed by his induction into the National Baseball Hall of Fame in 1964. Faber played with or against men whose major-league careers started as early as 1896 (Nap Lajoie) and ended as recently as 1950 (Luke Appling). He competed against nearly three dozen Hall of Famers.

And then there was Faber off the field. For most of his playing career, he endured an unhappy marriage to a woman beset by personal and medical problems. As a widower, he married at 58 and became a father for the only time when he was 59. Retired from the game decades before reserves commanded million-dollar contracts and received generous pensions, he went to work. The family needed the money. He owned a bowling alley. He tried to sell cars and real estate, but his honesty got in the way. Finally, Faber held down a full-time job on a county road crew until he was nearly 80 years old.

Still, he considered himself fortunate and went out of his way to help young-sters learn the game and to assist former ballplayers who were down on their luck.

Many of the facts of Faber's life and career were unknown to me on the first day of 2003, when I set my New Year's resolution to write a historical biography. I didn't know who the subject would be, but I wanted a Midwest-erner — preferably someone with a connection to the community I call home: Dubuque, Iowa. During my research, discovering that no one had published a full-length biography of Red Faber, Hall of Famer and native of Dubuque County, my choice became easy.

That decision was affirmed after I contacted the Tri-County Historical Society in Cascade, Iowa — Faber's hometown, just 25 miles from my front door. The organization's small museum does not have regular hours — or much heat — in the winter. But on a bright but frigid January day, Mary Lee Hostert and Lee Simon unlocked the place and showed me around. The museum's Faber collection, like the player himself, is modest. But what impressed me was Mary Lee and Lee's pride in their hometown star and their pledge to help my project any way possible. A slight, white-haired woman you'd love to have as your grandmother, Mary Lee carries out much of the historical society's work. She knows Cascade history — the famous, the infamous and the noto-rious — and refers to Faber on a first-name basis. The historical society board granted me complete access to its collection at virtually any time; Mary Lee would just meet me and unlock the place. Whenever Mary Lee came across mentions of Red or other members of the Faber family in back issues of the *Cascade Pioneer*, she sent me photocopies. It didn't take long for me to real-ize that the Tri-County Historical Society was *counting* on me. I hope they feel I did not let them down.

Most of my citations come from newspapers, from local journals in Cascade and Dubuque — the other Iowa city where the Fabers resided before Red became a major leaguer — to metropolitan papers and *The Sporting News*. Among the Chicago papers publishing during Faber's playing days, the *Chicago Tribune* provided the fullest coverage of the pitcher and his club — and, for-tunately, the *Tribune* was the most accessible to me. (Coincidentally, James Crusinberry, who covered the White Sox for the *Tribune* early in Faber's career, also was a Cascade native.) Faber appeared in nearly 700 major league games, including World Series and City Series contests. If I did not at least scan a box score or article about each one, it was an oversight. Enter the Society for American Baseball Research. For low annual dues, SABR provides its mem-bers a lending library, access to ProQuest's archives of several metropolitan newspapers, and a discounted subscription to view old issues of *The Sporting News*. Plus, SABR has a tremendous network of thousands of members whose willingness to help a novice biographer is astounding.

In the early 1920s, his Chicago team decimated by the Black Sox scandal, Red Faber was the best pitcher in baseball. A half-century later, he had outlived most of his baseball contemporaries, his fans and the sportswriters who remembered him best. When Faber died in 1976, he was 88 years old. His obituary was just inside-page news — even in the Chicago papers that once heralded his many achievements so prominently. My hope is that those of us who never met Red Faber or saw him pitch will, through these pages, get to know him and appreciate his achievements during what was a colorful, challenging and historic period for baseball.

Brian Cooper
Dubuque, Iowa
October 2006

1

Modest Hero

Fresh and white at the start, the baseball had become a sickly shade of brown. The sphere showed the effects of 8½ innings of abuse — from pitchers spewing saliva, tobacco juice and slippery elm; from collisions with white-ash bats; and from skids into the grass and dirt of the Polo Grounds. The spitball was legal, and there was no such thing as taking a baseball out of play; spectators had to return the ball after home runs and foul hits alike. Standing atop the pitching mound on that sun-drenched Monday afternoon in New York, Urban "Red" Faber gripped that baseball in his powerful right hand. Standing 6-foot-2 and weighing 190 pounds, the pitcher was just three outs from delivering for his Chicago White Sox baseball's biggest prize: the World Series championship of 1917.

Faber was no greenhorn. He was 29 and had four seasons of experience against the American League's best hitters. Nonetheless, Faber could not escape the sensation that his heart was trying to leap from his chest. His ears hummed from the din of 33,969 spectators; virtually every one rooted for him to fail. If Faber held Chicago's two-run lead against the host New York Giants, the White Sox would claim their second World Series title. (In 1906, the legendary "Hitless Wonders" won a "Subway Series" over the Chicago Cubs.) If Faber failed and the Giants won Game 6, the teams would decide the series the following afternoon. True, the White Sox had the American League's best pitcher, 28-game winner Eddie Cicotte, available for Game 7, but the New Yorkers, the pre-series favorite, would possess momentum and home-field advantage. Chicago desperately needed the series to end here. They needed Faber, a soft-spoken but gritty competitor from Cascade, Iowa, to deny the Giants, a team to which he was once loaned for an around-the-world exhibition tour.

This was Faber's fourth appearance in the 1917 World Series. Early on, Faber appeared destined to be remembered more for his ineptitude on the base paths than for his pitching prowess. In Game 2, he thought he had suc-

5

ceeded in stealing third base — only to find a teammate already occupying the base. However, Faber's pitching and a subsequent, more comical gaffe by the Giants made his blunder an inconsequential sidenote. In the first five games, he had won two — including Game 5, after two perfect innings of relief— and lost one. Now, entering the bottom of the ninth inning of Game 6, Faber guarded Chicago's 4–2 lead.

The White Sox's lead came gift-wrapped from the Giants, who committed a throwing error, dropped an outfield fly and then botched a run-down play during Chicago's three-run fourth inning. New York appeared to have Chicago baserunner Eddie Collins trapped between third and home. Somehow, however, catcher Bill Rariden and first baseman Walter Holke left the plate uncovered. That forced third baseman Heinie Zimmerman, ball in hand, to try to chase down the speedy Collins. Zimmerman, unfairly blamed by fans and reporters for a bone-headed play, could not catch Collins. The White Sox immediately added two runs on a single. The Giants closed the gap to 3–2 after five innings, but the White Sox gave Faber an insurance run in the top of the ninth inning. He might need that extra run in the oval-shaped Polo Grounds, a hitter's paradise (except for cavernous center field, where the wall stood some 500 feet from home plate).

Leading off the ninth, Dave Robertson stepped to the right side of the plate and dug into the batter's box. Though he hit only .259 during the season, Robertson was the series' hottest batter, with 11 hits in 22 at-bats. As he did on every pitch, Faber hid the ball behind his glove, close to his mouth. Did he "load up" for a spitball? Whatever the pitch, Robertson connected. He lofted the ball along the right-field line, toward the grandstand seats a mere 258 feet away. The nearly 34,000 fans in the park — and the thousands who lined Coogan's Bluff overlooking the park — roared in anticipation. They let out a sigh, however, when Robertson's drive landed foul. He returned to the batter's box. Faber wound up — his routine featured full extension of his arms above his head — and delivered his second pitch. It moved inside and hit *something*. Umpire Bill Klem, believing that the pitch glanced off Robertson's bat and landed foul, signaled Strike 2. That decision brought howls from Giants manager John McGraw, who rushed from the first-base coaching line, and Robertson, who claimed that the pitch hit him. Robertson showed Klem his evidence — a red and swollen finger. In a rarity, the umpire reversed his decision and awarded first base to Robertson. Despite a sore finger — later, doctors confirmed that it was broken — Robertson stayed in the game. After all, this was the World Series.

The cheers of Giants fans intensified as Holke, the switch-hitting first baseman, came to bat. Holke, who hit .277 during the season, represented the game-tying run. One of the few spectators *not* rooting for the Giants that afternoon was a Faber friend from Iowa, Dr. William Paul Slattery. Describing Faber's performance afterward, Slattery said, "In going and coming from the box, he was as cool as if going down the bridge at Cascade."[1] Faber had a different recollection. "Maybe it seemed that way — maybe I didn't show it — but I was praying before every pitch. All I could think of was what it meant to every fellow on the team."[2] Holke proved to be anxious, swinging at Faber's first pitch and hitting a slow roller to second baseman Collins. Instead of attempting a force-out — a double play was out of the question — Collins threw to first baseman Chick Gandil to retire Holke. Robertson advanced to second on the fielder's choice. One down.

Faber next faced Rariden, a .271 hitter who demonstrated more patience than Holke. Rariden managed to foul off a couple of pitches and pushed Faber to a full count. Faber then fooled Rariden, who watched Strike 3 go by. Two down.

Down to his last out, McGraw sent up Lew McCarty to pinch-hit against Faber. A back-up catcher, McCarty batted just .247 while appearing in only 56 games during the regular season. Further, McCarty was hampered by leg and shoulder injuries. Only this hobbled reserve stood between the White Sox and the championship. Faber delivered what would be the last pitch of the 1917 World Series. It produced another grounder to Collins. The future Hall-of-Famer took his time in gathering the ball and throwing it to Gandil at first base. "I'll never forget that sight," Faber recalled, "Chick, with one foot on the base, both hands holding that ball, shaking it at me out there on the mound."[3]

On the field moments later, McGraw himself was among the first to congratulate Faber. Four years earlier, after an international exhibition tour, the Giants boss tried to buy Faber's contract from White Sox owner Charles Comiskey. While the jubilant White Sox and the dejected Giants headed toward their clubhouses, working their way through the stunned New York fans who massed on the field, The Associated Press and telegraphic wires flashed the news to cities and towns all across the country. The dispatch reached Faber's hometown, Cascade, a tiny farming community in northeast Iowa; locals gathered at the Hotel Faber to congratulate proprietor Nicholas Faber, the father of the World Series star. The news also sparked celebrations in Dubuque, about 25 miles away from Cascade. The county seat and one of Iowa's leading cities, Dubuque was at various times home to Faber, team owner Comiskey and the new champions' manager, Clarence "Pants" Rowland. Back in Chicago, Mayor William Hale Thompson halted a contentious debate in the city council chambers. When he announced the news from New York, council members cheered and hastily approved a resolution congratulating the White Sox. Said the mayor, "Let the records show that for once the Council agreed unanimously on a subject."[4]

The day after winning the World Series, the White Sox defeated the

Giants *again*. The teams played a post–Series exhibition for the benefit of service personnel about to ship overseas for the Great War. Only after a fifth victory against the Giants did the champions board their train for Chicago. However, Faber was not among them. Uncomfortable in the spotlight, the modest hero of the 1917 World Series left New York a day ahead of his teammates. He preferred visiting family and embarking on a planned hunting trip in the Pacific Northwest. While the rest of the White Sox experienced a tumultuous celebration in Chicago, Faber quietly relaxed in Iowa. Though his name was Urban, this baseball star preferred the rural. Cascade was more to his liking. Cascade was home.

2

The Boy from Cascade

In the late 19th and early 20th centuries, Cascade was a quintessential Midwestern town. Straddling Dubuque and Jones counties on the undulating northeast Iowa landsca pe, Cascade's fortunes were symbiotically linked to agriculture. One of Iowa's oldest communities (1834), the town took its name from its Maquoketa River waterfall, which cascaded some 20 feet over limestone bluffs. Established on a former stagecoach trail and military road connecting Dubuque and Cedar Rapids, Cascade later became a stop along the Chicago, Milwaukee and St. Paul Railroad.

A visitor from Chicago, seeking respite from an August 1909 heat wave, provided a flowery description of Cascade. "The views from the bluffs along the river are enchanting to behold. The rolling prairies dotted with groves that shelter the large barns and dwellings from winter's blasts present a picture of peace and plenty, while along the cliffs are shady nooks where the tourist can assemble on the sands, collect clam shells and cast a line to the finny tribe." The author took refuge in the "shade of the many large spreading elms that line the streets and decorate the grassy lawns, on which is found sitting back from the streets many neatly painted dwellings. The houses are painted white, surrounded by a green plot of grass, decorated with climbing vines and creeping things of many colors, rare exotics that fill the air with their sweet perfume." The writer characterized Cascade residents as "a generous people who believe in entertaining strangers who come within their gates" and described "orderly crowds that assemble here from factory and forge beneath the electric lights and listen to the sweet music supplied by the Cascade Cornet band, speaks volumes for the refined and elevating influences exerted by the schools and churches of this locality."[1] A Cascade native in 1916 wrote, "Every one of Cascade's 1,500 citizens was content to live and die in comparative seclusion."[2] In those early days, however, Cascade was not always idyllic. It had its coarse side, and accounts in the local newspaper

9

Red's parents, Nicholas and Margaret Faber, constructed the Hotel Faber in Cascade, Iowa, in 1893. The building had on its main floor an office, lobby, dining room, "sample room" (where salesmen displayed and sold their wares) and a corner shop rented to small businesses. In 1944, after a half-century of ownership, the Faber family sold the hotel. In 2006, the building housed a retail establishment and apartments. (Courtesy of Judy Donovan, Cascade, Iowa.)

reflected that. "There was a lively discussion 'wid fists' at a threshing machine in Whitewater between one of Puck's Jokers and a lively granger," the *Cascade Pioneer* noted in 1888. "The discussion was called a draw."[3]

Years earlier, Cascade, like the rest of America, was a melting pot. It became home to waves of immigrants — mostly Germans and Irish, who, despite a mutual profession to Roman Catholicism, established separate Catholic churches, St. Martin's and St. Mary's, barely 250 yards apart. Luxemburgers were also part of the immigrant mix of Cascade, and one of the first was John Faber. Born in Kanich, in the parish of Remich, in 1824, he arrived in the United States in 1846 and soon found his way to Cascade.[4] On December 23, 1847, John Faber married fellow Luxemburg native Catherine May. Locals probably referred to her as an "old maid." She was 31; her husband was 23. By 1860, the Fabers were farming northwest of Cascade and raising five young children: Anna (8), Eliza (7), Matthias (5), Nicholas (3) and

Mary (1). A 13-year-old Illinois native named John Backous also resided on the Faber farmstead. The Fabers estimated the value of their land at $2,000 and their total estate at $5,000.[5] Described as "bright and intelligent," John Faber became a successful farmer. He was admired in Cascade, where he "held several local offices of trust and always acquitted himself creditably. He also had been entrusted with the affairs of large estates, which he handled honestly and profitably for the heirs thereof." At his death, the local newspaper described him as "a kind-hearted man, a good neighbor and friend and withal a consistent Christian."[6]

On New Year's Day 1883, John Faber's younger son, Nicholas, nearly 25, married 19-year-old Margaret Greif. Her father, Peter Greif, was one of the leading farmers of Cascade township."[7] After the couple exchanged vows in Worthington's St. Paul's Catholic Church, festivities moved to the Greif farmstead, "where a grand wedding feast was awaiting them and to which they did ample justice."[8] By this time, the groom's father had divided among his children his vast farm properties northwest of Cascade, in an area once called Spring Valley. It was there that Nicholas and Margaret took up residence, operated their farm and started a family. "There was a Christening at Nicholas Faber's in Spring Valley a week ago last Sunday," the paper reported. "To say that Nick is happy just about touches his heart, for it is the first boy baby born to his household."[9] He was not named in that article, but by adulthood the name of Nicholas Faber's son would appear in newspapers around the country. That first baby boy, born September 6, 1888, was Urban Clarence Faber. Baseball fans would know him as "Red."

The Nicholas and Catherine Faber family grew to include five children. Besides Urban, there was Lucille (born in 1883), Mae (1886), Celestine (1890) and Alfred (1893). Between the births of Celestine and Alfred, Nicholas decided to leave the farm and go into business. After considering prospects in nearby Dyersville, Nicholas in early 1891 selected Cascade. "Mr. Faber is a substantial citizen and will be a welcomed acquisition to the town," the local newspaper noted. Faber leased space for a saloon in the Doud building.[10] In 1893, he opened the Hotel Faber in a new three-story, red brick structure on National Street, part of the military road network and Cascade's primary thoroughfare.[11] National Street remained unpaved until 1923.[12] On the northwest corner of National and Spartan streets, the Hotel Faber featured on its main floor the office and lobby, a dining room, a "sample room"—a place where traveling men displayed and sold their wares—and a corner shop that Nicholas rented to small businesses. Over the years, its tenants included a jeweler, a stockbroker and a barber.[13]

The Faber Hotel had plenty of local competition. At the same intersection stood the Merchants Hotel.[14] In addition, there was S.M. Adamson's St. Elmo Hotel—it offered a central location, electric lights and "good service"

for $1 a night—and Miller's City Hotel. Nicholas Faber advertised that his hotel featured "heated rooms, electric lighted and sample rooms on ground floor."[15] The Hotel Faber served as a commercial center. Folks who needed their pianos tuned could leave their service orders at the hotel desk, and traveling medical specialists from Dubuque saw patients at the hotel every four weeks.[16] The Fabers resided upstairs most of the years they owned the hotel.[17]

A granddaughter, Mary Ione (Kurt) Theisen, remembers Nicholas Faber, a devout Roman Catholic, as "a religious nut" who believed all spare moments should be devoted to prayer. She recalls hearing of the time he chastised his daughter Celestine when she was drawing a picture. "You should be praying the rosary," he told her. "That [drawing] is the devil's work." To his young granddaughter, Nicholas was a man to avoid. She frequently walked by the open door of the Hotel Faber. "I would look in with one eye to see if Grandpa Faber was inside," she recalled. "If he was, I kept walking." If not, she went inside to visit her grandmother. "He was scary. I didn't like him," she said. "He was not a nice grandpa. Grandma made up for it. She was the sweetest thing. She could work all day and still have a smile. Grandma did all the work. Grandpa did all the praying."[18] If Nicholas felt that way about idle sketching, what did he think about his sons playing baseball, with its Sunday games and raucous behavior by players and spectators? A newspaper clipping suggested Nicholas disapproved of Urban turning professional. However, in later years, various accounts in the hometown paper referred to his parents' pride in their son's baseball achievements.

Cascade soon established its standing as a "baseball town"—a reputation that continues in the 21st century. In the late 1870s, the professional team from Dubuque, one of the nation's best nines, traveled to Cascade for an exhibition game, and the event was well received by the locals.[19] One of the stars on the 1879 Dubuque Rabbits was a first baseman named Charles A. Comiskey. Baseball's popularity in Cascade grew. The "baseball dance," a fund-raiser for the town team, was a major event in Cascade each winter.[20] In 1897, an estimated 5,000 spectators watched a baseball tournament in Cascade, where teams competed for prize money of $100, $60 and $40.[21] One of the spectators might have been an 8-year-old boy with red hair, Urban Faber.

He attended St. Mary's Catholic School, where all the classes were taught in German, the language regularly spoken in the Faber household. When he was 11, Urban's parents bought him a baseball bat, glove and ball of wound

Opposite: Urban "Red" Faber, circa 1898, when he was about 10 years old. He attended St. Mary's School in Cascade, Iowa, where all instruction was in the German language. It was about this time his parents bought him his first baseball equipment: a bat, glove and ball of wound string. (Courtesy of the Tri-County Historical Society, Cascade, Iowa.)

string. "As a result of the excellence of the ball I was able to organize and
manage one of the two best kid teams in the history of Cascade, Iowa," Faber
recalled years later. As the team's backer and manager, Urban appointed himself pitcher and clean-up hitter. In addition to learning baseball, he also
learned about sandlot politics. When Urban was 12, his team and the other
top boys' squad in Cascade met for the town championship. Neither team
scored for 11 innings. "Although it still was light, we decided to call it a draw,"
Faber said, "because loss of such a game would be too great a sorrow to the
losers." His first baseman, Chuck McQuillan, objected to the tie. Soon afterward, McQuillan talked his wealthy parents into buying three gloves, two
bats, a catcher's mitt and a *real* baseball. That changed the team's balance of
power. "In the next game, when I walked a batsman," Faber recalled, "Chuck
declared himself manager and backer and ordered me to the showers." Thus
ended Faber's career as a manager at any level.[22] The schoolyard provided
Urban other lessons as well: He learned about cigarettes; his lifelong habit
started at age 8.[23]

    As the son of a well-off businessman, Urban enjoyed a comfortable boy-
hood. He had few responsibilities and, when it came to work, little ambi-
tion.[24] After Urban completed eighth grade at St. Mary's, his father sent him
to a boarding school in Prairie du Chien, Wisconsin, a Mississippi River community about 80 miles north of Cascade. At the prep academy of Sacred
Heart College, a Jesuit school, Urban was uninspired in the classroom but an
enthusiastic member of the school baseball team. "It was there I began to suspect that a career on the diamond was a good way to avoid a career of milk-
ing cows at dawn and slopping shoats *ad infinitum*," he wrote years later. (It
was a curious choice for an example of an alternative career. Though he was
an Iowa native, he had not lived on a farm since age 5.) In the fall of 1904,
shortly before turning 16, he transferred from Sacred Heart to the prep academy of St. Joseph's College (now Loras College) in Dubuque, the county seat
and one of Iowa's leading cities. According to school records, he took only
two courses during the 1904–05 school year — Latin and Modern History —
and performed at an "insufficient" level.[25] Enrolled in classical courses, he was
admittedly an indifferent student. "I wasn't interested in it myself," Faber told
an interviewer, "but my father was. He was determined that his two sons
should have a better education than he had. I couldn't see where classical
studies were going to benefit me a great deal and I don't see as they have."[26]
Urban's name does not appear on rosters of his school's baseball squads in
1905. About that time, his family joined him in Dubuque. After more than
a decade operating a saloon and hotel in Cascade, 47-year-old Nicholas Faber
in late 1904 closed the saloon and in early 1905 leased the hotel to competitor S.M. Adamson. "Cascade regrets to lose them," a small item in the hometown paper stated, "and trusts that they will return at a future date."[27]

Fourteen-year-old Urban "Red" Faber (extreme lower right) poses with the Sparks baseball squad of Sacred Heart Academy of Prairie du Chien, Wisconsin, in 1902–03. Just a few years later, he was receiving $2 a game to pitch semi-pro ball on Sundays. (Courtesy of the Midwest Jesuit Archives, St. Louis, Missouri.)

(Simultaneously, Nicholas' brother, Matthias, moved his family to a wheat farm in Assinobia, Saskatchewan, Canada. Apparently, Canadian agriculture was unsatisfactory to Matthias, who returned to Iowa. In 1920, Matthias was the Farmer Labor Party nominee for governor; voters dealt him a crushing defeat.)

In Dubuque, Nicholas Faber held no job; apparently his investments and holdings provided sufficient income.[28] The Fabers had three addresses during the 9½ years they lived in Dubuque. They briefly resided just an outfielder's toss from the St. Joseph's campus.[29] The Fabers' final Dubuque residence, a two-story frame dwelling, was built on the Grandview Avenue, an upscale area then on the southwestern edge of the city.[30]

For the 1905–06 academic year, Urban took a full course load at St. Joseph's, received high marks for conduct and, except for a nosedive in algebra, held his own academically. He also pitched for the Invincibles, the

In the 1906 season, Red Faber (back row, middle) was not yet 18 but was one of the best semi-pro pitchers in Dubuque. The Tigers paid him $2 a Sunday. The next season, when the Tigers raised his pay to $5, Faber said, "I was certain as to my calling." (Courtesy of the Tri-County Historical Society, Cascade, Iowa.)

lowest squad in the school's three-team program.[31] (Whether the squads intermingled prep and college students is not clear.) After two years at Sacred Heart and two years at St. Joseph's, Faber completed his prep school career without a diploma.[32] His interest in the classics never ignited, but baseball was another story.

Urban's aspirations for a career in baseball intensified when the semi-pro Dubuque Tigers paid the 16-year-old $2 to pitch on Sundays. When the Tigers paid him $5 a Sunday the next season, he said, "I was certain as to my calling."[33] The games were intense and competitive. In a 1915 interview, Faber described for John J. Ward of *Baseball Magazine* how the semi-pro teams in Dubuque financed their games: "We used to chip in all 'round and thus put up a purse of perhaps $25 or $50. The opposing team would do likewise.

The winning club would thus have something to divide among the players. The losing team would pocket their losses along with the drubbing they received on the field."[34]

According to Dubuque newspapers' brief reports on local amateur games from 1907 through 1909, Faber pitched for multiple teams simultaneously, including the Dubuque Tigers, the Dubuque Grays, the Union Electrics, the Eagles and the town team in his native Cascade. In 1908, the 19-year-old Faber, pitching for the Tigers, struck out 20 Hawkeyes and allowed just three hits in a 5–1 victory.[35] He was nearly as dominant two weeks later, fanning 16 members of the Knights of Columbus team in an 8–1 win.[36] Later that season, in the city championship game against the favored Olympics, Faber won with a no-hitter.[37] The Olympics were less-than-gracious losers. They pointed out that they had lost only two local games — to the St. Joseph's College team and the city title game to Faber's Tigers — but had also competed favorably on the regional level, beating some teams that included professionals. "They claim that the Tigers' record does not compare with theirs either in the ability of the teams defeated or in the scores made, hence they feel that their championship of the city rightfully belongs to them," noted a newspaper article headlined, "War Among Local Amateur Clubs."[38] Toward the end of the 1908 season, Faber took the mound for the Eagles against the Olympics. The Eagles' center fielder that day was listed as "Rowland" — most likely Clarence "Pants" Rowland, who later influenced Faber's early professional career.

Even at the semi-pro level, teams often took the train to games. In 1909, Faber, pitching on a Sunday morning for Union

When he was a teenager, Faber split his high school years between academies affiliated with Catholic colleges — Sacred Heart in Prairie du Chien, Wisconsin, and St. Joseph's (now Loras) in Dubuque, Iowa. He admitted that he was uninspired academically. (Courtesy of the Tri-County Historical Society, Cascade, Iowa.)

Electric, held the Olympics to just one run on two hits through the seventh inning — at which point Mr. Rosenberg, the umpire, declared the game a 1–1 tie so that the Olympics could catch the train for Galena, Illinois, some 15 miles away, and their afternoon contest. Even local travel had its travails. One Saturday in 1908, a Galena team intended to briefly cruise the Galena River to Bellevue, Iowa, and then ride the narrow-gauge railroad to Cascade. Shortly after the launch pulled away from the Galena landing, a player lit a cigarette. His match landed in a pool of gasoline dripping from the engine. The resultant explosion caused a panic. The passengers rushed from the engine area and caused the boat to capsize. "Fortunately every man was able to swim," a Dubuque newspaper reported, "so they reached the shore without any fatalities."[39] That game was cancelled, but the teams met a few days later in Galena, and Faber started for Cascade. The score remained 1–1 after 16½ innings. In the bottom of the 17th, Faber suffered the 2–1 loss in dramatic fashion when Galena player-manager Monte Bales stole home.[40]

Despite his son's notoriety in the Dubuque semi-pro circuit, Nicholas Faber pressed Urban to continue his education. Father and son struck a compromise: Urban would attend Bayless Business College in downtown Dubuque — but he would continue to play baseball. He took classes in shorthand, typing and bookkeeping.[41] In the spring of 1909, the St. Joseph's College team needed a pitcher to succeed their star, named Palmer. Faber joined the squad. That he was not enrolled at the college was either poorly publicized or of little concern. The institution has no record that he actually attended college classes in 1909, and in subsequent years Faber never claimed academic standing at St. Joseph's.[42] Years later, Faber said that when he turned professional in mid–1909, he was taking a business class because he understood that bookkeepers could earn $40 a month.[43]

A "ringer," Faber helped the St. Joseph's nine hold their opponents to only four runs while completing their 1909 season undefeated in all five games.[44] (Other reports indicate an 8–0 season for St. Joseph's, including a victory over Cornell for the Iowa college championship, but that is not reflected in college records.) Faber opened St. Joseph's 1909 season in record-breaking fashion, striking out 22 St. Ambrose College batters in an 8–0 victory in Davenport, Iowa.[45] Faber was quiet but competitive, operating with controlled confidence but a fire for victory. He proved that the St. Ambrose game was not a fluke one week later when he struck out 17 batters from Sacred Heart College, his former school. In a pitchers' duel — Sacred Heart's Stoll whiffed 14 — St. Joseph's prevailed, 2–1.[46] St. Joseph's final game of the season, on June 5, 1909, was a rematch with St. Ambrose. St. Joseph's was so confident that a player named Kerwick started instead of Faber. However, in the fifth inning, St. Joseph's trailed, 2–0. Faber replaced Kerwick, and St. Ambrose scored no more. St. Joseph's tied the game with two runs in the bottom of the sixth and scored the game-winner on a sacrifice fly in the ninth. Faber received credit for the victory and St. Joseph's secured its undefeated season.

For the balance of 1909, Faber remained a pitcher for hire. On July 10, he pitched for Cascade but came out on the short end of a 2–1 decision to former major leaguer Charlie Buelow and his Manchester (Iowa) contingent.[47] Three weeks later, the tables turned; pitching for the Dubuque Tigers against Cascade, Faber recorded a two-hitter and a 2–1 victory.

Local college and amateur teams were not the only squads needing pitching help in 1909. Dubuque also was home to the Miners, a struggling entry in the Three-I League, a Class B professional league. By mid-summer, the Miners, led by player-manager Forrest "Rabbit" Plass, were mired in second-to-last place in the Three-I and begging for spectators. Newspaper articles regularly detailed the team's shaky financial status and campaigned for fans to turn out. "If Dubuque is to have baseball, the club must have support," the *Telegraph-Herald* stated. "The fans are the judges. What will the verdict be?"[48] The team's desperate need for pitchers was magnified as it moved into a period jammed with doubleheaders. By the first week of August, the Miners were so desperate that they took a chance and accepted Al Jones' offer to get back into a uniform. Jones had retired from baseball after 1907, when he was a little-used pitcher on the Dubuque roster. By 1909, he was a businessman whose baseball activity was limited to attending Miners' games.[49] His comeback was short-lived; all concerned agreed that Jones was of better service to the team in the grandstand. However, another mid-season acquisition for the Miners showed promise. He was a local boy — Urban Faber.

3

Hometown Professional

The man credited with bringing Faber and the Dubuque Miners together in 1909 was former owner Clarence "Pants" Rowland. Born in nearby Platteville, Wisconsin, Rowland's family moved to Dubuque when he was 1. He was managing the bar at the Wales Hotel when Faber signed. However, Rowland would soon be back in the game—he made baseball his life—and twice more would make significant contributions to Faber's career.

Soon after he signed with the Miners, a Dubuque newspaper previewed his professional debut: "'Red' Faber is scheduled to work in one of the games Tuesday afternoon. The big boy is ambitious and will be given a chance." That chance came July 27, 1909, when he started the second game of a doubleheader in Dubuque. Faber found himself in a jam in the very first inning of his professional career. Springfield's leadoff hitter reached on third baseman Dow Van Dine's error. The second batter laid down a sacrifice bunt, but an infielder failed to cover first base. After a successful sacrifice bunt, Springfield had runners on second and third with one out. The cleanup hitter Stieger stepped to the plate. "Then Faber tore loose and fanned Stieger and Bell," the newspaper stated. "The crowd gave him an ovation for his feat." The Miners then went on an uncharacteristic hitting binge to support the 20-year-old, who went the distance in a 12–1 victory. Faber allowed six hits, walked one batter and hit another. Four Senators went down on strikes. Reviews of Faber's debut were positive. "He had control and his curve ball broke fast," the *Dubuque Telegraph-Herald* stated. "He was not obliged to cut loose owing to the fact that the Miners took advantage of Patrick's wildness and also clouted the ball fiercely at opportune moments, scoring a dozen times. Faber was a master at all stages." The sportswriter was not one to gloss over the Miners' shortcomings, but he saw in the Cascade native someone special: "Red Faber showed class. He has more in a minute than a lot of these Three-I heavers have in a day. His beginning was pleasant."[1]

Still, things were not particularly pleasant for the Miners. Van Dine, whose error contributed to Faber's first-inning jam, left the team for a family emergency; his child died in early August. A few days later, player-manager and captain Plass quit over what he considered team directors' interference with his personnel decisions.[2] However, Plass had a change of heart, and he arrived in uniform at the Dubuque ballpark the next day. Unfortunately for Plass, the directors did not share his interest in reconciliation. Handed a written notice of suspension and $50 fine, Plass watched the game from the grandstand.[3] Within days, Dubuque native and fan favorite Charlie Buelow, who saw limited duty in the New York Giants' infield in 1901, arrived as player-manager. Dubuque's directors had been wrangling for Buelow's services since the previous off-season.[4] (Dubuque had not seen the last of Plass. In April 1911, he and Rowland bought the team.[5])

Meanwhile, Faber's status with the Dubuque Miners remained part-time. Even after signing a professional contract, he took a few turns on the mound on the local semi-pro circuit. "For testers of temper Faber's deceptive drops and shoots take the bakery," the *Cascade Pioneer* reported after he struck out a dozen Cascade batters in a 2–1 win for the Dubuque Tigers. 'They look easy, but they ain't,' as Lane and several of the others can testify."[6]

Professional baseball was a no-frills, hard-edged and raucous proposition in the early 20th century — especially in the minor leagues. Players, fans and sportswriters were tough on umpires. Especially unpopular was J.H. Malicoat, who turned to umpiring Three-I games immediately after retiring as a pitcher in the league (Cedar Rapids). A Dubuque newspaper headlined its report on a Miners' loss, "MALICOAT IS AN AWFUL UMPIRE." The sportswriter pulled no punches: "Aside from seeing 'em wrong, this former Bunny pitcher needs to have the cob webs wiped off his brain, for what he knows about rules would not fill a thimble." The author further criticized Malicoat for calling balls and strikes while standing behind the pitcher instead of crouching behind the catcher.[7] (At that time, umpires worked alone or, if they were fortunate, with one partner.) The next day, the sportswriter blamed Malicoat's casual acquaintance with the strike zone for frustrating Faber until he grooved so many pitches to Rock Island hitters that he suffered a 6–5 loss. In 1911, the season after Faber left the team, an arbiter named Guthrie barely escaped physical harm on at least three occasions in Dubuque. In early June, he abandoned the field and forfeited the game to Dubuque after Rock Island players swarmed around him to argue a close decision at third base. It was the first in his series of confrontations with fans and players. "It is probable that his resignation has already reached [league] President Tearney," a local newspaper noted, "and that Guthrie is through with the Three-Eye League umpiring for good."[8] The sportswriter was wrong. Six weeks later, Guthrie was back in town, and experienced two more episodes in three days. First,

Dubuque players swarmed the umpire after a close loss. Two days later, it was the spectators' turn. They surged onto the field in the sixth inning to confront Guthrie after an unfavorable call on a groundout. "To Manager [Clarence] Rowland, who had been banished from the grounds in the first inning for strenuous objection to one of Guthrie's crude decisions, and the Dubuque and Peoria players belongs the credit of saving the umpire from serious injury. The above mentioned finally induced the crowd to fall back to the stands while Guthrie screwed up sufficient nerve to continue the game."[9] Malicoat, who resigned before the end of the 1909 season, and Guthrie were not alone. Another umpire had had enough. "Jack Herbert did not last long as an umpire," the *Telegraph-Herald* noted. "Becoming disgusted over the roasting he received at Cedar Rapids, he resigned and players had to officiate in the closing game of the Decatur series."[10]

The acquisitions of Buelow and Faber in the last half of the 1909 season were among the few highlights of the Miners' lackluster campaign. In a doubleheader against last-place Cedar Rapids on August 7, Faber entered the first game as a reliever, struck out 11 and earned the 6–4 victory. In the nightcap, Faber started, struck out another 11 and surrendered just four hits in a 5–1 win. Two victories and 22 strikeouts — a nice day's work! Attendance at Dubuque's Athletic Park increased, surpassing 30,000 for the season. The dire mid-season predictions of Dubuque losing its franchise faded.

Faber's achievements caused the citizens and newspapers of two Dubuque County communities to become possessive of the pitcher. "The Dubuque baseball fans need not get 'chesty,'" the Cascade paper proclaimed. "'Red' Faber is a Cascade boy, son of Nicholas Faber, proprietor of the Hotel Faber. The family has been living in Dubuque for a number of years."[11]

The Miners staged Charlie Buelow Day in mid–September 1909. Though a bit wild (seven walks), Faber gave up just one run to Bloomington in nine innings. However, his counterpart from Bloomington, named Royer, was equally masterful. Despite the protests of some 3,000 spectators and the players, the umpire ended the game due to darkness with the score tied, 1–1. "The crowd was wildly enthusiastic and applauded everything from the game down to the umpire, all impartially."[12] Faber pitched the final Miners game of 1909 and defeated Davenport 7–4.

But Faber's baseball season was not yet over. Within a week of the Three-I finale, he pitched for the Dubuque Tigers in their rematch with the Olympics for the city semi-pro championship "and a substantial side bet."[13] The Tigers won 5–1. About 700 fans attended, and in their enthusiasm some lost control. "There was all kinds of excitement during the game," a newspaper reported, "the Olympic rooters becoming so demonstrative in the eighth inning that a couple of policemen were called to dampen their ardor."[14] Faber struck out 12, surrendered two hits and allowed only two balls to leave the infield. The Olympics' only run was unearned, in the eighth inning. Faber helped his cause offensively with two hits, a run batted in and two stolen bases.

Thus ended Urban "Red" Faber's outstanding 1909 season, during which he succeeded on the semi-pro, collegiate and minor-league levels. Faber's record in his first professional season was just 7–6 in 15 appearances. After Faber and player-manager Buelow entered the picture, the Miners played three games over .500 to finish the year with a winning percentage of .474. Team officials, no doubt valuing his earned-run average (1.60) more than Faber's win-loss record, reserved his services for the 1910 Three-I season.[15]

The hometown boy's surging popularity sustained itself over the winter. At Dubuque's Baseball Fair and Bazaar, a multi-day event staged in the local armory, one evening was declared "Faber Night" (as well as "First Ward Night"). It must have been a curious blend of attendees that evening: friends and fans of Faber — many of whom spoke German as their primary language — mingled with the Irish of Dubuque's First Ward. This occurred in a city where people defined a mixed marriage as the union of a German Catholic and an Irish Catholic. In any case, according to press reports, a good time was had by all who jammed the Shamrock-adorned armory. "Twirler Faber, banked on all sides by a legion of friends and admirers, was on hand from early in the evening until Baron von Hoffmann's Venetian musicians had wafted forth the very last strain of 'Home Sweet Home,' and his supporters came not alone from the First Ward, but all parts of the city as well."[16]

Midway through the 1910 campaign, his first full season as a professional, Faber established himself as a major league prospect. By the end of July, no other Three-I League pitcher had appeared in as many games as Faber — but his heavy workload was cited for a July slump. "That Red Faber is to go up is the latest sensation in the base ball line. Of course, this is not certain, but when Roger Bresnahan of St. Louis announces that he is going to take a trip to Dubuque to see the lanky one work out there must be something doing," the *Dubuque Telegraph-Herald* reported. "Of late the auburn haired one has had a lot of hard luck but he is right now as good as any pitcher in the league in the line of having stuff. Red has most everything and all he needs is a little training and experience. If Roger Bresnahan secures him he will get just the training he needs and should make good easily."[17] However, Bresnahan, the player-manager of the Cardinals, was not alone. The Pittsburgh Pirates sent scout Howard Earle to Dubuque, and the Cincinnati Reds also indicated interest. St. Louis and Pittsburgh planned to wait until the Aug. 20 opening of the draft period to pursue Faber. That way, they could purchase his contract from Dubuque for the standard draft fee of $1,250.[18]

The *Telegraph-Herald* of August 18, 1910, carried this one-sentence item: "Faber's arm is back in shape."[19] Later that day, Faber proved it: He threw a perfect game against the host Davenport (Iowa) Pretzels. Not only did all 27 batters who faced Faber fail to reach first base, only one managed to hit the ball beyond the infield. Faber struck out seven and recorded five pitcher-to-first assists. Among the Pretzels shut down that day was Ray Chapman, who a decade later became the only major league player to die from being hit by a pitch. Faber's feat was only the fourth perfect game recorded in the high minors — but the second in less than two weeks. Nine days earlier, Chester Carmichael of Buffalo turned the trick against Jersey City in the Eastern League.[20] Faber's achievement made national news, albeit of the filler variety. *The New York Times, Chicago Tribune* and *The Washington Post* were among the major newspapers picking up the wire dispatch.[21] Over the next quarter-century, there would be thousands of additional articles mentioning Urban "Red" Faber.

Faber's perfect game came just two days before the draft period opened, and his feat changed the clubs' strategy. "If Rog Bresnahan wants this boy," a Davenport newspaper noted, "he had better grab him quick, for when the noise of this feat gets around, somebody else is liable to hook him."[22] The "somebody else" was Pittsburgh manager Fred Clarke. The day between the perfect game and the start of the draft, Clarke acquired Faber's contract for $1,750 — $500 over the draft price.[23] The transaction particularly pleased Dubuque baseball fans for two reasons: First, one of their favorites — and a local boy at that — was about to "make good" in the majors. Secondly, Pittsburgh's check went a long way toward easing the Dubuque club's financial struggles.

Despite his perfect game and the interest of major-league clubs, Faber's record in 1910 was only so-so. He was saddled with early-season physical problems and some of the Three-I League's worst hitters for teammates. (Lack of offensive support plagued Faber through most of his career, but he was no batsman, either. Faber batted .065, third-worst in the league.) He pitched 37 complete games in 44 appearances but posted a record of just 18–19, placing him in the middle of the Three-I pack. However, his earned-run average of 2.03, 200 strikeouts and 242 innings — while pitching for a middling club — established his credentials as major league material.

The most career-influencing development of the 1910 season was not his perfect game or anything evidenced in box scores or league statistics. During his time on the Dubuque roster, Faber started toying with the spitball. That was not particularly unusual; the pitch was legal, and pitchers were constantly trying to come up with ways to stay ahead of hitters. However, history would show that Faber would become among the few who could control the pitch in game situations. The spitball would save his playing career and eventually earn him a place among baseball's greatest players.

However, at that time, the Pirates were more interested in his fastball, his best pitch, than the unpredictable spitball. "When I was with the Pirates, they wouldn't let me throw no spitters," Faber told an interviewer four decades later. "I don't know why, but they wouldn't let me do it."[24] At the time, Faber did not necessarily need the spitball in his repertoire; his "drops and shoots" were his stronger pitches.[25] The opportunity — indeed, the need — for the spitball would come later.

Late in the 1910 season, the talk around Dubuque was that Faber would join the Pirates for the balance of the campaign. Aware that it could lose their hometown hero at any time, the Dubuque team staged "Faber Day" in early September. After the ceremonies, Faber pitched well — he gave up only four singles — but Dubuque's porous defense and offensive ineptitude saddled their star with a 6–0 loss to Rock Island. "It was sad, awfully sad, but to tell the honest truth, it wasn't Red's fault," the *Telegraph-Herald* reported. "At least it may be said there is some real booster spirit in the city, judging from the big delegation who paid respects to the lanky one."[26] However, a late-season call-up to the major leagues did not materialize.[27]

4

One Season, Three Teams

Red Faber's first chance to show his stuff on the major-league level came in the spring of 1911. He reported with the Pittsburgh Pirates' pitchers and catchers in West Baden, Indiana, and then joined the rest of the team in Hot Springs, Arkansas.[1] At that time, and for decades afterwards, players received no salary during training camp. There was a story that Faber reported to camp without any money — unlikely, considering that his family was far from impoverished — and that his manager, the hard-nosed Fred Clarke, loaned the pitching prospect $5. Faber scrimped to stretch the five-spot as long as he could, but he finally had to approach Clarke again. The player-manager said: "You must be gambling."[2]

His spendthrift ways notwithstanding, Faber impressed Clarke enough to remain on the Pirates' roster when they concluded spring training. However, his position was perilous. The roster still included 26 men — one more than the league would allow after May 5. Further, Clarke said he intended to carry 10 pitchers on his final roster; Faber was one of 13 hurlers.[3] Nonetheless, Faber was in uniform on Opening Day 1911. He watched his teammates defeat the Reds 14–0 in Cincinnati's Palace of the Fans. He watched the second. And the third. And the fourth. Faber remained on the bench the entire next month, never throwing a pitch in a regular-season game. Four decades later, Faber's mentor, Clarence Rowland, said Faber developed a sore arm after Clarke tried to make him abandon his three-quarter-arm delivery in favor of pure overhand style.[4]

The inactivity of their favorite son frustrated Faber's boosters back home. "Dubuque fans are divided in their opinions as to whether 'Red' would be doing better pitching regular for a club like Indianapolis instead of warming the bench at Pittsburg," the *Telegraph-Herald* noted. "The old time fans, however, are more than satisfied to see Faber get his daily workout with the great Pittsburg team, maintaining that he is gaining more actual experience in the manner than pitching every fourth or fifth day for the Indiana club. Manager Clark [sic], himself, has great confidence in the Dubuque boy, and it is only the great number of pitchers on the Pirate staff that has kept him out of the game for this length of time."[5]

When the Pirates had to trim their roster further, they tried to send Faber to the Indianapolis Indians of the American Association.[6] However, one report said the transfer was rescinded when a couple of teams tried to claim Faber off the waiver wire.[7] Another story had Indianapolis refusing the transaction because it wanted another player in addition to Faber.[8] After a week, Pittsburgh sent Faber to another American Association team, the Minneapolis Millers, but retained its option for his future services.

Faber caught up with the Millers in Columbus, Ohio, where his American Association career started on a positive note — an 11–3 complete-game victory on May 20.[9] Fred R. Coburn of the *Minneapolis Tribune* told his readers that he had yet to see Faber pitch but reported that "scribes in other cities assert he is quite a twirler."[10] Representing adjacent cities in the same league, Minneapolis and St. Paul were spirited rivals, and the St. Paul fans had a reputation for incessantly showering the opponents with taunts and abuse. The teams met May 31 in St. Paul's Lexington Park. The most noteworthy hits that afternoon occurred *off* the field. According to the *Minneapolis Journal*, some St. Paul fans considered it "great sport" to purchase a front-box ticket for a particular African-American man, who boisterously heckled visiting players. Finally, Minneapolis catcher Hubert Dawson had had enough. Newspaper accounts noted that Dawson came from Kentucky — "a part of the country where a Negro does not take any liberties with a white man" — and Dawson charged into the stands and assaulted the heckler. Minneapolis manager Joe Cantillon, carrying a bat, and Rube Waddell followed Dawson. The manager bloodied the heckler with the bat, but authorities intervened before Waddell could do further damage.[11] Police arrested Cantillon, who was taken to his arraignment in an ambulance, and Dawson on charges of disorderly conduct.[12] Patched up by a doctor, the heckler returned to the ballgame and accepted cheers from the St. Paul faithful.[13] "The whole affair is unfortunate but the blame cannot attach entirely to the Minneapolis contingent," the *Minneapolis Journal*'s J.H. Ritchie wrote. "St. Paul has long furnished the worst class of rooters of any city in the league, barring Louisville."[14]

When they weren't posting bond for their uniformed personnel, baseball clubs in that period staged skills contests. At field meets players competed in such events as fungo hitting, fastest running out a bunt and accurate throwing home plate to second base. In one such event featuring World Series participants, Ty Cobb raced from home to first base in 3⅕ seconds and was fastest circling the bases (13⅘ seconds). Another popular contest was long-distance throwing; the record was 435 feet, set in 1908 by Larry LeJeune (who, like Faber, once played on Dubuque's minor league team). Faber entered the distance-throwing event. His arm might have been bothered by Clarke's tampering, or it might have been due to a body-weakening cold, but Faber strained his pitching arm in the exhibition. After that, his pitching suffered and the Millers did not take him on a road trip.[15] In mid–June, despite two weeks of rest, Faber still experienced intense pain and barely lasted one inning. The Millers sent Faber home to Iowa for longer recuperation.[16] A Dubuque sportswriter, seeing the 22-year-old Faber for the first time since the off-season, noted a physical transformation. "Training in the warm southern climate has effected a change in Red's appearance, the player being brown as a berry, while several pounds of avoirdupois have vanished from the youngster's manly frame. Outside of the injured throwing member, Faber is in splendid physical condition, and declares he never felt better in his life." (The article also referred to Faber's "new home" in his native Cascade, to which the family returned after six years in Dubuque.[17] His parents held onto the Dubuque residence a couple of years longer.) After a couple of weeks in Iowa, Faber thought he was ready to pitch again. "False rumors that Faber's arm was in awful shape, and that he would be out of the game for the remainder of the season, were current upon the twirler's return to Dubuque," a local paper reported, "but these will be quickly dispelled when 'Red' appears on the mound for the Millers in the near future."[18] That statement proved to be little more than wishful thinking.

Pitching the second game of a doubleheader on Independence Day, Faber lasted only two innings. His arm still was not right. Minneapolis officials needed pitchers, not problems, and they notified Pittsburgh to that effect. The Pirates, who retained the rights to Faber, shipped the injured hurler to Pueblo, Colorado. Faber's Minneapolis career consisted of six games (one as a pinch runner), and he mustered only one inning of work between Memorial Day and Independence Day. Even with his complete-game debut — his lone decision — Faber gave up 33 hits, 19 runs and 10 walks in only 24⅓ innings.

The only positive result of Faber's few weeks with Minneapolis was that he received advanced instruction in the spitball from teammate Harry Peaster. (Decades later, Faber had trouble recalling his tutor's name.[19]) Peaster, who pitched in 17 games for Minneapolis that season, threw a spitball "in baffling style."[20] Peaster's instruction changed Faber's career, but its significance was not immediately evident.

In Pueblo, the owner and manager was Frank Isbell, a former White Sox infielder, who had moved his Western League team from Wichita to Pueblo during the season to avoid the Kansas community's prohibition on Sunday baseball.[21] Less than two weeks after leaving the field in pain, making his Pueblo debut, Faber struck out 15 Sioux City batters and allowed just two hits. The performance inspired a Denver sportswriter. "The new Steelworker is still a youngster, but he has made his mark on the diamond and friends predict that he will be a second Christy Mathewson if luck breaks even for him.... Wildness is his only drawback. He has an assortment of curves and shoots that cannot be excelled, and when he is right the heaviest hitters are at his mercy. His strikeout record is little short of marvelous."[22] Those reviews notwithstanding, Faber had lost arm strength. His baseball future in jeopardy, he worked on his spitball. Through the years, Faber claimed that throwing a spitball exacted less strain on his arm. With time, he regained his strength and performed well for Pueblo the balance of 1911. Toward the end of the season, Faber started and completed both games of a doubleheader sweep against Omaha. He gave up just three runs on 11 hits all afternoon.[23] In his final appearance for Pueblo, a complete-game victory, he gave up four hits and two runs to Des Moines, the doormat of the Western League.[24] The victory boosted his record to 12–8. In his 29 appearances over 180 innings, he posted an earned-run average of 1.89, gave up 191 hits and walked 39. Faber's strikeout total fell one shy of triple-digits.[25] Despite this, the Pirates, who initially exercised their option to reserve Faber for 1912, lost interest.[26] Fearing that Faber's arm would never be the same, they released him to Isbell's new team.

5

The Spitball

As soon as there was baseball, pitchers and batters worked to gain the advantage against each other. Pitchers studied the aerodynamics. They learned that altering the spin of the thrown baseball caused it to curve and dip. Similarly, they discovered that pitched balls with irregular surfaces — through cutting, scraping or smoothing, for example — also baffled batters.

The spitball, delivered with the fingers or the ball (or both) moistened with saliva mixed with the juice of chewing tobacco or slippery elm or who knows what, behaved erratically when cruising toward home plate. (Pitchers also used emery boards, nails and all sorts of items to rough up the ball's surface to create an aerodynamically unpredictable pitch.) Old-timers said that the split-fingered fastball, popularized in the late 1970s and 1980s, behaves much like a spitball.

The spitter has a long history; references to it occur as early as 1868. The spitter never gained the popularity of the fastball or curve, and some players and fans for years called for its prohibition. But at the time the spitter remained legal, and it served as an effective "out" pitch for hurlers who could control it. A pitcher did not need to throw the spitball often; knowledge that it was in the pitcher's repertoire was enough to keep hitters guessing.

One long-time opponent of the spitter was Washington manager Clark Griffith, a former pitcher who admitted that in his playing days he scuffed the ball against his spikes. In a 1917 article, Griffith claimed the spitball was unnatural, caused wild throws by fielders and was unfair to hitters. "There is only one objection to reading the spit ball off the boards without delay. A number of pitchers have developed the spit ball and it would be a hardship to deprive them of the results of their study and practice without warning." Griffith advocated setting a future date upon which the spitball would be prohibited, thus giving spitball pitchers time to "learn the regulation delivery of the ball" so the wet pitch "could be exiled from the game forever." Griffith concluded, "And it would be mighty good riddance."[1]

In the winter of 1919–20, the major leagues followed Griffith's advice — sort of. Prior to the 1920 season, the Joint Rules Committee decided that declared spitballers (two per team in the American League) could use the pitch through the upcoming season only. After that campaign, however, the major leagues, noting the potential adverse impact on current pitchers' livelihood, softened their stance. They allowed designated spitballers to continue to throw the pitch for the duration of their careers. Faber was among the 17 such "grandfathered" pitchers. One, Ray Fisher, retired after the 1920 season anyway. Faber's teammate Eddie Cicotte would have been on the 1921 list had he not been suspended pending the Black Sox case.

At the time of the change, Faber was the major leagues' leading spitball practitioner and one of its staunchest defenders. He disputed critics' contentions that the pitch was unfair, unsanitary, dangerous and too stressful on a pitcher's arm. However, he also cautioned against pitching too much too often. (It seemed sound advice, regardless of whether a pitcher threw the spitter. When he was 40 years old and still winning ballgames for the White Sox, Faber advised, "Take your regular turn and there is nothing to worry about. But try to squeeze a few relief jobs in between your starts or attempt to warm up in the bull pen without proper rest and the arm quits functioning." Faber cited the career of Hall-of-Famer Ed Walsh, a White Sox ironman (1904–17): "A few years back everybody said Ed Walsh's arm finally fell apart because the spitter placed too great a strain on the elbow. What killed Walsh was overwork. One season I tried to duplicate some of his stunts. I worked in eight games in nine days, and for a time after that I thought my arm was gone.")[2]

In a 1922 interview, Faber repeated his story of how he came to add the spitball to his repertoire, explaining that in the minor leagues he suffered arm problems from throwing too many curveballs. (He failed to mention the 1911 distance-throwing exhibition.) Of the challenge in throwing a spitball, Faber said, "It took me two years before I could control it."[3] After much experimentation, Faber found that tobacco juice produced the consistency of saliva that made his wet pitch most effective. He kept a chew of tobacco in one side of his mouth and a stick of gum in the other side. "By moistening the tips of his fingers he could slip the ball off those fingers so that it had little, if any, spin," his hometown weekly explained. "The result was a sharp-breaking ball much like a knuckler only that it could be thrown much faster."[4] In a 1922 interview, Faber said, "Slippery elm doesn't work with me. It's too slippery and I can't control the ball. I have tried chewing gum, but that was not slippery enough." A lifelong cigarette smoker, Faber noted that his relationship with chewing tobacco was purely professional: "I don't chew it because I like it. In fact, I never chew except when I am pitching."[5] In any case, Faber com-

Before every pitch, Faber hid the ball between his glove and mouth. Sometimes he would "load up" for a spitball, but most times he would not. Could the batters ever be sure? Some claimed they could tell by watching movement of Faber's Adam's apple. (Courtesy of the Tri-State Historical Society, Cascade, Iowa.)

pared the speed of the pitch as being only slightly slower than the fastball, much faster than the curve or knuckler.[6] "Thrown overhand it comes up with absolutely no spin, almost like a knuckler, except it doesn't wobble, then breaks down real sharply like it was falling off a table," he explained. "I sometimes threw it sidearm and it broke away real sharply. At no time does it spin. You can see the seams on the ball."[7]

Faber did not use the spitter extensively, but the fact that he *might* throw one at any time kept hitters a bit off-balance. Though the rules changes nearly cost Faber use of his most-effective pitch, some experts thought he would be hurt less than his peers. Veteran umpire Billy Evans told *The Sporting News,* "Of the American League pitchers using the spitball, I would say Faber of Chicago and Shocker of St. Louis would be most effective minus the spitball." He explained, "A good fast ball is essential to the success of any pitcher.

Faber has a puzzling side arm fastball, delivered in a peculiar manner. This, coupled with a fairly good curve that he possesses, should enable him to be a fairly consistent winner."[8] Long into retirement, Faber acknowledged, "I had a sinking fastball that really was my main pitch."[9]

Another change in 1920 concerned the baseball itself. Manufacturers switched to Australian yarn, which was said to be stronger than its American

Faber learned the finer points of the spitball in the minor leagues, but, he said, "It took me two years before I could control it." (Chicago Historical Society, *Chicago Daily News* collection SDN-068992.)

equivalent and thus able to wind tighter. The result produced a sphere that was believed to be harder and thus flew faster and farther off the bat.[10] However, other experts contend that it was the change in rules — not in the baseball — that was largely responsible for major league baseball's transition from the "Deadball Era."[11] Faber was among a handful of pitchers who excelled in both periods.

With time, the grandfathered spitballers disappeared from major league diamonds. Faber lasted through 1933 and Burleigh Grimes hung around into 1934. Two decades later, debate flared over whether to make the pitch legal again. Its most prominent proponent was Commissioner Ford Frick, who in 1966 said he would support the change. Faber, of course, supported it. The argument that the spitter was so unpredictable that it posed a hazard just didn't stand up. "Slobberers like Spittin' Bill Doak, Clarence Mitchell, Red Faber and Frank Shellenback weren't notorious for braining batters," observed Red Smith of *The New York Times*, "and if Burleigh Grimes occasionally tucked one under a guy's chin or stuck it in his ear, it was due more to venom in his soul than the slippery elm in his mouth."[12] Ultimately, nothing came of the campaign to restore the spitball to baseball's good graces. The pitch remains on the shelf (at least officially).

6

Des Moines

Late in the 1911 season, Chicago White Sox owner Charles A. Comiskey saved Des Moines' financially foundering Western League franchise by purchasing it.[1] Former Sox veteran Frank Isbell, who had just sold his Pueblo team, came to Des Moines to become president, manager and, with Tom Fairweather, part-owner.[2] Isbell made a deal to bring Faber with him to Des Moines.[3]

The Boosters conducted their 1912 spring training in Des Moines and Wichita. One noteworthy event occurred in Kansas, where Isbell suffered cuts and scratches from broken glass when first baseman Jack Thomas accidentally discharged a shotgun in the lobby of the Geuda Springs hotel.[4] (The newspaper account failed to mention *why* the player had a loaded shotgun in the hotel.)

Isbell ticketed Faber as his starting pitcher for Opening Day 1912, a road game in St. Joseph, Mo. Before the game, players for both teams participated in a 200-car parade through a decorated downtown district. At the ball field, Faber took a 4–1 lead into the eighth inning. He was denied a larger lead in the top of the eighth, when the umpire failed to notice that the St. Joe catcher dropped the throw on a bases-loaded force-out. The Drummers of St. Joseph rallied in the bottom of the eighth, when fielding miscues and Faber's wildness resulted in four runs and a 5–4 victory for the home team.[5]

In 1912, Des Moines barely broke .500, but it was a vast improvement over the previous season's .302. Faber went 21–14, posted an earned-run average of 2.08 and was hailed for placing the Boosters in the first division by winning both games of a late-season doubleheader.[6]

Just before the opening of the 1913 season, the White Sox sent their second team to Des Moines for a couple of exhibition contests. Chicago star Eddie Cicotte, who played in Des Moines before advancing to the White Sox, faced Faber and his roommate, Clint Rogge. The minor-leaguers shut out the Sox on just two hits. (An apparent third hit, a double by Ping Bodie, was nullified after the batter failed to touch first base.) Des Moines scored all of its runs in the eighth inning against Cicotte, who took the 3–0 loss.[7]

Faber was a popular, hard-working and hard-luck pitcher his two seasons in Des Moines. He suffered through game after game with losses or no-decisions because his teammates failed him. For example, early in 1913, with two out in the bottom of the ninth at Omaha, Faber's left fielder misjudged an easy fly ball, and the tying and winning runs crossed the plate.[8] Such miscues seemed to cost Faber victories through most of his professional career. However, the 6-foot-tall, 190-pounder was a workhorse who refused to back down. Illustrative was his performance the afternoon and evening of Saturday, June 28, 1913, when Faber faced league-leading Denver. The Midwest was wrapped in a killer heat wave. The temperature peaked at 94 degrees and remained 90 at 7 P.M., as the game churned on. After Des Moines tallied twice in the first, Denver tied it at 2–2 with single runs in the third and fourth innings. Then Faber and King, Denver's starter, took turns shutting down their opponents. Despite the sauna of an Iowa summer, Faber returned to the pitcher's slab inning after inning, hour after hour. The big right-hander kept the game 2–2 through nine innings, through a dozen innings, through 15 innings. For his part, King held the Boosters at bay. Shadows crept across the field — then covered it. As goose egg after goose egg went into the extra pages of the scorer's book, the evening's twilight gave way to darkness. Sportswriter R.E. Bales, covering the epic for *The Des Moines Register and Leader*, wrote that it was so "gloomy that the ball looked like a mere speck and the outfielders were almost lost in the shadows." The game should have been called after 16 innings, Bales wrote, but umpire Colliflower continued it, as "both managers and the crowd were anxious to fight it out to a decision." Faber was partly to blame for letting the game go so long. In the 10th inning, he ripped a double to right center but "went to sleep" and allowed himself to be picked off second base by the catcher. In the 17th, Des Moines had a couple of opportunities to end the affair, and Faber nearly was the hero. With Des Moines' Andreas on first after an infield hit, Faber lofted a shot into the darkness. The ball struck one foot below the top of the outfield wall, but Andreas — probably squinting into the gloom to see whether the ball would be caught — advanced only to third base. The next Des Moines batter hit a foul pop-up behind first base. Andreas tagged up and tried to score after the catch, but he missed home plate and was tagged out. That was Denver pitcher King's 17th and last inning of work; his reliever was Casey Hagerman, the Western League's leading pitcher. Hagerman and Faber blanked their opponents in the 18th, and umpire Colliflower finally declared the battle a draw four hours and 10 minutes after the first pitch. Faber pitched all 18 innings, striking out 14, walking seven and uncorking one wild pitch. At the plate, the usually light-hitting Faber went 3-for-6, including a double. For his efforts, he received a no-decision. However, his gritty performance only solidified his standing as a fan favorite.[9]

Earlier that season, Faber proved that he could not be intimated, even when his control was suspect. Leading Sioux City in the seventh inning, Faber found himself in a jam. After a walk and a teammate's error, Faber loaded the bases by delivering a pitch to the head of one Mr. Rapp. A Des Moines sportswriter described what happened to Faber after that: "The Packers charged on him like a pack of snarling wolves, trying to get his nerve by accusing him of beaning Rapp purposely. Red helped revive his victim and then struck out Young on three pitched balls and forced Smith to lay down an easy roller for Reilly." Faber went on to pitch a one-hitter and post a 9–0 victory.[10]

Many days, however, Faber was less fortunate: Several times he was stuck with the loss despite outstanding pitching. "Red Faber essayed the role of 'Iron Man' yesterday, pitching his second game in as many consecutive days," the *Register and Leader* reported. "That the lion hearted hurler failed to deliver was due entirely to the shortcomings of his teammates, who not only failed to hit behind him, but accorded him bum support." A hometown sportswriter labeled Faber "easily the champion hard luck pitcher of the league." He continued, "Scarcely a game that he has worked this season but has been turned out in workmanlike fashion. Something always happens, though. The team either fails to hit or had a bad day in the field. In the last four games he has pitched his mates have made just two runs behind him."[11]

In 1913, Faber's record in Des Moines was 21–20 in 49 games with a 2.48 earned-run average. He placed just second on the team in victories and fourth in winning percentage — evidence of his status of a hard-luck pitcher. Faber's modest record did not dissuade Charles Comiskey, owner of the Chicago White Sox. In late August, the Old Roman signed Faber for the 1914 campaign; various reports placed the purchase price at $3,500 to $4,000.

Des Moines fans were happy for Faber but sorry to see him leave. A *Des Moines Register and Leader* sportswriter put it this way: "Red has been one of the most popular players who ever wore a Des Moines uniform. He is one pitcher who went through one of the most disastrous losing streaks possible without hearing a word that was otherwise than friendly from either the grandstand or bleachers. Not one once in his two years service here has Red heard the cry 'Take him out!' when he was on the mound. Game to the core, he fought every minute with every ounce of energy that he could give. The fans realized and appreciated it. That he is a wonderful pitcher goes without question. Red will have a lot of competition in making the White Sox staff, which is already filled up with high class pitching talent. If given a fair chance, he will make good, because he has every requisite for a successful major league career."[12] Ring Lardner, the *Chicago Tribune*'s sportswriter and columnist, noting that the prospect's last name was the same as that of a leading manufacturer of writing instruments, reported the Chicago owner's optimism about the Iowan. "Commy expects Red Faber, his new pencil — no, no, we meant pitcher — to make his mark."[13] When the Western League announced its all-star team, Faber was among its six pitchers.[14]

At the season's end, Faber returned to his family's Dubuque home, no doubt optimistic about the 1914 season, when he would receive another chance to prove himself worthy of the big leagues.[15] As circumstances developed, however, Faber's off-season was severely abbreviated. He did not even have to wait until spring training to pitch against baseball's best.

7

World Tourist

After two successful campaigns with Des Moines, Faber was barely two weeks into his off-season in October 1913 when he received a message from the Chicago White Sox: Report the next day to Ottumwa, Iowa, and spend the next four months playing around the world with the White Sox and New York Giants. The exhibition tour promoted itself as featuring top professionals, but Faber had yet to appear in a regular-season major league game. However, the White Sox needed another pitcher, and the show was already on the road.

Starting in December 1912, two of the biggest names in baseball, representing the largest two American cities, planned the game's biggest exhibition ever. Charles A. Comiskey, owner of the White Sox, and John McGraw, fiery manager of the Giants, agreed to take their players on a four-month worldwide tour during the 1913–14 off-season. The Comiskey-McGraw tour would be more ambitious and competitive than that staged 25 years earlier by baseball executive and sporting goods magnate A.G. Spalding. Unlike Spalding, whose touring team routinely routed overmatched local squads, Comiskey and McGraw intended to recreate the major league experience as much as possible. Comiskey and McGraw, assisted by Ted Sullivan, a long-time Comiskey friend and aide, made arrangements throughout the 1913 season. The upcoming tour fueled much speculation: Who would receive invitations? Who would sacrifice their off-season and time with their families, forego their winter jobs and endure the rigorous travel and game schedule for the chance to see the world, all expenses paid? Outside of the Giants and White Sox, whose teams would allow their players to risk illness or injury on a tour that was expected to fatten the pocketbooks of McGraw and Comiskey? For those reasons and others, many players declined invitations. For those making the trip, that was not necessarily bad news. Traveling day and night, month after month, with Detroit star Ty Cobb — arguably the most disliked person ever to wear a baseball uniform — was unfathomable to some players. Thus, no one shed a tear when the "Georgia Peach" declined his invitation.[1] As the "tourists" departed Cincinnati for the month-long domestic leg of the tour, the rosters remained in flux.

The 25-year-old Faber had a booster in Clarence "Pants" Rowland, owner-manager of the Dubuque minor league franchise, a Comiskey friend and, most of all, a knowledgeable baseball man. If Faber needed any convincing to turn professional in 1909, he received it from Rowland, whose resume would eventually include managing a World Series champion, scouting and umpiring in the major leagues, serving as a major league general manager, and holding the presidency of the Pacific Coast League.[2] As the tour was about to begin, Comiskey, noting that a couple of White Sox pitchers declined invitations, asked Rowland for recommendations. He suggested Des Moines roommates Clint Rogge and Red Faber.[3] Apparently receiving just one day's notice — did Faber really pack that quickly for a four-month trip, or had Rowland advised him to be ready at any time?— the Iowan traveled from Dubuque, in northeast Iowa, to Ottumwa, in southeast Iowa, to catch up with the entourage. (Rogge did not make the trip.) Some references state that Faber was initially expected to play only in the stateside games. However, Chicago and Dubuque newspapers reported that he was ticketed for the full tour.[4]

Domestically, the tour generated plenty of excitement. The Giants, featuring pitcher Christy Mathewson, won the 1913 National League title before losing the World Series to the Philadelphia Athletics. Meanwhile, the White Sox finished in the middle of the American League at 78–74. People who had never ventured to a U.S. city for a major league game — St. Louis was the westernmost outpost — flocked to see the stars as they played their way west. Fans traveled great distances — by rail or horse-drawn wagon or automobile — to see "Matty" in Blue Rapids, Kansas, Sox infielder Buck Weaver in Bisbee, Arizona, and defrocked Olympic champion Jim Thorpe in Medford, Oregon. By the response of the fans at every stop, the leading attractions were Mathewson and Thorpe.

The tourists were booked for three dozen games in little more than a month in the United States before sailing for Japan to start three months of international visits. The basic itinerary: Arrive to the sounds of the local brass band. Cheering fans. Speechifying dignitaries. A brief city tour. A lavish luncheon. A parade to the ballpark. A mid-afternoon game. Time permitting, a celebratory banquet hosted by local officials. Finally, a rush to the railroad depot for an overnight trip to the next destination. Repeat it all the next day.

In Ottumwa, Faber, little concerned about fashion, made a less-than-favorable first impression on Chicago manager James "Nixey" Callahan, a snappy dresser.[5] "Callahan took one look at him and told [Comiskey] that he didn't want him on his team," Rowland said years later.[6] Nonetheless, Faber stayed and joined a small contingent with ties to Dubuque, where the pitcher lived in Dubuque the previous eight years. Comiskey started his professional career there and married a Dubuque girl, Nan Kelly, who was also part of the tour. Ted Sullivan was more than a business aide, friend and former coach to "Commy." The men had been brothers-in-law: Sullivan was, for apparently a short period, married to another of Dubuquer Lawrence Kelly's daughters, Nellie.

In his first week on tour, Faber saw how the exhibitions contributed to tragedy. In Tulsa on October 28, some 4,000 fans jammed South Main Street Park in anticipation of witnessing baseball history. Two future charter members of the Hall of Fame, Walter Johnson and Mathewson, were to have their first head-to-head meeting ever. A half-hour before game time, the bleachers in right field collapsed, spilling fans and burying a contingent of soldiers walking underneath. A private died after suffering a broken skull. Of the 50 other people injured, half required hospitalization. Among those narrowly escaping injury were Oklahoma governor Lee Cruce, who had arrived to throw out the ceremonial first pitch, and three Giants' wives. Incredibly, after the casualties and fractured lumber were cleared, event organizers acceded to the wishes of the survivors (including the governor) and decided to play the game. The tragedy set back the schedule just a half-hour. Signed just for this contest, Johnson pitched for the White Sox. The Washington Nationals (Senators) great went the distance against an arm-weary Mathewson, who departed in the fourth inning. The 6–0 game lasted just 70 minutes.[7]

Faber's first action on tour came in the fourth inning of a scoreless contest on a raw day in Kansas City. Rain and snow made the field a quagmire. The Giants immediately racked up three runs. Though Faber gave up only one hit in that frame, he contributed to his own problems with a walk and participation in a botched run-down play between third and home. A stolen base, passed ball and teammate's fielding error in the inning didn't help matters. Two innings later, the Giants scored three more runs, again on a single hit, and Callahan yanked Faber with one out in the sixth inning. New York coasted to a 6–2 victory.[8]

Despite pitching on an empty stomach — the railroad somehow failed to resupply the tourists' train — Faber fared better in his next outing in Beaumont, Texas. Before being relieved in the eighth inning, he gave up but a home run and an unearned run. However, the Giants prevailed again, 3–2.[9] Two days later, the New Yorkers jumped to a big lead and then roughed up Faber, who worked the final couple of innings of the 11–1 contest. In Bisbee, Arizona, miners received the day off so they could attend the game. Faber started and struggled as the Giants cruised to a 9–1 win. His only highlight came at the plate, where he stroked a triple.[10]

In Los Angeles a couple of days later, Faber showed more promise — despite participating in arguably the worst-played game of the tour. The contest featured numerous physical and mental errors as well as lineup oddities. New York's left-fielder Lee Magee lost track of the number of outs. Catching a fly ball and believing he had recorded the final out of the inning, Magee tossed the ball to the spectators as a good-will gesture. However, the real gift went to the White Sox. Magee's catch was only the *second* out. The Chicago base runner tagged up and scored before Magee could recover from his gaffe. Injuries depleted the White Sox bench, so Callahan, who had just nine at-bats in 1913, entered the game in the fourth inning. He rose to the occasion. The 39-year-old smashed a triple and a single, stole a base, scored twice and drove in the tying run. Meanwhile, Faber pitched brilliantly. In relief, he held the Giants to one hit and one run over the final four innings, during which time his Callahan-led White Sox teammates scored six unanswered runs to tie the game. After nine innings, it was too dark to continue, and the contest was declared a 7–7 tie.[11]

Meanwhile, speculation grew over which players would drop out of the tour — some voluntarily and some due to management's decision. The *San Francisco Chronicle* listed a handful of Sox players likely to be cut from the tour; it included Faber.[12] Meanwhile, as the tourists worked their way up California, toward Victoria, British Columbia, and their departure for Japan, more players made it known that they would not go overseas. They offered various reasons, but Chicago American sportswriter Bill Veeck Sr. — his pen name was Bill Bailey — revealed the unspoken concern: seasickness. Veeck reported that Chief Meyers, Hal Chase, Ray Schalk "and a few others" found the prospect of seasickness too unpleasant. The sportswriter listed one more key name among the seasick-sensitive players: The marquee player, Christy Mathewson.[13] McGraw did his best to get Matty to reconsider, but the tired star could not be dissuaded. The tour's No. 1 attraction would not cross the ocean.

McGraw suddenly had too few pitchers while Comiskey had too many. Between November 16, when Faber pitched a complete-game victory for the White Sox, and 5 P.M. November 19, when the tourists boarded the luxury ocean liner RMS *Empress of Japan*, Comiskey loaned Faber to the Giants. Instead of being sent home, Faber received his international ticket and the assignment to fill in for the day's most popular athlete. Later reports on the World Tour, noting his last-minute "trade" to the Giants, claimed that Faber sailed for Japan without a passport.[14] But that is improbable. In early November — more than two weeks before departure — a wire service reported that tour organizers had submitted passport applications to the U.S. State Department.[15] James Elfers, author of a 2003 book on the tour, found no reference to Faber having trouble involving travel documents.

Soon after the 298-foot-long Canadian liner shoved off from Victoria, Faber and the other 18 players in the 67-member entourage received envelopes containing $550— reimbursement of their $300 deposits to hold their places on the tour plus a bonus of $250. Many players considered the bonus a pittance. The sum was less than one-third of the winners' share for the Chicago City Series. Even for Comiskey, who had a reputation as a skinflint toward players, the miserly amount insulted the athletes.[16] The tour was financially successful; a McGraw aide revealed that receipts from the stateside swing already were sufficient to pay for the entire tour. The players received no salary; Comiskey and McGraw considered expense-paid travel and first-class accommodations (where available) sufficient.[17] (After the tour, during spring training, Sox players Buck Weaver and Jim Scott pouted in the belief that Comiskey should have shared more of his proceeds from the expedition.[18])

However, the lack of cash would soon be the least of the tourists' concerns. In their first full day at sea, Faber and everyone else aboard the *Empress* must have believed that Mathewson had the right idea by staying on land. Off the Alaskan panhandle, a horrific storm rocked the ocean liner, and nearly everyone on board became seasick. During a visit to the ship's rail, umpire Jack Sheridan became so violently ill that he lost his "store-bought teeth." (Misfortune dogged Sheridan in 1914. He missed a train and was separated from the entourage for nearly three weeks. After the tour, during the 1914 season, Sheridan suffered heat stroke on the field. He never recovered, succumbing to a heart attack several weeks later at age 63.[19]) The ship's crew reported never seeing so many seasick passengers. One of the leading sufferers was Tris Speaker, who had made up his mind to go overseas just two hours before departure. However, Faber had the dubious distinction of leading the tour in seasickness.[20]

The seas remained rocky through most of the 6,000-mile voyage. Rain, wind and hail regularly buffeted the ship. Day after day, Speaker, Faber and several others remained in their cabins or leaned over the deck rails. During one storm, a huge wave crashed into the ship, breaking loose a steamer trunk that slammed into Giants pitcher George "Hooks" Wiltse's right hand. Fortunately for the curveball specialist, Wiltse was a southpaw. The worst weather of the excursion hit November 29, 1913, when a typhoon — packing snow and huge, unrelenting, crashing waves — struck the *Empress*. The storm was so severe that the officers declared an emergency as the ship suffered damage and took on water. Observing the frightening battering sustained by the *Empress*, moviemaker Frank McGlynn wrote: "How she ever kept her head up is a mystery that can only be answered by the brave men who stuck to their work through cold and wet and impending disaster; but she rose on each occasion and gradually up, up, up till near the top when, crash!" Somehow, the captain of the *Empress*, W. Dixon-Hopcroft, avoided ordering the passengers to take to the lifeboats in the roiling waters. After two long days, in which minutes felt like hours, the storm finally passed. In a letter to his parents, Faber reported that winds exceeded 90 miles an hour during some of the storms and that he had been "awful sick" aboard the rocking ship.[21] For Comiskey, it got worse: Intestinal flu or food poisoning hit the White Sox owner, and he felt less than 100 percent the rest of the tour.[22]

During calmer periods, the tourists engaged in leisure pursuits, including card games, shuffleboard and music. Thanks in part to the duration of the crossing — it lasted 17 days, and the storm blew the ship hundreds of miles off course — and the adage that "misery loves company," the two teams, whose on-field rivalry had left them barely on speaking terms at the start of the voyage, became civil and sociable.

The grand receptions staged for the players in the United States were matched overseas, starting upon their arrival in Japan. Several of the leaders of welcoming committees were familiar with baseball, but many of the hosts knew nothing about the game. However, they did know that baseball was wildly popular among Americans, and that was good enough for them to roll out the red carpet. One player did not partake in the opening festivities: Red Faber. Still weak after extended bouts with seasickness, the Sox-turned-Giant, under orders of the ship's doctor, remained on board the *Empress*.[23]

Faber recovered, but he did not see action in the first week in Asia. He took the mound in Hong Kong, where his newly adopted team, the Giants, edged the White Sox in a five-inning contest, 7–4. The tourists enjoyed the various receptions and endured the travel, closing out 1913 with stops in Shanghai, Hong Kong and Manila. The week before Christmas, they boarded another ship, the *St. Albans*, and headed for Australia. They welcomed 1914 in the Land Down Under.

In his letter home, Faber indicated that he had a camera and promised to have many pictures to share with family and friends upon his return to Iowa.[24] Unfortunately, his snapshots apparently have not survived the subsequent nine decades. What scenes and events they would have captured! They would have shown a fantastic array of experiences, including rickshaw rides in Asia, a visit to the pyramids and Great Sphinx of Egypt, an audience with Pope Pius X and a luncheon hosted by Sir Thomas Lipton (then the richest man in the world) and a climactic final game before the king of England. His photos might have also shown the travails of travel, including the tourists' brief quarantine during a close encounter with smallpox (and another round of painful vaccinations), rides in sedan chairs and the run-in with police over a barkeeper's mistaken complaint that some players had stolen his pool table's cue ball. Later, the tourists had a run-in of sorts with Italian authorities, who had to see a demonstration of baseball to be satisfied that it did not violate their law forbidding brutal games. (The officials had heard such references as

"Weaver smashed the ball through Doolan," and, "Crawford died at home.")
After receiving an official permit to stage the contest, the tourists were rained
out.[25]

With the exception of the final game, in London, Faber was largely a
footnote on the excursion. The major league veterans commanded the attention of fans and reporters. Faber received only occasional mention in newspapers (outside Iowa), and his name and photograph rarely appeared in a
documentary booklet about the tour. One of the few Faber photos shows him
on December 17 or 18, 1913. In Manila, he sits on the New York bench but
wears his Chicago uniform. The pitcher sports the beginnings of a mustache,
evidence of the tourists' vote of no confidence in their ship's shaky-handed
barber.[26]

The tour's first series of 1914 was in Australia, where Faber went 2–1.[27]
In the final game on that continent, on January 8, he pitched all 11 innings
for the Giants in a 4–3 victory.[28] The tour staged just one game (in Ceylon)
over the next three weeks, when the entourage trekked to Egypt. Faber won
again, in Cairo, in early February. The entourage experienced rainout after
rainout; only one of eight games scheduled for Italy and France was contested. The game was played in Nice, France, where hundreds of American
tourists added excitement to the proceedings. The most expensive ticket of
the tour was sold in France — 20 francs, or $4.[29] The tourists moved on to
London for the final stop of their adventure. Wet and chilly weather and
McGraw's ill-advised comments to London reporters nearly ended the tour
prematurely. A few days before the game, McGraw expounded on why British
soldiers were inferior to their American counterparts. In McGraw's view, the
Brits lacked athletic discipline because they did not play baseball. He explained
to the writers why baseball was superior to cricket. If that were not enough,
McGraw suggested that England was losing her edge. In the ensuing furor,
some papers called for a boycott of the game. McGraw kept his mouth shut
the next couple of days. A lavish pre-game banquet went off without incident (and without Comiskey and McGraw, both of whom were ill) and the
weather cooperated. Steering clear of reporters and nursing a severe cold,
McGraw chose his pitcher for the tour's final game: Red Faber.

The newspapers' opposition notwithstanding, thousands of people
showed up for the game at Chelsea Football Grounds in London on February 26, 1914. Attendance estimates varied wildly — from 5,000 to 30,000.
Whatever the number, expatriate and visiting Americans represented a substantial portion of the crowd. The spectator of honor was King George V,
who arrived wearing a dark suit and black derby hat. The U.S. ambassador
to Great Britain, Walter Hines Page, introduced the king to Comiskey,
McGraw, Callahan and tour director M.D. Bunnell. The players lined up
before the Royal Box and were introduced en masse (no handshakes). King

The Chicago White Sox and New York Giants visited Egypt during their 1913–14 world tour. Though Red Faber (back row, fourth from left) had yet to appear in a major league game, the White Sox belatedly added him to the tour and then loaned Faber to the Giants for the international contests. Afterward, New York manager John McGraw failed to persuade Chicago owner Charles A. Comiskey to sell him Faber's contract. (Courtesy of the Tri-County Historical Society, Cascade, Iowa.)

George threw out the ceremonial "first pitch" — sort of. Ambassador Page handed a baseball to the monarch, who passed it to umpire Bill Klem, who threw it to White Sox starter Jim Scott. After Giants leadoff hitter Mike Donlin's at-bat, Comiskey accepted the "first pitch" baseball from McGraw and Callahan.[30] The king impressed Faber as "a real guy."[31] Before the afternoon ended, Faber impressed the king.

King George appeared to enjoy the tight battle. He followed each pitch and each play intently. Sportswriters noted that even when a foul ball smashed a stadium window above him, the king barely noticed the falling glass.[32] Knowing it was their final game, and aware of their enthusiastic and royal audience, the Giants and White Sox held nothing back. "They brought out a contest that could not have been bettered as an attraction beneficial to baseball," noted *Chicago Record-Herald* sportswriter G.W. Axelson.[33] The game featured several fielding gems and tough pitching. As the Giants starter, rookie-to-be Faber picked a great time for his best performance of the tour. He gave up two runs in the bottom of the third inning, but the Giants tied it in the top of the fourth. In the top of the sixth inning, with the score 2–2, Faber found himself in a bases-loaded, one-out jam. The Iowan managed to retire the next two White Sox batters without giving up a run. "His Majesty applauded Faber as enthusiastically as did any of the American fans," a London paper reported.[34] Scott gave way to Joe Benz in the seventh inning, but Faber kept pitching.

The game remained tied after the regulation nine innings. In the top of the 10th, the Giants notched two runs against Benz. In the bottom of the 10th, holding a 4–2 lead and with no opponents on base, Faber stood just one out away from a royal victory. Whether it was due to nerves or fatigue or just bad luck, Faber walked Buck Weaver to keep the White Sox's hopes alive. That brought to the plate "Wahoo" Sam Crawford, then of the Detroit Tigers and a future Hall-of-Famer. A native of Wahoo, Nebraska, Crawford proceeded to slug a Faber offering for a home run. Suddenly, the game was tied 4–4. After Benz held the Giants scoreless in the top of the 11th inning, Faber faced 22-year-old catcher Tom Daly. At that point, Daly's official major league experience totaled exactly one game.[35] A Canadian and thus considered one of the king's subjects, Daly launched a Faber pitch high over the left field fence for a game-ending home run.[36] Final score: White Sox 5, Giants 4. (As a major leaguer, Daly, a little-used reserve, hit no homers and only 20 extra-base hits in 540 major league at-bats in a career that stretched into 1921.) Despite taking the loss by giving up home runs in the 10th and 11th innings, Faber impressed the king and baseball experts alike. "Too much credit cannot be given to young Faber," McGraw said. "It was the youngster's day of triumph, and I'll bet he will remember it until the last day he lives."[37] McGraw put his money where his mouth was — or at least he tried to. He made Comiskey a cash offer for Faber's contract. Reports of the amount bid vary from $3,500 to $50,000. Comiskey, whose ample pitching staff was considered the best in the major leagues, probably considered McGraw's proposal seriously. Ultimately, however, Comiskey declined. He kept Faber for the White Sox. In less than four years, sportswriters would have occasion to recall the transaction that *wasn't.*

Faber and the tourists on February 28 boarded the *Lusitania* and steamed toward New York. Unlike their tumultuous Pacific crossing three months earlier, this cruise lacked incident or seasickness. As they gazed out over the Atlantic, the players' thoughts no doubt turned toward their homes and the start of the 1914 regular season. Back in the United States, spring training was under way. When the *Lusitania* approached New York harbor March 7, players were surprised to see several smaller vessels race out to pull alongside. Representatives of the upstart Federal League jockeyed with those from the National and American leagues to get unsigned players under contract. The Federal League would last but two seasons.

McGraw and Comiskey staged self-congratulatory banquets in their home cities — in New York the evening of their return and in Chicago on March 10. (Dubuque physician William P. Slattery attended both banquets.[38] Slattery might have been Dubuque's preeminent baseball enthusiastic of the era. As a spectator at the Cubs-White Sox World Series of 1906, he left the stands to provide medical assistance to Eddie Hahn, a White Sox outfielder, after a pitch struck him squarely in the face.[39] Eleven years later, Slattery was on hand in New York to see Faber achieve World Series glory.[40])

Faber rode the Illinois Central and received a hero's welcome in Dubuque at 7 the following morning. Clarence Rowland and Slattery were part of the traveling party.[41] Faber soon found himself in local baseball headquarters, surrounded by friends who peppered him with questions. In his quiet and calm manner, Faber tried to answer each query individually, but, before he could finish, someone else would blurt out another question. "It really was such a wonderful trip, that I could talk for weeks and still be unable to tell you how much I appreciated it," Faber said. "There was a hearty welcome and interest in our exhibitions everywhere we landed, and the treatment accorded us was splendid. Mr. Comiskey, Mr. McGraw, and all of the members formed such a congenial party that I seem to miss their company already. Of course, I'm glad to be back home again, and it feels good to meet all the boys in Dubuque."[42] A sportswriter observed that Faber looked to be in the best of health, adding that the pitcher saw just enough action to "keep his throwing arm limber and prevent staleness" so he would be ready when he joined the White Sox for the balance of spring training camp. Another sportswriter asked the hometown hero about his prospects of making the Chicago's major league roster and whether he was "hopeful." His reply was a sample of

Faber braggadocio: "I feel better than that about it." The writer, noting Faber's "usual custom," said the ballplayer "likes to talk about himself about as much as Ban Johnson likes the Federal league or Cubs owner Charley Murphy." Faber preferred to talk about the tour rather than his on-field performance. He cited the audience with Pope Pius X as "the most impressive occasion of my life. I can't describe my feelings when I first saw the pope and heard his voice ... I'll remember that experience as long as I live."[43] The interviews completed, Faber returned to his Dubuque parents' home on Grandview Avenue, where he immediately prepared for the trip to California for what remained of spring training. His "leave" lasted barely 24 hours. The following noon, St. Joseph's College (now Loras College), honored Faber at a luncheon. Again, his modesty was evident. "Although Faber has had much experience in facing crowds," one account stated, "he never received a greater ovation nor appeared to be more embarrassed than when he was called upon to address the student body." The college president's glowing introduction of Faber before some 450 students left the athlete "practically non-plussed."[44] (Fifty years later, the college honored Faber again by naming its baseball field after him.)[45] Shortly after a huge ovation closed the luncheon, Faber boarded the Illinois Central to Chicago, where he reconnected with Manager Callahan and other Sox players from the world tour. Together they would join the team at spring training in Paso Robles, California.

Red Faber's official major league career was about to begin.

8

White Sox Rookie

After spending five grueling months traveling the world, Faber probably considered his half-week train trip to California training camp a breeze. For the second straight spring, the White Sox trained in Paso Robles, a resort community midway between Los Angeles and San Francisco. Paso Robles was noted for its therapeutic hot springs and varied recreational opportunities. In 1913, the world-renowned pianist Ignace Paderewski reported experiencing relief from his arthritis after three months' treatment in the mineral waters of Paso Robles.[1] While manager James "Nixey" Callahan, Faber and the other world tourists were abroad, the White Sox opened training camp under the direction of coach William "Kid" Gleason. Floods in California disrupted railroad service, and the team arrived three days behind schedule. Gleason divided the team into two squads, one practicing for two hours in the morning and the other for two hours in the afternoon. After each workout, the players relaxed in the baths — hot and cold — and received rubdowns.[2] In the 21st century, hosting a major league team is a financial boon and matter of prestige for a lodging establishment. In the early 20th century, when the baseball and its participants were less refined, some hoteliers did not see it that way. For example, after receiving the team's request for lodging, a Washington hotel responded to the White Sox office: "The management has nothing but admiration for baseball players, but believes it would be bad policy to accommodate the Chicago, or any other, baseball club."[3]

Though technically just a prospect with no official major league appearances, Faber arrived in California in condition and with world tour experience. He was among 17 pitchers in training camp, but few doubted that he would make the cut.[4]

The White Sox split the team as they played exhibition games and worked their way east toward Chicago. One squad started from San Francisco and the other from Los Angeles. The teams played poorly, and the fans knew it.

"Oh, base ball, what crimes are committed in thy name," a California journalist wrote. "Oh, Charley Comiskey, how many more years do you propose to pass out this kind of stuff to Pacific Coast fans?" *The Sporting News* predicted that by 1916, after three years at Paso Robles, the White Sox would not be training in the Golden State. The high expenses associated with a California camp and locals' interest in seeing new teams every three years or so were the main reasons.[5] (The prognostication proved correct: After three years at Paso Robles, the White Sox in 1916 returned to Mineral Wells, Texas, their 1911 training site.)

For the second time, Faber's name appeared on a major league team's Opening Day roster. The White Sox paid him $1,200 for 1914. Unlike his 1911 experience with Pittsburgh, Faber did not just ride the bench. The 25-year-old made his official debut on Friday, April 17, 1914, when he started against Cleveland in Comiskey Park. The White Sox jumped to a 4–0 lead after four innings, but Cleveland rocked the rookie for three runs in the fifth inning, when Callahan summoned Sox sophomore Reb Russell to rescue Faber. In his first 4⅓ innings in the majors, Faber gave up four hits, two walks and a wild pitch while striking out four. Cleveland tied the game with two out in the top of the ninth inning, thanks to a Jack Lelivelt triple and Chicago infielder Buck Weaver's "daily error."[6] However, with two out in the bottom of the ninth, John "Shano" Collins legged out an inside-the-park homer to give the White Sox a 6–5 victory and a season record of 4–0.

Even though future Hall-of-Famer Ed Walsh struggled with arm problems, the White Sox had a strong pitching staff—"perhaps unequaled in the history of the game," in the opinion of a *Sporting News* writer.[7] Eddie Cicotte, Joe Benz and Jim Scott and Russell (21–17 as a rookie) opened the season as the starters. During April and May, Faber saw limited action, starting once and relieving only occasionally. He also appeared in a May 11 exhibition game in Pittsburgh, where Walsh, in a test of his arm, struggled in four innings against the Pirates. "It was apparent from the first ball pitched that Big Ed was not the old Big Ed," the *Chicago Tribune*'s I.E. Sanborn observed, "but Manager Callahan kept him on the firing line long enough to make sure." Facing the team that released him three years earlier, Faber completed the game and surrendered only one hit in his four innings of relief.[8] Though it was not recognized as such at the time, the exhibition contest represented a changing of the guard. Walsh, the one-time "Iron Man," pitched in only 17 major league games from 1914 to 1917. However, by the end of June 1914, sportswriters were heralding Urban C. "Red" Faber as the new "Iron Man."

On June 1, at Navin Field in Detroit, Callahan gave Faber his second start. "For nine innings ... Faber held the Tigers to four hits, two of which were measly infield scratches," Sanborn reported. "In spite of a tendency to wildness this graduate of Des Moines was so good in the pinches that the

Tigers did not even look as if they could score a run off him." The White Sox blew their chance to win in the ninth inning, and the game went into extra innings. Faber demonstrated his durability and tenacity by battling the Tigers into the bottom of the 13th inning, when Detroit prevailed, 2–1, saddling Faber with a loss "instead of what ought to have been a brilliant victory." Nonetheless, Faber's gutty performance against veteran Hooks Dauss caught the notice of players, fans and other sportswriters.[9]

On June 7, a steamy Sunday afternoon in Chicago, Faber posted his first major league victory — and he did it in convincing fashion, limiting the New York Yankees to three hits in a 4–0 contest. Though the Iowan displayed some wildness — he walked three and forced one Yankee from the game with a fastball to the knee — no New Yorkers reached third base. He also retired 13 consecutive batters early in the game and struck out five. "While Faber pitched beautiful ball, his roundhouse curve, spitter and fast one being too much for the opposition, he was helped in a way by steady support," the *Chicago Record-Herald* reported. "His infield co-workers were continually digging them out of the dirt, while the outfielders, 'Ping' Bodie in particular, performed wonders with long, hard drives. Not a slip was made behind the globetrotting recruit."[10] A *Tribune* sportswriter (probably Sanborn) noted, "U. Red Faber probably earned a regular turn on the slab by yesterday's performance on top of his unlucky 13-inning game in Detroit last week."[11] He was correct.

On June 17 in Chicago, Faber barely missed the record books. He held the Philadelphia Athletics, the defending world champions, hitless through eight innings. To that point, the only base runners reached on a walk and infielder Lena Blackburne's error. In the top of the ninth, leadoff hitter Jack Lapp hit a grounder to the right of Blackburne. According to a wire-service account, the infielder, instead of charging the ball, stepped back to play it on a big hop. Apparently underestimating Lapp's running speed, Blackburne threw easily to first base. Lapp beat the throw and spoiled Faber's no-hit bid. "Had Blackburne fumbled the ball temporarily or made a bad toss," an observer wrote, "Faber would have gone through with the record, for previous to this time the Sox's 'keystone king' had handled four or five chances in the same spot off speedier men and had thrown them out without trouble."[12] *The Sporting News* concurred, describing Lapp's hit as "not a clean one by any means." However, the *Tribune's* Sanborn saw it differently: "There was no question about the hit."[13] The decision of the scorer did not bother Faber as much that of the umpire. More than three decades afterward, Faber said that he was upset because he thought Blackburne's throw beat Lapp. However, he added, "Time heals everything."[14] Faber completed the one-hitter, a 5–0 victory. As *The Sporting News* put it, "Any pitcher who can hold the Athletics to one hit is entitled to a seat with the mighty."[15] Faber followed his

Red Faber (foreground, wearing jacket) shows off the gift he received during a Chicago White Sox exhibition game in Dubuque, Iowa. Sox owner Charles Comiskey, who played in Dubuque in the late 1870s, brought the Sox to Dubuque in 1914, 1915 and 1916. Faber was a Dubuque resident in 1909 when he signed with Dubuque's minor league team. In addition, Sox manager Clarence Rowland (1915–18) and Comiskey's wife, Nan, were raised in Dubuque. (Courtesy of the Tri-County Historical Society, Cascade, Iowa.)

one-hitter with a four-hit, 5–3 win over Boston, where two errors by Buck Weaver contributed to all the Red Sox's runs.[16]

While not as significant as his first major league victory, his first shutout, a one-hitter and his exploits on the world tour, another memorable event of Faber's 1914 season occurred June 23. Comiskey used an open date on the American League schedule to take his White Sox to Dubuque, Iowa. It was the city where Faber lived when he turned professional and where the Old Roman's in-laws resided. The city was abuzz all day. Its annual Sunday School Parade and Picnic, involving thousands of Dubuque and area residents, took place earlier in the day. The Chicago, Milwaukee and St. Paul railway put on a special train to accommodate fans, and the other railroads serving Dubuque publicized their schedules for arrivals and departures around game time.[17] The White Sox — minus Faber, who came to town earlier in the day — arrived at Dubuque's Great Western railroad depot at 1:30 P.M., just 75 minutes before the game. The players changed into their uniforms at the YMCA because the city's brand-new ballpark still lacked locker rooms. Thousands of visitors, their numbers were swelled by Sunday school participants, jammed Dubuque's streets, restaurants and four railroad depots. They bought up the last seat more than an hour before the first pitch; after that, folks paid to stand.

Some 6,189 spectators — including several hundred from Cascade — filled the grandstand, jammed bleachers and stood on the field three to six deep along the first-base line and in front of the grandstand. The turnout was a record for a baseball game in Dubuque.

The White Sox asked their hosts to bat first, and Sox starter Henry "Hi" Jasper, a 33-year-old rookie, easily retired the Dubuque minor leaguers in the top of the first inning. However, in the bottom of the first, the White Sox leadoff hitter did not immediately step to the plate. A Dubuque newspaper reported, a "few mysterious murmurs around the Sox bench caused the white-hosed players to remove their hats and surround the home plate. Faber was in the center of the gang, which was augmented by the players who wear the garb of [Dubuque manager Forrest] Plass. Just about that time George Bennett and several Knights of Columbus stepped into the limelight and headed towards the plate. In the course of the next few moments 'Red' had been presented with a handsome solid-gold, diamond-studded Knights of Columbus pendant worth $159. After the crowd discovered what was going on, that 'Red' had been shoved another notch in the direction of the income tax collector, there was a bundle of cheers unloosened."[18] Faber, Dubuque County's favorite son, pitched the final three innings of the exhibition, won by the White Sox, 11–2. The exhibition turned out to be profitable for all concerned. Of the $2,492.05 in receipts — the average paid admission was 40 cents — Comiskey took home $1,465. The Dubuque Hustlers' cut ($977.05) took some of the sting out of their eight rainouts on their Three-I League schedule.

Faber resumed his winning ways on the major league mound June 26, when he went the distance in a 2–1 win over Detroit's Jean Dubuc. The Iowan held Detroit to three hits and smacked an RBI double in the sixth inning to plate Chicago's first run. Faber's "Iron Man" reputation took shape as he pitched smartly in relief the next three days. In his fourth appearance in four days, Faber entered in the bottom of the eighth inning, snuffed a Detroit rally with one pitch and then threw a perfect ninth inning to save a 3–2 victory for Joe Benz.[19]

The 1914 White Sox saved their worst for last. As late as July 9, after a seven-game winning streak, Chicago was only two games out of first place with a 41–33 record. However, the White Sox went 29–51 thereafter and finished 70–84, in seventh place, far ahead of AL doormat Cleveland (51–102).

On August 9 in Chicago, Faber outlasted Washington legend Walter Johnson over 11 innings. The White Sox rookie scattered 10 hits and won, 2–1. "Faber may not be in Johnson's class," a Dubuque sports editor noted, "but he isn't a half-bad pitcher at that."[20] Five days later, during or immediately after his 6–4, complete-game victory in St. Louis, pain radiated from Faber's right elbow. Callahan sent him to the legendary healer "Bonesetter" Reese, of Youngstown, Ohio. Reese treated Faber's arm, said the problem was not serious and prescribed a week of rest. Faber used the recuperation time to visit friends and family in Cascade and Dubuque, where he reported that Reese "put his arm in good condition and he felt he could go at any time."[21] The seriousness of the injury must have been understated, because Faber missed 3½ weeks instead of one. In his next appearance, a start in the second game of a Labor Day doubleheader in Detroit, Faber lost to the Tigers 3–0. His manager was criticized for the injury and lackluster performance the remainder of the season. Sportswriter Sanborn already blamed Callahan for former star Ed Walsh's arm injury due to overuse. "That grand old slab staff [of the White Sox] will be a thing of the past, however, unless Callahan revises his methods of working it. This season he has put an awful crimp in the career of one promising youngster, Faber, who looked like the find of the decade until overwork sent him to the Bonesetter, and he has not yet demonstrated that he can recover from the setback given him."[22]

In 40 games, evenly divided between starts and relief, Faber went 10–9 — 2–2 in relief and 8–7 in 20 starts — with 11 complete games. Among White Sox pitchers, Faber and Mellie Wolfgang (9–5), another rookie with the nickname "Red," were the only ones with winning records.

As early as 1903 — the year of the first World Series — the White Sox and Cubs met in a post-season Chicago City Series (if neither team was involved in the World Series). Bragging rights and the prospect of the winner's share of gate receipts gave the players ample incentive to treat the games as much more than mere exhibitions. (Some years, the winner's share from the Chicago City Series approached that of the World Series champs.) In the 1914 City Series, the Cubs won three of the first four games in the best-of-seven series. In the fifth game, the Sox scored twice in the bottom of the fifth to pull ahead, 2–1. Faber relieved Jim Scott in the sixth and two-hit the Cubs over the final four innings to deny the North Siders the city title. The White Sox proceeded to edge the Cubs in the sixth game 5–3, to force a seventh game. The White Sox won their fourth straight game to claim the city title in dramatic fashion with a 3–2 victory at Comiskey Park. For Faber, whose save contributed to the championship, it was an exciting conclusion to an extended rookie season.

In his first year as a major leaguer, Faber joined The Baseball Players' Fraternity, whose directors included Ty Cobb, Sam Crawford, Johnny Evers, Ed Reulbach and Fred Merkle. In the issue of *Baseball Magazine* listing Faber's addition to the membership rolls, an article in from the organization warned of unwise spending by ballplayers. Headlined, "A Growing Evil in the Life of the Baseball Player," the story noted, "One very glaring instance of this among ball players is the growing tendency to purchase and maintain automobiles." Faber was among that group. When he returned to Iowa, friends and family seemed to take as much interest in his new automobile as in its owner. Newspaper items reporting his visits often mentioned the make and model of his latest vehicle. "For the ball player who has the required principle, there is, of course, no more objection to his keeping a machine than there is for anyone else doing so, but the player who is spending any considerable amount of his salary for this purpose will some day, without doubt, regret his foolish extravagance."[23] There is no record of Faber ever having second thoughts about owning motor cars.

For the Faber family, 1914 was noteworthy for reasons other than Urban's achievements on the baseball diamond. The player's parents, Nicholas and Margaret, reacquired the Hotel Faber and moved back to Cascade.[24] His younger brother, Alfred — some accounts called him Albert — opened a pool hall in Cascade and took a bride, Miss Lulu Mae Lane.[25] His younger sister Celestine married M.F. Kurt, a Cascade banker. (The ballplayer was absent because the White Sox were playing in Washington.)[26]

There were other occurrences in sports and global affairs that made 1914 significant. The upstart Federal League opened play that year, with the Chicago Whales, playing in Weeghman Park (later renamed Wrigley Field), representing the Windy City's third major league team. In late June, an assassin shot Archduke Francis Ferdinand of Austria, setting off a chain of events that led to World War I in Europe. That same month, the Boston Red Sox gave a 19-year-old pitcher his introduction to the major leagues. The prospect's prowess with a bat matched that of his pitching arm. Eventually, he was moved to the outfield to take full advantage of his slugging abilities and then traded to the New York Yankees. The star's name was George Herman Ruth. Over the next two decades, "Babe" and "Fabe" would come to respect each other as tough competitors and formidable adversaries.

The offseason of 1914–15 provided Faber his first extended break from baseball in a year and a half, and he spent much of it in his native Cascade. Immediately after the City Series, Faber motored toward Cascade in his red Ohio Speeder.[27] During the off-season, Faber hunted and fished during the day and at night he drank whiskey with the traveling men frequenting his parents' hotel. He also could be found manning the cigar counter in his brother Alfred's pool hall a few doors from the hotel. Though the local newspaper regularly noted his accomplishments and adventures overseas and in the American League, at least one local was out of the loop. On the street one day after his outstanding rookie season, Faber encountered one of Cascade's senior citizens, who said, "Well, well, Red, my boy, where have you been all summer?"[28]

9

Sophomore Sensation

In late January 1915, the Cascade newspaper joked that if Urban "Red" Faber started spring training "in the pink of condition," thanks should go to local resident Cy Conlin. "Cy's course of treatment is to say something of a caustic nature to Urban and then the latter proceeds to chase Cy around the billiard and pool tables in Al Faber's pool hall. The exercise has kept the big athlete busy most of the past winter," the paper noted. "Cy may ask to have a small clothes cleaning bill reimbursed, as he did a good deal of rolling around on the floor in his efforts to keep the White Sox twirler in training."[1] In mid–February, amateur fitness coach Conlin might have been among the guests at a farewell "stag party" for Faber in the home of E.D. Hogan, an attorney engaged to Faber's sister Mae.[2] (Hogan's first wife died in late 1913 when she jumped from a moving automobile in the mistaken belief the vehicle was on fire.)

The White Sox's free-fall in the last half of 1914 cost manager James J. "Nixey" Callahan his job. "To the utter and be-dazed surprise of all the baseball world, Charles Comiskey, instead of retaining Jimmy Callahan or appointing Eddie Collins to the position, announced the appointment of Clarence Rowland, a hitherto obscure minor leaguer, as the leader of the White Sox for 1915," *Baseball Magazine* noted. "This was indeed a stunner. With veterans like Callahan, Gleason, Sullivan and Walsh at hand and with Collins just secured, Commy goes and pitchforks a Three-I man from Peoria into the place of supreme command! Can you beat it for a novelty or for a big surprise?"[3] Comiskey defended his selection of a 35-year-old who never played even Class A ball. "I have considered it carefully. Rowland is by no means a new man to me. I have been watching his work most carefully in the minor leagues for the past seven or eight years, and have been greatly impressed with his aggressiveness and his judgment," Comiskey wrote in *Baseball Magazine*. "He is particularly good at picking ball players, and has sent up quite a few to the White Sox during that time."[4] One of those picks was Urban Faber. A half-dozen years earlier, when they both lived in Dubuque, Rowland scouted Faber and encouraged him to sign his first professional contract. Four years later, it was Rowland who recommended to Comiskey that he take the untested Iowan on the 1913–14 world tour. Eventually, Faber would repay those favors by helping Rowland, the so-called "busher from Dubuque," stand atop the baseball world.

In August 1914, Comiskey invited Rowland, then manager of Peoria of the Three-I League, to Chicago for a conversation. "He asked me about the league in general," Rowland recalled four decades later. "Then he told me, 'Tell your bosses in Peoria you won't be back next year. You're going to be with me.' That's all he said — nothing about what he had in mind." Rowland learned more later in the season, when the Old Roman invited him to join him at a City Series game. "He asked me, 'You're not afraid to take my club, are you?' I told him, 'No. And if you think I'm kidding, I'll go down on the field and take charge right now." That convinced Comiskey, but he did not reveal his decision for another couple of months.[5]

After training camp in Paso Robles, California, Rowland opened the regular season on the road. The White Sox won their first two games but lost six straight before limping into Chicago. Comiskey pulled out all the stops for the home opener. There were three automobile parades from the Chicago Loop to the ballpark, where entertainers included a cabaret quartet and three bands, including that of Faber's alma mater, Dubuque College (formerly St. Joseph's). It was a special day for Dubuque, hometown of the new White Sox manager. Many Iowans — including friends of Rowland, Faber and Comiskey — traveled to Chicago for the occasion. The Iowans among the 22,000 in Comiskey Park were excited to see Faber enter the game in the fourth inning, but at the time they wished that the circumstances were more favorable. St. Louis had battered starter Hi Jasper for three runs in the third. Browns starter Carl Weilman baffled the Chicagoans, who managed only one hit through eight innings. Faber struggled at times but did not allow a run until the sixth inning. The Browns held a 4–0 lead entering the bottom of the ninth. In a thrilling rally, the White Sox solved Weilman and rallied for five runs to snare the victory. Faber was the winning pitcher.

Less than a week later, the major league sophomore displayed some gamesmanship in a pitching battle against Detroit's Jean Dubuc. "Red crabbed and stalled and pulled up grass and argued with his mates and the umpires and apparently did everything but pitch," the *Chicago Tribune* reported, "but just the same when the game was over it was found that the hard-hitting Tigers had made only three base hits off him. All the time he was doing the other things, he was pitching ball. He had a purpose in his actions and had [manager Hughie] Jennings' men guessing and outguessed all the time."[6] His teammates broke through in the eighth for a 4–1 victory. In early June, after Faber beat his Tigers by another 4–1 score, Ty Cobb said of the Chicago hurler, "No question about the stuff he's got. But do you think he'll last? It looks to me as if he pitched unnaturally. He arm snaps and I don't see how he can keep it up. And he's always got a sore spot in it somewhere."[7] Cobb was at least partially right: Faber occasionally suffered arm problems. But he lasted 20 seasons. Cobb exacted some revenge on a rainy Independence Day in Detroit, where Faber was pitching the bottom of the 10th inning of a tie game. A Cobb hit, an error and an intentional walk filled the bases with one out. As the rain intensified, Faber failed to find the strike zone on four straight pitches. As the hometown fans celebrated, Cobb trotted in from third base and registered the winning run by jumping on home plate with both feet.[8]

New acquisitions keyed the White Sox's 23-game improvement over the previous season,

Hall of Famer Sam Rice once described Red Faber's pitching technique against him: "He steps toward first base and breaks that spitter low and outside, and I can't lay off it. I just dribble balls to the infield." (Courtesy of the Tri-County Historical Society, Cascade, Iowa.)

including Eddie Collins, former member of Connie Mack's "Million Dollar Infield," and outfielder Oscar "Happy" Felsch. Midway through the season, the Sox purchased veteran outfielder Eddie Murphy from the Athletics. However, Comiskey's biggest "catch" of 1915 was a 28-year-old pure hitter acquired from Cleveland: "Shoeless" Joe Jackson.

In June 1915, Faber achieved a record that escaped notice at the time — and for nearly 60 years. On June 18 in Philadelphia, as he posted an easy 11–4 win over the Athletics, Faber as a batsman received four walks in four plate appearances. In his next start, four days later in Cleveland, Faber again pitched a victory, 9–6 — and again drew passes. He walked in his first three visits to the batter's box, establishing a streak of seven consecutive walks.[9] It was a mark all the more remarkable because of Faber's paltry record as a batsman. However, Faber's feat apparently escaped the notice of the *Tribune* and other papers at the time. Billy Rogell of Detroit was credited with setting the record 23 years later (1938), but in 1983 baseball researcher Al Kermisch discovered that Faber reached seven straight walks first.[10]

Under Rowland, and with new personnel, the White Sox moved from sixth place to third in 1915. Propelled by victories in the last 11 games of the season, Chicago finished just 9½ games behind eventual World Series champion Boston. Faber collected two victories during that streak, including the season finale, to finish 24–14 and tie Jim Scott (24–11) for the team lead in victories. Though he led Sox pitchers in strikeouts (182 in nearly 300 innings), Faber's forte was getting hitters to beat his offerings into the ground. That skill was best demonstrated on May 12, 1915, in Comiskey Park, where he held Washington to just three hits in a 4–1 victory. The Nationals (also called the Senators) scratched across their lone run with two outs in the ninth inning. "His strong side arms soakers swooped across the plate with deadly effect," fellow Cascade native James Crusinberry wrote, "and when eight innings had been completed only one hit had been made off him, that being a scratch hit which Weaver knocked down with his bare hand but couldn't recover in time to make a play."[11] A Washington sportswriter gave Faber his due, but he also cited the ineptitude of his opponents. "But from the way the Nationals have been going of late it does not take a real pitcher to defeat them. Poor hitting does not describe it. There is no word we know of strong enough to express it."[12] Faber retired the side on three pitches in the third and fifth innings. His busiest inning was the eighth, when he tossed 13 pitches.[13] That evening, Faber's achievement acquired greater notoriety. A Washington boy who operated an electronic scoreboard simulating the game pointed out that Faber threw just 67 pitches to the 32 batters he faced — reportedly a record. Christy Mathewson was said to have required just 72 pitches seven years earlier. The boy, Frank Saffell, said that his tally showed that Faber delivered 50 strikes and 17 balls.

Immediately after that record-setting victory in Chicago, Faber hopped a train for Iowa. While his teammates staged a ninth-inning victory over Walter Johnson and the Nationals, Faber visited family and friends in Cascade. A newspaper reported that, after arriving in Dubuque, the pitcher "was seen riding in a buzzwagon pointed towards Cascade and going like 60."[14] The next day, a Friday, was an open date throughout the American League. (It was not a travel day for the Nationals, who cooled their heels in Chicago before resuming their series against the White Sox.[15]) Instead of granting his team the day off, Comiskey shepherded his charges to Dubuque, where they engaged the local minor leaguers in their second annual exhibition game. As rookie manager of the White Sox, Rowland, who grew up in Dubuque, was the main honoree. Ex-Dubuque residents Faber, Comiskey and pitcher Hi Jasper shared in the local adulation. Further, the exhibition was a homecoming for *Chicago Tribune* sportswriter James Crusinberry, who, like Faber, was a native of Cascade. "One has to visit Dubuque or Cascade to learn just how great some of the Sox athletes are," Crusinberry wrote from Dubuque. "Manager Rowland is about the biggest fellow in this county, and Red Faber drew a big crowd of his own from Cascade, 30 miles away. Hi Jasper, who is kept in the background, is called by his first name by every fellow he meets on the streets here. Such famed men as Eddie Collins, Ray Schalk and Jack Fournier got nothing more than a wee bit of applause."[16]

The Hugo Brothers circus played in Dubuque the same day, giving locals entertainment options of the three-ring and four-base variety. The city effectively observed a half-day holiday for the various festivities, with shops, factories and railroad offices closing for the day at 2 P.M. Fathers and sons were said to prefer the ballgame, while wives and daughters headed for the circus grounds. However, many folks chose neither because of thunderstorms. At the municipal ball park, weather delayed the first pitch for the better part of an hour, and the contest occurred in alternating rain and sunshine. Though Faber had just pitched two days earlier against the Nationals, Rowland assigned him to work the final three innings. It just would not do to have an exhibition game in Dubuque without an appearance by the Dubuque County native. (Besides, Faber should have been well rested, requiring only the aforementioned 67 pitches to beat Washington.) The pre-game downpour cut attendance to 1,800, just one-fourth the turnout for the previous year's exhibition. As a Dubuque sportswriter quipped, "One thing that rain doesn't make grow — gate receipts!"[17] The precipitation paused long enough for the game to begin, but it resumed during the first inning. Between innings, the Dubuque College brass band presented Faber a college pennant and sweater of his alma mater (when it was called St. Joseph's). Despite the treacherous conditions and the contest's exhibition status, Rowland played his regulars. However, the White Sox took it easy and coasted to a 4–1 victory. The defensive star was Chicago right fielder Shano Collins, who twice robbed Dubuque hitters of clean singles with lightning throws to first base.[18] (The White Sox played another Iowa exhibition on July 8 in Muscatine, where Chicago prevailed in an error-filled contest, 3–2.[19])

By the middle of the 1915 season, Faber was recognized as one of baseball's up-and-comers. F.C. Lane, editor of *Baseball Magazine*, included the major league sophomore among interviewees for an article, "When Pitcher Meets Batter in a Duel of Wits." Apparently through correspondence, Lane quizzed various stars — hitters and pitchers — about whether they try to outguess the other. In a breakout summary of pitchers' quotations accompanying the article, Faber was the third player quoted — after Christy Mathewson and Walter Johnson and before, another future Hall-of-Famer, Ed Walsh. Pretty fast company. Unlike the other three, Faber admitted thinking about what the batter might be thinking. In his reply to Lane, Faber had this to say:

> I try to outguess the batter a good deal of the time. I should say, off hand, about a quarter of the time. I think most pitchers try to outguess the batter at least to some extent, but I can readily understand why the greatest batters don't try to outguess the pitcher. They don't have to. They are so good that they can stand back there and hit any thing that comes. The weaker hitter can't do that. He has to study out what he can expect and hit accordingly. If he is wrong he doesn't hit, but, on the other hand, he wouldn't hit anyway if he didn't try to guess what was coming and guess right a fair share of the time. I can also understand why some pitchers are so good that they don't have to use guesswork at all. Walter Johnson, for instance, burns them over the plate with sheer speed and tries to put them over so fast that they can't be hit. When he is at his best he can do this and he is the only pitcher who can. The batter knows what is coming well enough, but he can't hit it. Such men as Johnson don't need any frills on their work.

Lane said he considered Faber's view "substantially correct."[20]

Americans had more on their minds in 1915 than the length of baseball games. World War I raged in Europe, where hostilities claimed the lives of hundreds of thousands of people, including civilians. News from the Irish coast no doubt gave Faber pause. German torpedoes on May 7 destroyed the RMS *Lusitania*, the British ocean liner upon which he traveled to New York on the final leg of the world tour. About 125 Americans were among the nearly 1,200 passengers to perish aboard the *Lusitania*. The attack stoked simmering anti–German sentiment in the United States. Many Americans treated people, businesses and institutions of German extraction with suspicion if not hostility. In Faber's native Iowa, the state made it illegal for people to speak German in public, and schools were prohibited from teaching in that language. Among the schools affected was Faber's former elementary school, St. Mary's in Cascade, and the public schools in Dubuque dropped the practice of teaching immigrant children in German. Faber, the grandson of Luxemburgian immigrants, spoke German as well as English. In these early years of the war, at least, Faber was not outspoken but made no secret of his allegiances. In 1915, he gave a *Baseball Magazine* interviewer a vigorous argument for the Germans in the European war.[21] There is no evidence that the ballplayer experienced any discrimination or hostile attitudes because of it. He just went out and played baseball.

Though he had broken the record for pitch economy, Faber, as he had proven in the minors, could throw lots of pitches when required. In a May 21 battle against Boston, he pitched the final 10 innings of a 17-inning Chicago victory, allowing just two hits and no walks. "At the finish he appeared able to continue another 10 rounds, if necessary," the *Tribune* reported. Taking in the 3–2 thriller were long-time friends of Comiskey from Dubuque, Dr. William P. and Anna Slattery. The physician told a reporter it was "the greatest game of ball they ever had seen."[22] That a hometown boy pitched it made it even better. On June 24 in Cleveland, Faber entered in the ninth inning of a 4–4 game and almost immediately found himself in a bases-loaded jam. He wriggled out of the predicament to send the game into extra innings. Faber proceeded to pitch the next 10 innings until his teammates pushed across a run in the top of the 19th inning. He shut out the Indians in his 11th inning of work to seal the 5–4 victory. In his afternoon's labors, Faber surrendered just four hits while striking out nine.[23]

Those endurance feats, his second career one-hitter and at least one victory over each American League team put Faber in the White Sox record book.[24] Faber's second career one-hitter came in Boston on September 15, 1915. The hit occurred in the fifth inning, when Tris Speaker shot a single between the shortstop and third baseman in Chicago's 3–1 victory.[25]

The light-hitting Faber, never noted for his foot speed, also found his way into major league history for an offensive exploit in 1915. He stole second, third and home in the same game. However, of the few players to achieve the feat — Ty Cobb has done it the most — none was **less** deserving of honor than Red Faber. What made it even more unusual was that Faber was trying to accomplish just the **opposite**. Thunderstorms threatened Chicago the afternoon of July 14, when the White Sox hosted Connie Mack's Philadelphia Athletics. In the top of the second inning, with the score 2–2, rain halted play for 20 minutes. By the time the White Sox pulled ahead 4–2 after three innings, rain had returned. The precipitation made conditions unpleasant but not severe enough to cancel the contest. At that point, Mack decided his goal was to deny the first-place White Sox a victory — not by outscoring them but by preventing completion of the fifth inning; otherwise, the game would be considered official. His Athletics, convinced that a game-ending deluge was imminent, in the bottom of the fourth inning employed every delaying tactic in Mack's bag of tricks. Mack knew that no matter how many runs the Sox might score in the fourth, all would be erased if rain washed out the game before the Athletics went down in the top of the fifth inning. Rowland realized that too. He instructed his players to quickly put themselves out; he counted on Faber to quickly retire the Athletics in the fifth and seal a rain-shortened victory.

With thunder rumbling in the distance, the game became a farce. The Chicago offense tried to make outs, but the Philadelphia defense would not cooperate. Athletics pitcher Joe Bush tried to walk Lena Blackburne but the Chicago hitter managed to strike out on three wild pitches. One out. Faber, the next batter, did not get a chance to strike out; Bush plunked him in the ribs. Faber's run for the record books then began. He kept on trotting—past first to second, past second to third, and around third to home—all to the Athletics' indifference. As Faber approached third, Bush threw the ball to third baseman Wally Schang, but Schang, with Faber within tagging distance, simply tossed the ball back to the pitcher. Though contemporary scorers would not credit stolen bases under such circumstances, Faber entered the record books as having stolen second, third and home in the same game. For someone so slow to hold a piece of that record underscores the circus-like events of that afternoon. In any case, the White Sox led 5–2.

The bottom of the fourth inning continued with Harry "Nemo" Leibold struggling to strike out. The ridiculous situation grew testy when Bush nearly beaned Buck Weaver, who responded by letting his bat fly in Bush's direction on the next two pitches. Rowland came out to settle down Weaver and remind him of his assignment—to quickly make an out. He nearly failed. Weaver lifted a lazy fly ball to right field and kept running. Outfielder Eddie Murphy let the ball drop. But Philadelphia, apparently threatened with being assessed a forfeit, retired Weaver at third base for the final out of the fourth. Faber retired the Athletics in the fifth. But the game continued. Mack proved to be a better manager than a meteorologist: The anticipated storm skirted Comiskey Park, and the Athletics lost in a full nine innings to Faber and the White Sox, 6–4.

Ten days later, the White Sox did experience postponements, but the reason was tragic. On Saturday morning, July 24, 1915, nearly 2,600 people—Western Electric employees and their families looking forward to a picnic—boarded the excursion steamer *Eastland* at a Chicago River dock. As soon as the *Eastland* cast off, it listed and rolled onto its side, trapping hundreds of men, women and children. The death toll reached 844. Upon hearing of the tragedy, Comiskey postponed that afternoon's home game against the Yankees. He planned to make up the game as a doubleheader the next day, but when the acting mayor asked for all amusements to shut down in respect to the dead, Comiskey complied. Few other Chicago establishments honored the request. Many baseball fans did not know of Comiskey's decision, and they complained when they arrived at the ballpark to find the gates locked.[26] Though make-up of the postponements necessitated five games over three days during the Yankees' next visit to Chicago, the White Sox won four of those games.

Though unable to catch Boston for the 1915 pennant, Rowland's team ended the season on a hot streak. The White Sox finished 13–3, including wins in their final 11 games. Faber pitched the season finale in his league-high

50th appearance. The white-hot White Sox kept on winning in the postseason, taking four out of five from the Cubs for the Chicago City Series title. Faber won the third contest, 5–2, thanks to his teammates' five-run rally in the bottom of the eighth inning.

His sensational sophomore season completed, Faber returned to Cascade for his favorite off-season pursuits. "If the farmers don't bar all of the territory against hunters," the *Cascade Pioneer* said, "the first thing he'll do will be clean up his trusty shotgun and meander afield in search of the festive game products."[27] While hunting and fishing in the Iowa countryside, or traveling to Dubuque to visit friends, he no doubt contemplated the White Sox's prospects for 1916.

10

"Feared by Every Batsman"

Five days before Faber was to meet the White Sox in Chicago and depart for spring training, his friends threw him a farewell bash at his brother Al's pool hall. Two days later, Faber was confined to bed. This was no case of "bottle flu." The diagnosis was tonsillitis, and the subsequent surgery caused Faber to report to spring training a week late and not at full strength.[1] It would not be the only time that illness sidelined him in 1916.

After three springs in California, the White Sox trained in Mineral Wells, Texas, site of their 1911 camp. As the regular season approached, the White Sox were considered contenders — perhaps the favorites — for the American League pennant.[2] Facing top minor league teams in spring exhibitions, the Chicagoans won all 15 contests, further boosting fans' optimism. However, in the season opener, on April 12 in Chicago, Detroit pitcher Harry Coveleski beat the White Sox with his arm and his bat. Meanwhile, owner Charles Comiskey incurred the wrath of thousands of fans. Shortly before the opener, workers applied a fresh coat of green paint to the Comiskey Park chairs and railings. The paint had yet to dry completely when unsuspecting patrons took their seats. Comiskey received numerous bills for garment cleaning.[3]

For the third consecutive season, Faber and Rowland returned "home" when the White Sox played an exhibition game in Dubuque. The previous two years, the Sox played the local minor league team, an entry in the Three-I League. However, Dubuque lost its professional team after 1915, so the White Sox agreed to play Dubuque College (previously St. Joseph's College and today Loras College.) As was the case in 1914 and 1915, the game sparked excitement among fans in Dubuque and the region. Al Faber predicted "all Cascade will be in Dubuque ... if the weather is right." Hundreds of people, many of them students from the college, participated in a parade from the campus to the ballpark. College alumni in Waterloo, 90 miles west, arranged a car caravan. Game organizers announced that, in anticipation of a record crowd, there would not be room for automobile owners to park their vehicles inside the ballpark. The *Dubuque Telegraph-Herald* explained the arrangement: "All cars will be parked outside the fence along Fourth street, where there will be room for several hundred cars and where policemen will guard them."[4] Comiskey and his advance party, which included William K. McKay, the *Chicago Post*'s managing editor, and Howard Mann, the sports editor, arrived in Dubuque about 7 A.M. Meanwhile, the White Sox rode the overnight train from St. Louis to Chicago, and on game day, accompanied by "a bunch of Chicago rooters," stepped off the Illinois Central in Dubuque at 1:40 P.M., less than two hours before the 3:30 contest.[5] The players changed into their uniforms at a nearby hotel (probably the Julien) and proceeded to the ballpark nearby. By prior agreement, the White Sox provided the pitchers and catchers for both teams. (Catcher Ray Schalk was absent, attending his grandfather's funeral back home in Litchfield, Illinois[6]) Local organizers hoped that Faber would see action, but that appeared unlikely earlier in the week when a rainout pushed the spitballer's scheduled start in St. Louis to the afternoon preceding the exhibition. However, the Browns cooperated by knocking Faber from the game in less than three innings, so Rowland penciled in the Dubuque County native to pitch three innings for the college team. Despite rainy weather, the fans turned out — 2,700 or 5,000, depending upon which Dubuque newspaper one believed. "In characteristic fashion Charles A. Comiskey appeared at the park shortly after the game stared, and accompanied by a few friends, lingered at the outskirts of the crowd, endeavoring to keep as far as possible from the spotlight of public attention," the *Dubuque Times-Journal* reported. "He was marked promptly, however, by scores of admirers and soon was surrounded by a host of fans. The band serenaded the Old Roman with several stirring pieces and his car was marked for further attention on the march from the park back to the business district."[7] The professionals, paced by four hits by Eddie Collins and three from Joe Jackson, easily defeated the collegians 8–0. (The *Chicago Tribune* reported a 9–0 score.[8] Perhaps the *Tribune* gave Jack Fournier credit for the home run he deserved. Umpire Ernie Matz was the only person in the ballpark who believed that Fournier's smash over the right-field wall was a foul ball.)

In the bottom of the third inning, as Faber stepped up to bat, the game stopped. Players from both teams gathered around home plate. Cascade mayor J.F. Keefe and five constituents — Faber's brother-in-law E.D. Hogan was among them — presented the pitcher with a bouquet and a gold watch valued at $100.[9] A Chicago sportswriter noted, "Faber was as tickled as the juvenile with his first pair of long trousers."[10] Rowland likewise received a warm reception. "Manager Rowland appears to know everybody here," the *Tribune* reported, "for he spent most of the day and evening shaking hands."[11] A "motion picture camera man" named Orin Stribley shot 300 feet of film at the game and associated festivities. "The pictures are so clear that practically every person in the picture can be recognized without difficulty," the *Telegraph-Herald* said. The film debuted a month later in Dubuque's Dreamland Theater.[12] The players, bushed from all the travel and due to play the next afternoon in Chicago, skipped the post-game banquet honoring Rowland. They ate supper, adjourned to their sleeper car and departed for Chicago at midnight.[13] Instead of attending the banquet, the Old Roman dined at the summer home of Dubuque businessman William Klauer.

Comiskey apparently took a personal liking to Faber, because he named a moose residing in his Wisconsin game preserve after the right-hander. In September 1916, the moose escaped and startled a couple of youthful hunters. When word of the incident reached the Chicago newspapers, headline writers had some fun. One wrote: "Red Faber killed in self-defense."[14] Another teased, "Shoots Red Faber/ Pride of Comiskey!/ Moose, not pitcher."[15]

Meanwhile, war still raged in Europe. The Battle of the Somme spanned the entire baseball season and claimed 1.2 million British, French and German lives. Across the Atlantic, Americans speculated whether their country would — or should — stay out of the fray. (That November, U.S. president Woodrow Wilson won re-election because of his neutrality stand — a position he later abandoned.) Eventually, the war greatly impacted American citizens and institutions — included their beloved baseball.

When the White Sox got off to a slow start in the regular season, observers cited indifferent play. Their malaise continued through the opening third of the campaign, and speculation grew that Comiskey would fire the "busher" Rowland. In a clubhouse meeting, the players resolved to go all out for Rowland, whom they considered their advocate with the frugal Comiskey. Soon after the meeting, the Sox went 11–10 during a doubleheader-heavy road trip. Fourteen of the 21 games on the trip were part of doubleheaders; the Sox *twice* had three straight days of doubleheaders. Finally, the Sox returned to Chicago for a 22-game homestand, during which they opened 11–2, including nine straight wins to climb atop the American League standings. Faber was just returning to action after missing nearly two months with various ailments, including a sore thumb and rheumatism. (Many observers speculated that Faber would not come back at all in 1916.) With the White Sox trailing the Yankees 5–0, Rowland summoned Faber to pitch the ninth inning. After giving up a single, Faber fired a pick-off throw to first baseman Jack Fournier. The infielder was not ready. "Jack didn't see it, but felt it as it bored into his stomach," the *Tribune* noted. Though he "dropped to earth for the count," Fournier stayed in the game.[16] The next day, Faber received his first starting assignment in nearly two months. His six-hit, 6–1 victory over the Athletics launched Chicago's nine-game winning streak. Faber also claimed the final game of the streak August 4 by defeating Walter Johnson

3–2. "Red outpitched the famous Washington hurler," the *Tribune* reported, "though it was a close and hot fight from start to finish." Faber allowed five hits and Johnson seven.[17] However, by the end of the homestand, Rowland's crew was ill and injured, and the White Sox slipped to third place. On September 17, during another long homestand, Faber lost a pivotal game against eventual AL champion Boston; his mound opponent, who claimed his 20th win of the season, was Babe Ruth.

The tension of the pennant race, which at one point involved five teams, produced some particularly bad behavior. By early July, American League president Ban Johnson had suspended several players and managers. Within a one-week span, Detroit's Ty Cobb assaulted a fan in St. Louis and, after a being called out on strikes in Chicago, flung his bat into the Comiskey Park grandstand. His light punishment — three days' suspension and a $25 fine — sparked charges of special treatment. "The [White Sox] players argue that if any one else had tossed a bat into the stands he would have been ruled off for life," *The Sporting News* noted. In one raucous contest, players from Chicago and Cleveland rumbled frequently after repeatedly attempting to spike each other. The period also included some exhibitions of a positive nature. One occurred on Independence Day in Chicago, where Joe Jackson hit an inside-the-park homer, banging his head during his slide at the plate. Knocked out for an instant, Jackson awoke before the fans had stopped hollering its appreciation. The dazed hitter asked, "What are they cheering about?"[18]

Jackson was among the players to speak up for Rowland after their pivotal clubhouse meeting early in the season. "Rowland is the greatest manager I have ever had," he said. "He knows how to get the best results out of a bunch of fellows better than any leader I have ever seen and there is always harmony on his ball club.... He has proved to us fellows that a man doesn't have to have played baseball in the big leagues to manage a major league club."[19] Nonetheless, in mid–August Comiskey convinced the popular Kid Gleason to end his retirement (inspired by a contract dispute) and assist Rowland by coaching on the baselines and working with pitchers and catchers.[20]

In his first assignments after his illness and long layoff, Faber performed inconsistently. However, when he was good, he dominated. Consider the end of his four-hit win over the Tigers in mid–August. "That Faber had a lot of speed and a lot of stuff on the ball was quite evident from the mode of attack of the enemy," the *Tribune* reported. "Even in the ninth inning, with two out, three runs needed to tie and a man on first base, [Ralph] Young attempted to bunt, figuring he had a better chance to reach first that way than by hitting the ball."[21] Sportswriter George S. Robbins noted, "The comeback of Red Faber last week was the biggest boost pennantward the Sox have had this year. This great curve ball artist is feared by every batsman of prowess in the circuit."[22]

White Sox owner Charles Comiskey (left) and Clarence "Pants" Rowland con-
fer before the 1915 season. The Old Roman shocked the baseball world in December 1914 by hiring Rowland, who lacked any major-league experience, as his new
manager. Just a few years earlier, Rowland was a mentor and advocate for Faber.
The so-called "Busher from Dubuque" managed the White Sox to the 1917 World
Series title. Fired after the 1918 season, Rowland remained in baseball throughout his life, including turns as an umpire, scout, minor league executive and
major league general manager. (Chicago Historical Society, ICHi-20773.)

On September 11, Faber registered his 50th career victory — a five-hit-
ter against St. Louis, 5–2. Never known as a strikeout artist, he nonetheless
retired on strikes all three Browns he faced in the fifth inning.[23] His 51st
win — and final victory of the season — came three days later in Comiskey
Park, where he threw a complete game against Washington, 7–5, and brought
the White Sox within a half-game of the American League lead.[24]

In their final 100 games, the Sox went 63–37. Their overall 89–65 was
four games worse than their 1915 mark, despite losing the services of pitchers Faber and Russell and several position players for extended periods.
But they finished second, just two games behind Boston. Their last hope of

catching the Red Sox expired on the last day of the season, when host Cleveland beat Faber 2–0 in the first game of a doubleheader. Despite being inactive nearly two months, Faber appeared in 35 games and posted a 17–9 record with a 2.02 ERA. His .654 winning percentage was fourth in the league and only .003 behind runner-up Ruth.

After falling just short in their bid for the pennant, the White Sox took on the Cubs, who were reinforced with players from the Chicago Whales of the defunct Federal League, in the City Series. The Cubs-Whales squad was no match for the Sox, who swept the series in four games. With his brother, Alfred, in attendance, Faber went the distance to win the second game 3–1. The city title was the sixth straight for the White Sox. The city series would not resume for five years, for reasons both positive and negative.[25]

His season concluded, Red and Alfred Faber roared home to Cascade in the pitcher's new roadster. The car was manufactured by the H. A. Lozier Co.; it probably was the 12-cylinder model.[26] Again, Faber spent the off-season hunting, fishing and socializing. The local newspaper reported the comings and goings of many of its citizens, not just baseball stars. However, the editor took care to report when Faber traveled or played host. The *Pioneer* noted when he took a day trip to Dubuque with George Patterson and when he accompanied his sister Mae Hogan to Chicago, where they spent a couple of weeks with their sister Lucy Dailey. The paper added that, while in the Windy City, Faber also "circulated around the haunts of the White Sox." Though they were later to be cast in separate White Sox cliques, Faber hosted teammate Lefty Williams for a week of hunting and socializing in early January 1917. They probably reflected upon what might have been had Faber and several teammates stayed healthy throughout the 1916 season. "The days were spent hunting the cottontails and nimble squirrels of the region with fine success," the local weekly noted. "Mr. Williams is a splendid and companionable fellow and made many friends while here."[27] The paper did not report on their nocturnal activities, but it is likely that they involved visits to Alfred's pool hall and the Hotel Faber bar. Raising their drinks, they might well have toasted the new year with this vow: The 1917 season would belong to the White Sox.

11

American League Champs

The previous three seasons, major league baseball played under the cloud of the war. Would the war in Europe impact professional baseball? Less than a week before Opening Day 1917, U.S. involvement in the conflict became certain: the United States declared war on Germany. With military enlistments lagging, the government enacted the Selective Service Act of 1917, which made men 21 to 30 years old subject to the draft. The law allowed exemptions for men who had dependent families or physical disabilities or who performed indispensable duties. Organized baseball officials hoped to avoid losing their players to the military while still appearing patriotic. They argued that playing baseball was indispensable for the psyche of fans — hardworking civilians and service personnel alike. The sporting press, similarly interested in self-preservation, promoted that message. "Public turning to it as a relief in these trying times," noted a headline in *The Sporting News*, which reported a huge turnout — more than 10,000 fans — for an August exhibition game featuring the Cubs and Tigers in Toronto, which already had lost many sons and brothers in the Great War. "No better proof that baseball is needed in this country could be had than that game in Toronto," Cubs president Charlie Weeghman said. "Canada is head over heels in the war yet it is turning out to see ball games. That crowd at Toronto was an eye-opener for me." Meanwhile, Comiskey and Ban Johnson, the American League president, separately arranged for thousands of copies of *The Sporting News* to be sent to baseball fans in the military. (In addition, a reader who affixed a 1-cent stamp to his used copy of *The Sporting News* could send it to U.S. servicemen overseas.) "These things are mentioned to show that war is not killing interest in baseball," *Chicago Daily News* sportswriter George S. Robbins wrote in *The Sporting News*. "Rather it makes the hunger for it greater and if these incidents show the trend the great conflict is sowing the seeds for the greatest comeback the game ever knew."[1] Meanwhile, the U.S. military randomly assigned draft numbers and scheduled physical exams for players, most of whom sought exemptions. By mid–August, at least a half-dozen White Sox players had undergone physicals. Pitcher Jim Scott was a willing participant; he applied for officer training school.[2]

Red Faber, unmarried and 28 years old, most likely was an unenthusiastic prospect for the U.S. military. He was of Luxemburgian descent, and German was spoken at home and in his Catholic elementary school. He was not alone. With its significant population of German immigrants, the Americans in the early years of the war found their allegiances divided. Eventually, the U.S. government came to support Great Britain, France and the Allies, and the public and private sectors acted to remove German influences from American society. In the years preceding U.S. involvement in the Great War, Faber did not conceal the side for which he was rooting. *Baseball Magazine*'s John J. Ward stumbled onto that fact in during a 1915 interview. "Personally, Faber is blond, very unassuming, and apparently unambitious. Much of this, no doubt, is due to his easy-going way. The name Faber, so he says, is Latin for Carpenter. It sounded French to me, and as the conversation drifted inevitably toward the great European war, I ventured diplomatically, I thought, to extol the chances of the allies, but I waited in vain for any enthusiastic response from Faber. Instead, after listening to me for some few stolid minutes, he launched out into a vigorous counter argument in favor of the Kaiser. 'I take it Faber is of German extraction,' I suggested. 'Yes,' replied the leading twirler of the American League, and we switched on to less dangerous subjects."[3]

In addition to working on throwing, catching and hitting, major league players in 1917 practiced close-order drills under the supervision of military instructors. Game days took on a militaristic flavor. Pre-game activities included players performing their drills. Toward the end of the season the American League sponsored a competition offering $500 to the best drill team in the league and $100 to its instructor. Though a doormat in baseball, the St. Louis Browns won the pennant for drill.[4] Fans attending the game between Washington and Cleveland saw more than baseball. The players competed in bomb throwing, tossing dummy grenades from home plate to second base — the approximate distance involved in actual hostilities. The judge, an Australian Army instructor, reported that the American baseball players were more adept at the bomb toss than cricket players in England.[5]

Ranked only fourth in drill, the White Sox nonetheless led the American League in baseball most of 1917. Occasionally, Chicago slipped behind Boston, the defending World Series champion. Faber, who missed nearly two months of the 1916 season with rheumatism, suffered a strained shoulder ligament in 1917; he did not start between April 29 and June 22. During his recuperation, Faber's teammates failed to get a hit in two games on consecutive days. On May 5, Ernie Koob of the Browns was belatedly credited with a questionable no-hitter in his 1–0 win. The feat was tainted: The hometown scorer awarded the 24-year-old the no-hitter by switching Buck Weaver's first-inning infield chopper from a hit into an error. The scoring change was so late, morning newspapers around the country reported the game as a one-hitter. The game's only run scored after Swede Risberg failed to catch a pop-up.[6] The next day, in the opener of a doubleheader, the Chicagoans' defensive blunders handed the Browns an 8–4 win. St. Louis' Bob Groom relieved in the final two innings and held the Sox hitless. Manager Fielder Jones decided to start Groom in the second game. The 32-year-old responded by throwing an undisputed no-hitter. Groom walked three and hit a batter in his 3–0 win.[7]

On Saturday, June 16, just before Faber's return to the lineup, the White Sox found themselves engaged in an on-field battle of a different sort. On a drizzly day in Boston, Chicago led 2–0 with two out in the top of the fifth inning. If five innings were completed, the game result would count, even if the balance of the contest were washed out. As the rain picked up — but still not hard enough to halt play — the game was halted briefly while bleacher fans sought refuge under the grandstand roof. They took the most direct route — scurrying across the outfield. Boston gamblers, who lately had come out on the short end, stepped in — literally. "When they saw they were likely to get another trimming and that it might be averted by breaking up the ball game," Chicago sportswriter Jim Crusinberry reported, "they incited the fans to riot." The first interruption featured about 500 people swarming from the gamblers' section in the right field pavilion. They streamed onto the outfield and walked to the edge of the diamond. That interruption ended peacefully after the umpires and Boston player-manager Jack Barry informed the intruders that if play did not resume, the game would be declared a Chicago victory by forfeit. However, gamblers soon incited another wave of trespassers to storm the field, and this time they were riotous. As undermanned and overmatched police officers went through the motions of attempting to clear the field, Boston and Chicago players headed for their clubhouses. While making his exit, Ray Schalk gave the head of the police detail an earful, and teammates Buck Weaver and Fred McMullin slugged some spectators. After a delay of 45 minutes, sawdust was spread over the soggy infield and the game was played to completion. Chicago's four-run rally in the ninth inning sealed a 7–2 victory.[8] "The situation in Boston has been a scandal on which the lid has been kept long enough," Robbins fumed in *The Sporting News*. "When a horde of gamblers, permitted to run riot in a major league ball park, seek to stop a ball game, and urge hoodlums to attack visiting players to save their dirty coin. . . ." Referring to problems at National League games in Boston, Robbins added, "If this had been the first time that gamblers had staged a disturbance in a Boston park, the club management might have some excuse for saying it was unexpected, but it was not the first time, not by several years."[9] The White Sox, who won despite the mayhem in Boston, showed they had the mettle to battle their way to the World Series. On August 18, they took first place for keeps.

Faber was not consistently dominant when he returned. In the morning game of a Labor Day doubleheader, the visiting Tigers roughed him up for 11 hits in 4⅔ innings. Chicago scored three unanswered runs late to win, 7–5. That afternoon, manager Pants Rowland started Faber again. "I still believed Faber good enough to work," Rowland explained years later.[10] However, the right-hander was no better in the afternoon. He retired only one batter in the Tigers' four-run second inning. However, the White Sox rallied again, posting a 14–8 victory. Rowland still stuck with Faber. He started him in St. Louis the next day, and this time Faber won. (Since 1900, only seven major league pitchers started three consecutive games. Faber was the last to do it,

Red Faber in 1917, the year the Chicago White Sox became world champions. The 29-year-old Faber won the American League pennant-clinching game against Boston; the contest ended on pinch-hitter Babe Ruth's groundout. Though he was not the White Sox' top pitcher during the regular season (16–13), Faber emerged as the pitching star of the World Series by winning a record three games (and losing one) against the New York Giants. (Courtesy of the Tri-County Historical Society, Cascade, Iowa.)

and the only one to start three games in two days.[11])

The doubleheader sweep over Detroit was Chicago's second in two days. Those four victories, coupled with two Boston losses to New York on Labor Day, gave the White Sox a six-game lead over the Red Sox. September 19–20, Detroit helped douse Boston's hopes of catching the White Sox by winning three straight games — the last two by identical 1–0 scores. The losses dropped the Red Sox nine games behind the White Sox, who came to Boston the next day needing only one more victory to clinch the American League pennant. According to some accounts, Chicago players had already discussed collecting money for the Detroit players. In the final days of September, with a slice of the World Series pot assured to the White Sox, Arnold "Chick" Gandil collected $45 from every teammate but one. Buck Weaver did not contribute but said he would send his third-base counterpart Oscar Vitt a Christmas present, Gandil said.[12] "Some of the fellows didn't have this cash with them, and I told Red Faber that I didn't have the money but had promises for all," Gandil stated years later. "So Red gave me a check for $500 to cover the money that had been promised but was not paid. He cashed the check himself in the Ansonia hotel [in New York] and gave me the money in currency."[13] This story first came to light in May 1922, courtesy of Oscar "Happy" Felsch, then banned from the game as a Black Sox conspirator. Felsch said the money was a payoff to Tiger pitchers for "laying down" in the back-to-back doubleheaders Labor Day weekend. Faber, Ray Schalk and Eddie Collins issued a statement that the money was a "present" to thank the Tigers for dousing Boston's pennant hopes by winning three from the Red Sox September 19–20.[14] The incident resurfaced nearly five years later when two other Black Sox defendants, Risberg and Gandil, renewed the claim that the White Sox paid Detroit to throw four consecutive games. In January 1927, Commissioner Kenesaw Mountain Landis, already investigating gambling allegations involving stars Ty Cobb and Tris Speaker, conducted hearings on the claims by Risberg and Gandil. Landis made it clear that he put the word of Faber, Rowland and other "Clean Sox" above that of the banished players. However, the commissioner also let it be known that any such "reward" pools would not be tolerated.

In any case, Chicago won five straight games after Labor Day to extend its victory streak to nine. The eighth win in the streak came on a forfeit. With the game tied 3–3 in the tenth inning and darkness looming, umpire Brick Owens, having already warned the argumentative Indians about their time-wasting tactics, awarded the game to the White Sox. The last straw was Cleveland catcher Steve O'Neill demonstrating his disgust with an Owens decision by hurling the ball into left field.[15]

On September 21, only the host Red Sox stood between the White Sox and the victory required to clinch the pennant. Through nine innings, the Bostonians, with Dutch Leonard on the mound, made it clear that they would not roll over against Red Faber and Chicago. In the top of the 10th inning, the White Sox pulled ahead, 2–1. After retiring the leadoff hitter on an infield pop-up, however, Faber gave up consecutive singles. With the potential tying run on third and winning run on first, the Red Sox sent up a pinch hitter — star pitcher Babe Ruth. Respectful of Ruth's power, the White Sox infield played back, effectively conceding the tying run, should Ruth hit a slow roller. Ruth ripped a grounder toward second base. Eddie Collins snagged the ball and tossed it to Buck Weaver, who fired the relay throw to first baseman Gandil. The ball slapped into Gandil's glove barely ahead of the hard-charging Ruth. With that, the White Sox owned the American League pennant.

Comiskey did not make the trip to Boston to see his team clinch the pennant. He received the news over a special telephone line; telegraph reports would not be fast enough to suit him.[16] The owner spent freely on himself and cronies, but he had a reputation as a skinflint toward his players. When the team traveled, he paid them only $3 a day toward meals when nearly all major league teams paid $4. Comiskey's usual strategy in contract "negotiations" was, "Take it or leave it." During the 1917 pennant race, Comiskey promised his players a bonus for an American League championship. When they succeeded, Comiskey's "bonus" was a case of champagne for the victory party.[17]

Faber's regular-season record was a modest 16–13, but his earned-run average was a stellar 1.92. That figure masked his teammates' defensive negligence. Forty-two percent of the 92 runs opponents scored off Faber were unearned — making him the worst-supported starter in the major leagues.[18] Faber won the pennant-clinching game, but he would play a bigger role in the 1917 World Series, facing John McGraw's New York Giants, the team for which he was a "loaner" during the 1913–14 world tour.

12

World Series Hero

Baseball fever gripped Chicago. The Auditorium, Dexter and Coliseum theaters erected electronic scoreboards. Featuring light bulbs illuminated on a baseball field diagram and, in some cases, facsimiles of players, the boards simulated the positions of base runners and recorded balls, strikes and outs. Patrons paid from 50 cents to $1 for a ticket — almost as much as a bleacher ticket to the game itself. These scoreboards were common in the days before radio and television broadcasts of the Fall Classic. In Dubuque, fans paid 25 cents each to watch the scoreboard in the Grand Theater. Proceeds were divided among the Knights of Columbus and two Dubuque newspapers, which donated the proceeds to servicemen.[1] In Cascade, locals gathered in the railroad depot, outside the telegraph office, to hear the translation of Morse code clicks and follow the progress of their local hero.[2] The Associated Press provided virtually "real time" reports. Using its longest continuous circuit ever, the AP connected some 600 newspapers directly with Comiskey Park. "'Ball One' or 'Strike One' was known to each and every one of them before the echo of the umpire's voice had died out or the catcher had returned the ball to the pitcher," *The Sporting News* explained.[3]

In the pre-dawn hours outside the hastily expanded Comiskey Park, hundreds of fans queued outside the ticket windows. Some men built fires to ward off the autumn chill. Later that Saturday morning, the line of fans extended for blocks. Men sitting on crates passed the time by playing poker and speculating about that afternoon's game. Inside the ballpark, some 32,000 fans, including a large contingent from Cascade, roared when the White Sox emerged for pre-game practice. The players wore new uniforms. In recognition of U.S. participation in the war and the wave of patriotism, the uniforms were trimmed in red, white and blue.[4]

In Game 1, Chicago's top pitcher in the regular season, Eddie Cicotte

(28–12), continued his dominance in the post-season. He limited the Giants to seven hits and outpitched lefty Harry "Slim" Sallee 2–1.

Before Game 2, Rowland picked Faber as his starting pitcher after observing the sore-armed Reb Russell struggle during warm-up. George Burns, the New York leadoff hitter, tried to trick his way to first base. He ducked away from Faber's third pitch and came away holding his wrist. The raucous fans, who were riding the visiting Giants from the start, weren't buying it. Neither was umpire Billy Evans. Burns stepped back in into the batter's box and rapped out a single.[5] In his first couple of plate appearances, Faber tried a little trickery of his own. A natural left-handed batter who rarely switch-hit, he surprised the Giants by batting right-handed a couple of times against the Giants' left-handers. He coaxed a walk from southpaw Ferdie Schupp in the second inning but fouled out in the fourth against righty Fred Anderson. Faber displayed his own moments of distraction during the contest. His failure to back up outfielder Joe Jackson's throw home contributed to a Giants run; Jackson's throw eluded catcher Ray Schalk. Faber made up for that with a spectacular play in the third inning, when he grabbed Benny Kauff's weak roller and dove to touch first base an instant ahead of the diving Kauff.[6] However, Faber's most memorable mental lapse occurred on the basepath. With two out in the bottom of the fifth inning and teammate Buck Weaver on second base, the light-hitting Faber — this time, he batted left-handed — connected against Pol Perritt for a clean single to right field and took second base when outfielder Dave Robertson threw to the plate. Somehow, Faber failed to notice that coach Kid Gleason had stopped Weaver at third base. Faber didn't consider the possibility that Weaver would not score from second on an outfield single. Standing on second, Faber did not notice Weaver leading off from third. "Somewhere in my frenzied flight I caught a glimpse of Weaver rounding third and as I reached second safely I supposed he had scored," Faber explained. "True, I didn't look toward third to see if he was there. I didn't need to. I *knew* that he had scored."[7] Rowland had instructed his White Sox to "run wild" against Perritt, the third Giants pitcher. Faber was shocked when Perritt went into a full wind-up to Nemo Leibold. "Now, I don't claim to be a world-beater in speed," Faber wrote later, "but any dub can steal third when the pitcher starts to wind up." Except when third base is occupied by a teammate. Faber, thinking Perritt was committing a "bone head play," took off to steal third base. He slid into the bag — and his teammate Weaver. The Giants' Heinie Zimmerman, bemused by the proceedings, tagged both Chicagoans, and Faber was the one adjudged the final out of the inning. "I am not much of a wisecracker," Faber said, "but when I went into third Weaver yelled, 'Where the hell are you going!?' And I replied: 'I'm goin' to pitch.'"[8]

Faber's gaffe would have been less amusing for the Chicago side had the

White Sox not held a 7–2 lead, thanks to a five-run rally the previous inning. Neither team scored after that, and Chicago grabbed a 2–0 Series advantage. The newspapers credited Faber with a well-pitched game, but they also had a great deal of fun at Faber's expense over the attempted steal of an occupied base. But that did not faze him. "Red Faber has a disposition that no amount of kidding can spoil," his hometown newspaper stated, "and no laugh will be as hearty as his own."[9]

After a one-day postponement due to rain, the White Sox and Giants squared off for Game 3 on October 10 in the Polo Grounds. Did the extra day of rest help the Giants regain their confidence after two straight losses? Did it allow the White Sox to cool off? How would it affect the betting line? (Newspapers in this period routinely referred to the presence of gamblers in the stands; the World Series was no exception. Gamblers were known to plant false reports about injuries, managerial changes and even train wrecks, all in an attempt to sway the betting line.) In any case, Giants left-hander Rube Benton allowed White Sox batters just five hits and outdueled Game 1 winner Cicotte 2–0.

Game 4 the next day pitted the Game 2 starters, Faber and Schupp, the Giants lefty who four days earlier could not survive two innings. In their rematch, however, Schupp scattered seven hits to shut out Chicago 5–0. In his seven innings on the mound, Faber gave up seven hits, including a Benny Kauff shot that was scored as an inside-the-park home run after White Sox outfielder Happy Felsch repeatedly fumbled the ball while trying to retrieve it from under a tarp.[10] Not only had the White Sox squandered their two-game Series advantage by losing shutouts on consecutive days in New York, they also lost momentum and confidence. With the World Series now tied 2–2, team owners Comiskey and Harry Hempstead participated in a coin toss to decide the Game 7 site, if the game became necessary. Comiskey called it wrong, but then boasted that New York would not need to host a seventh game because his White Sox would win the Series in six.

Snow flurried over Chicago on the teams' travel day, and the weather remained gray and raw the afternoon of October 13, when the players took the field for Game 5. Ticket scalpers, who a week earlier commanded the astounding sum of $10 (worth more than $152 in 2005) for a Comiskey Park grandstand seat, had trouble unloading their wares for $2.[11] Emotions ran high in the stands and on the field. Play turned rough on a couple of occasions, and the men in uniform nearly came to blows. As they did in the first two games, the Chicago faithful at every turn hooted and taunted the Giants, particularly Heinie Zimmerman. At the time, such behavior by a World Series crowd was considered unusual. "There was more personal ill-feeling started in these games than in any past world series," a *Chicago Daily Journal* reporter observed.[12] *The New York Times* absolved Giants fans of bad behavior but did acknowledge that Chicago's Eddie Collins was the locals' target.[13] Bench jock-eying and epithets flowed freely, with Artie Fletcher taking a leading role for the Giants. Zimmerman targeted Faber. "He'd started to ride me right from the start," the pitcher recalled years later. "He'd tell me I didn't have a thing. And I'd tell him what a great hitter he was."[14] (Zimmerman did not get a hit off Faber the entire series.) Rowland's decision to start sore-armed pitcher Reb Russell was, in the manager's own words, "a lousy guess."[15] Russell failed to retire the three Giants he faced, giving up a walk and two hits. The Giants scored once and had a runner on third base when Rowland pulled Russell in favor of Cicotte. The Giants scored once more, but they missed their chance to break the game open. Twice in the first, White Sox infielders gloved Giants grounders and threw out base runners at the plate. In his third appearance of the Series, Cicotte pitched through the sixth inning; after 5½ innings New York led 4–1. When the Sox scored a run in the third inning, they ended 24 straight innings of offensive failure against McGraw's lefties.

The turning point of the game and, according to many sportswriters, the entire World Series occurred in the bottom of the sixth, when dirty play by Giants infielders Artie Fletcher and Buck Herzog stirred the White Sox from their doldrums. With Weaver on first, Ray Schalk singled to the outfield. Herzog, the second baseman, and Fletcher, the shortstop, impeded Weaver's dash from first base to third. Weaver wrestled his way to third safely, but Rowland, coaching at first base, argued for Weaver to be awarded home. The umpires disagreed, deciding that, even without interference, Weaver could not have advanced three bases on Schalk's single. Weaver later scored anyway, on pinch hitter Swede Risberg's single. But New York still led 4–2.

In the top of the seventh, Chicago's Claude "Lefty" Williams took the mound and found himself in a jam immediately. He escaped after yielding only one run but now the Giants held a 5–2 lead. In the bottom of the seventh, the White Sox staged a three-run rally against starter Slim Sallee, sparked by a Chick Gandil double, to forge a 5–5 tie. The hometown fans went into frenzy. "Wild demonstrations have been seen in previous World's Series, but nothing ever beat that one at Comiskey Park," reported sportswriter William G. Weart. "So terrific was the din that reporters in the scorers' boxes who were describing the plays over special wires had to yell into the ears of the operators and the operators had to put their ears down on their keys to make sure that they were sending the words correctly. It was a baseball crowd gone fairly mad with joy."[16] Chicago pinch hitter Byrd Lynn fanned to end the seventh inning, and as the teams changed sides, Rowland confronted Fletcher. It took the intervention of first base umpire Bill Klem to keep the Chicago manager and New York shortstop from coming to blows.[17] Comiskey Park still buzzed as Faber took the mound for the top of the eighth in the tie game.

After striking out Herzog on three pitches, Faber fielded Benny Kauff's comebacker. As Faber tossed the ball to first baseman Gandil, the crowd's roar intensified. The volume increased further as Chicago fans' favorite target, Zimmerman, stepped to the plate. After working Faber deep into the count, Zimmerman flew out to Shano Collins for the third out of the eighth. Faber's performance added fuel to Chicago's fire, and White Sox hitters resumed their rally. New York boosters criticized Manager John McGraw for not pulling starter Sallee sooner, but pitching was not the Giants' only problem in the inning. Zimmerman's throwing error contributed to another three-run rally by the White Sox, who took an 8–5 lead into the ninth.

Faber had a three-run cushion, but he didn't need it. Two groundouts sandwiching a fly ball to Joe Jackson ended the game and gave Chicago a 3–2 Series lead. Faber received credit for his second victory of the Series. The players boarded their trains for New York and Game 6. On the way, Rowland and coach Kid Gleason asked Faber whether he could pitch the next afternoon. "Heck, I never heard of anybody refusing to pitch unless they knew something was wrong with 'em and they couldn't help the ball club," Faber said years later. "I'd rather be pitching than sittin' on the bench. There was always more of a strain for me on the bench than pitching, especially in a tight spot. I was pitching every ball anyway — at least, figuring what I would do just then."[18]

While Game 5 in Chicago was played in near-wintry conditions, the weather for Game 6 in New York had a scent of summer, featuring bright sunshine and temperatures in the mid–60s. In the top of the fourth, Chicago jumped to a 3–0 lead, thanks to one of the oddest plays in World Series history. Again, New York third baseman Zimmerman played the role of the goat. The inning opened with Zimmerman fielding Eddie Collins' grounder and throwing the ball to the stands, permitting Collins to advance to second. Joe Jackson lifted a fly ball that right fielder Dave Robertson dropped. Collins moved up to third while Jackson stopped at first. The Giants infield moved in, hoping to hold Collins at third while executing a double play. "Collins' strategy was to break for home to compel a throw," Rowland recalled. "That would leave men on first and second with just one out instead of two men out and a man on third." Happy Felsch hit a comebacker to pitcher Rube Benton, who ran at the trapped Collins. Meanwhile, Collins motioned for teammates Jackson and Felsch to advance while he tried to postpone being tagged out. As Collins moved toward third base, Benton tossed the ball to his third baseman, Zimmerman. Collins changed directions and dashed for home. Instead of throwing ahead to the plate, Zimmerman engaged in hot pursuit of Collins. The Chicago base runner won the race to score the game's first run. Many observers blamed Zimmerman for overestimating his speed and underestimating that of Collins. The New York fans were clearly angered.[19] However, others pointed out that during the rundown catcher Bill

Rariden had moved up the baseline and left the plate unattended. That is how Zimmerman saw it: "Who the hell was I going to throw the ball to? Klem [the umpire]?"[20] *Chicago Herald* sportswriter G.W. Axelson agreed, as did Faber: "It wasn't Zim's fault — it was the catcher and first basemen who were to blame," Faber said years later. "Neither of them covered the plate; Heinie didn't have anybody to throw the ball to; so all he could was try to catch Eddie, and he couldn't do it."[21] Rowland, however, said Zimmerman called off Rariden, shouting, "Get out of the way, I'll get the blankey-blank myself."[22]

The next batter, Gandil, scored Jackson and Felsch but was thrown out trying to stretch his single. Though the Sox continued to threaten — Schalk singled and Faber walked — they finished the fourth inning with a 3–0 lead.

Faber, who had given up just three hits over the first four innings, remained in command. He opened the fifth inning in dominating fashion, striking out No. 7 hitter Walter Holke on three pitches. However, the next batter, Rariden, coaxed a walk, and then pinch hitter Joe Wilhoit did the same. Suddenly, Faber appeared vulnerable. After an infield force-out, New York closed the gap to 3–2 when Buck Herzog cracked a low line-drive to right field, where outfielder Shano Collins missed his attempted diving catch. The ball rolled to the fence for a triple. "I was so mad [at Collins], I couldn't see," said Faber, who nonetheless held the Giants in check. After three scoreless innings, Chicago scored in the top of the ninth to make it 4–2. However, the Giants refused to concede anything. In the ninth inning, New York shortstop Artie Fletcher kept it personal, spitting at Rowland. The 38-year-old Chicago manager challenged 32-year-old Fletcher to a fight after the game.

Faber was in command before and after the fifth inning, but he did permit the Giants and their fans one last hope. The first batter in the bottom of the ninth, Dave Robertson, was credited with being hit by a pitch after appearing to hit it foul. "The crack of the bat was heard all over the stand," Chicago sportswriter G.W. Axelson reported. "Davy claimed he had his finger in between, and after [umpire] Bill Klem had called it a foul he reversed himself and sent the batter to first." Robertson suffered a broken finger. "He showed it to me years later," Faber said. "It was all smashed up." The potential game-tying run stepped into the batter's box. However, the next three Giants never rapped the ball out of the infield. With two out, pinch hitter Lew McCarthy ripped a grounder to second baseman Eddie Collins. The future Hall-of-Famer made certain of his catch before flipping the ball to first baseman Gandil for the final out of the 1917 World Series. Decades later, and perhaps forgetting the walks and hit batsman, Rowland described Faber's game as the best pitching performance he had ever seen. "Red never wasted a single pitch. He had beautiful control and was hitting the corners with both his fast one and curves."[23]

The Chicago White Sox were the World Series champions!

It was their first title since the "Hitless Wonders" beat the Cubs in 1906, and it would be their last until 2005. The Associated Press and telegraphic wires flashed the news to cities and towns all across the country, including Cascade, Red Faber's hometown, and Dubuque, which promoted its connection to three White Sox principals. "Not to celebrate would have meant that the three ringleaders in conducting the event — Charles Comiskey, Clarence Rowland and Urban Faber, former citizens of this city — had been ignored," a Dubuque newspaper stated, adding that there was another reason for celebration. "The outcome of the series caused thousands of dollars to change hands, hundreds of Dubuquers being enriched, temporarily at least, while the Giant contingent vows that the American eagle is a migratory bird."[24]

Back at the Polo Grounds, the White Sox and Giants worked their way through the stunned New York fans to their clubhouses. (No security lines of ushers and police were considered necessary in 1917.) Rowland did not get his fight with Fletcher, whose gentle off-field persona contrasted sharply with his hard-edged manner between the lines. A Chicago newspaper reported that Fletcher was "the first man to the clubhouse and the last man out."[25] McGraw located Faber, the pitcher he tried to acquire three years earlier, to congratulate him. "It was a hearty sincere handshake," *The New York Times* reported, recounting how Faber was loaned to McGraw for the international leg of the 1913–14 world tour. "The Giants manager took a great liking to Red. He taught him many tricks and gave him good advice," The *Times* continued. "Little did McGraw think at that time that one day this same awkward Red Faber would beat his Giants out of a world's championship." How did McGraw respond afterward to his managerial counterpart, Rowland? The same *New York Times* article had McGraw pushing through the crowd to find and congratulate Rowland. "There were tears of happiness in Rowland's eyes as McGraw grasped his hand, and he was happier still when McGraw told him he had won with as game and fair a team as he had ever played against."[26] *The Sporting News* had a similar account.[27] The *Chicago Herald* likewise reported that McGraw rushed over to congratulate Rowland.[28] Those accounts differ greatly from that in a McGraw biography published three decades later. Biographer Frank Graham stated that it was Rowland who found McGraw, and Rowland who attempted to shake the legendary manager's hand. "Mr. McGraw, I'm glad we won, but I'm sorry you had to be the one to lose." In Graham's account of the exchange, McGraw snarled, "Get away from me, you _____ busher!"[29]

The "busher" label lost credence after Rowland's teams just missed the pennant in 1916 and then won it all in 1917. After the first two games, *The Sporting News* featured Rowland on its front page. Under the headline, "SO HE'S A BUSHER, IS HE?" and a two-column portrait of Rowland, *The*

Sporting News reported that "experts" observed that Rowland, in his handling of the White Sox, had "outgenerated" McGraw and had silenced the naysayers.[30] Harvey Woodruff of the *Chicago Tribune* recalled a 1915 conversation with Rowland, who said, "I am a bush leaguer. It's no disgrace. But if you call me a bush leaguer at the end of 1916 ... I might regard it as a reflection."[31]

A pocket watch commemorates the 1917 Chicago White Sox, winners of the 1917 World Series. Red Faber, the pitching star of the series, appears in the 11 o'clock position. (Chicago Historical Society, *Chicago Daily News* collection SDN-061301.)

Nonetheless, there remained whispers that White Sox players put more faith in veteran coach Kid Gleason and that he was really the one responsible for Chicago's success.

However, there was no disputing the 29-year-old Faber's role in the White Sox's success. On its front page, under a two-column photo of Faber warming up, *The Sporting News* declared, "Taking the whole Series and comparing the work of the pitchers, Faber was THE pitcher of the Series."[32] *Baseball Magazine*'s William A. Phelon concurred.[33] *The New York Times* added: "Upon Red Faber was showered all the admiration for carrying the White Sox through. It was this massive country lad from Cascade, Iowa, who proved to be the salvation of Rowland's pitching staff instead of Eddie Cicotte...." The Chicago papers, as expected, were effusive. "Faber won the pennant in Boston for his mates. He won the world's championship today," the *Herald*'s Axelson wrote. "They should at least name the town pump for him at Cascade, for he came back purely on his nerve after his wild spell in the fifth."[34] James Crusinberry, the *Chicago Tribune* writer, said of his fellow Cascade native, "It was a great victory for Cascade, Dubuque and Chicago, and Red Faber is one of the big heroes of the champions tonight, for he was credited for three victories in a world's series. As a matter of fact, it seems that no one is a bigger hero than Faber, now that it is all over. Even though he was defeated in one game and even though he pulled the biggest boner of world's series history in stealing third when third was occupied, there is no one on the team deserving of more credit for the factory than the redhead from Cascade."[35]

The World Series was lucrative for Faber. Reports on the size of a winner's share ranged from $3,528.13 to $3,929.72.[36] A baseball web site set the figure at $3,669. Whatever the amount, it represented roughly half a season's salary. In 2005 dollars, his share was worth more than $62,000. Contrast that with the 2005 White Sox, whose winning share was $324,532.72.[37]

The end of the World Series was not the end of the 1917 baseball season for the White Sox and Giants. The day after the World Series ended, the combatants played an exhibition game in Garden City, New Jersey, before 6,000 U.S. soldiers, most of them from New York and Illinois.[38] The White Sox won 6–4, then boarded their train for Chicago, where a tumultuous welcome awaited them. The pitching hero, Red Faber, missed the whole thing.

13

The Lost Season

As the rest of the White Sox attempted to sober up for their post–World Series exhibition against the Giants — their championship celebration brought "bedlam" to New York's Biltmore Hotel — Urban "Red" Faber boarded the New York Central's 20th Century Limited.[1] His services would not be required in the exhibition, a Great War benefit for U.S. military personnel, and he was anxious to get to the Pacific Northwest for hunting season.

By passing through Chicago a day ahead of his teammates, the modest star avoided the pandemonium when the team made its triumphant return to the Windy City. An estimated 5,000 White Sox fans broke through police lines outside the LaSalle Street station to mob their heroes as they disembarked from the train. A brass band from the Naval Reserve added to the festivities. The first to step onto the platform was manager Pants Rowland, who was hoisted on fans' shoulders and paraded into the street. "From track to track and for almost the entire length of the train shed it was one joyous, hand-grabbing mob, bent on making the homecoming one which would make New York jealous," the *Chicago Herald* reported. "Dodging Polo Grounds mobs was nothing compared to the gauntlet which the returning Hose were compelled to run before they got into their taxis."[2] The horde brought traffic outside the station to a standstill for about 20 minutes.

Faber's welcoming committee in Iowa was smaller, but that was no reflection on the level of excitement and local interest. All the previous day, Illinois Central Railroad ticket agents in Dubuque fielded inquiries about the itinerary of one particular passenger. "Everybody wanted to know when 'Red' Faber was coming, who was coming with him, and how long he was going to stay," a Dubuque newspaper reported. "The phone was busy all day but the limit was reached when some nocturnal individual called the night agent from his cozy cot at 3:30 in the morning and wanted to know 'if Faber was in yet.'" The baseball star arrived shortly before 7 A.M. "He was met at the station by a good-sized crowd of fans and friends, but nothing compared to the large throngs that would have greeted him had he arrived at a later hour." He was accompanied by two friends who were on hand to see his heroics in New York, former Cascade area resident Fritz Moes, of Pilot Rock, Oregon, and William P. Slattery, a Dubuque physician and leading baseball enthusiast. Faber told a Dubuque reporter he felt "never better," but added, "I'm a little tired, and I'm going to take a long sleep." He enjoyed breakfast with a few friends before his brother, Al, drove him to Cascade. After a few hours at home, Faber returned to Dubuque. At 10:30 P.M., he and Moes boarded a train for Oregon and a hunting trip.[3]

The World Series star stayed in the Pacific Northwest nearly two months, during which time he bagged two trophy deer in the Blue Mountains.[4] This probably was the excursion he described as his most memorable hunting trip. *Baseball Magazine* interviewed various stars for its series, "The Greatest Hunting Trip I Ever Had." The article was written in Faber's "own words" by a magazine staffer. Faber admitted that he was not much of a "cave man" when it came to roughing it. "I don't mind climbing mountains or roaming all day through brush woods," he said, "but neither do I object to a stone fireplace and a blanketed bunk under a roof at night." Faber referred to bagging a couple of deer — "one of them a really magnificent head that I consider my very best trophy." He also bagged his quota of coyotes, and intended to have a fur rug made. "I made a poor job of skinning the animals, and when the pelts were delivered to a taxidermist, he pronounced them unfit for use. That, however, was only a minor disappointment." What also made the trip memorable was a blizzard. "Three days that storm raged, and when it cleared, you could not have recognized the landscape. It was one blanket of white," Faber said. "The snow, I should judge, was nearly three feet deep on the level, only there wasn't any level. There were huge drifts and hollows." To reach town several miles away, they had to dig out and push their snow-choked car down the mountain road. After struggling in that fashion for four miles, "we were forced to abandon the undertaking and confess that we had bitten off rather more than we could chew." Fortunately, the weather took a positive turn, providing warm Chinook winds that made quick work of the snow. "What had been impassable drifts became only smooth patches of snow into which you would sink a little above your ankles," he recalled. The party was able to drive the rest of the way into town. "The big game hunter who likes a thrill of danger will find none in this little exercise," Faber concluded. "Perhaps in the simple way I have told it, it will not seem very interesting to anyone. But it lingers in my recollection as the most enjoyable trip I have ever made."[5]

Soon after returning to Cascade, Faber received his World Series championship award: a button of solid gold about three-fourths of an inch in diameter, with a diamond in the center. On the front was inscribed "World's Champions, 1917." Faber's name was etched on the back. "It is a beauty," the Cascade paper noted, "and the champion is proud of the decoration."[6]

While Faber avoided the limelight, his manager spent the off-season in it. Rowland contracted to appear in vaudeville, where his "act" consisted of a monologue about baseball. He made his vaudeville debut at the Majestic (now Five Flags) in Dubuque. He was warmly received by full houses all four days in his hometown. Rowland's schedule included dates in Cedar Rapids, Iowa; Peoria, Illinois; Moline, Illinois; Chicago; Cleveland; and several Eastern cities.[7]

One January day, after a heavy snowstorm, Faber drove toward Dubuque. Bursting through snowdrifts, his Lozier roadster broke down. The car wound up buried in a huge drift near the Peter Johnson farm. Faber and friend George Patterson spent many hours trying to dig out the car. It was futile. It was April before the roadster was towed into town, and Faber had been at spring training nearly a month.

While Faber, Rowland and other baseball men engaged in their off-season diversions, other Americans engaged in the Great War. Despite the close-order drills, donation of gate proceeds toward war relief and patriotic trim on uniforms, professional baseball felt the pressure to do more toward the war effort. It had already lost a few players to military service during the 1917 season, some through the draft and some through enlistment. Pitcher Jim Scott abruptly left the White Sox in September, during the pennant drive, when the Army accepted his application for officer training. His teammates shared with Scott a portion of the post-season proceeds.[8]

As U.S. involvement in European combat increased, the 29-year-old Faber was among the baseball stars that sportswriters identified as likely candidates for conscription. "The Sox are reasonably certain to lose Red Faber," George S. Robbins reported in November 1917. "Red is single, able-bodied and escaped the first draft for the simple reason that his number was up in the thousands instead of 500 or lower."[9] The status of hundreds of players depended on whether the U.S. government viewed baseball as essential during wartime. With military service looming, Faber nonetheless reported to the White Sox's 1918 spring training camp in Mineral Wells, Texas. Despite being roughed up in relief against the lowly St. Louis Browns in the season opener — two hits in just one-third of an inning in a no-decision — Faber was impressive in his fifth major league season. He built a 3–0 record. Later, in a relief appearance, he pitched the final seven innings of a 6–4 victory but, according to the scoring rules of the day, credit for the win went to starter Joe Benz.

Faber's prospects for completing the season in a White Sox uniform changed significantly May 22, 1918, when Gen. Enoch H. Crowder, provost marshal general, announced a work-or-fight amendment to the Selective Service regulations: effective July 1, every man of draft age had to be in the military or engaged in some occupation useful to the war effort. (Faber's brother, Alfred, 25 and married, opted for the latter by taking a job at the arsenal in Rock Island, Illinois.[10]) Crowder postponed a decision on how his order affected professional athletes. Secretary of War Newton Baker exempted theatrical performers, and baseball officials hoped for similar consideration.[11] August Herrmann, chairman of baseball's national commission, walking the tightrope between patriotism and professional interest, made the case that baseball, like theater, was entertainment vital to Americans. He said that if Crowder's order held, major league teams would lose 258 of their 369 players.[12] American League president Ban Johnson professed amazement that the government might consider baseball non-essential. "I cannot understand that statement [by Crowder] the game is nonproductive when the two major leagues will deliver to the Government a war tax in the neighborhood of $300,000," Johnson said. "The ball players, umpires, club stockholders and officials have bought more than $8 million of Liberty bonds and have subscribed thousands upon thousands of dollars for the Red Cross and other war charities. Where is there another class of men earning so much for the government?"[13]

Faber, with an A-1 draft classification, did not wait to see how it all played out. On June 7, the American League's leading pitcher enlisted as a chief yeoman in the U.S. Navy. The next day he briefly visited family and friends in Cascade. "He did not desire to be drafted," the Cascade newspaper reported. "His number was likely to be called very soon, hence his decision in resigning his position on the pitching staff of the White Sox."[14] Before turning in his White Sox uniform, however, Faber took two more turns on the mound. On June 11, he posted a complete-game 4–1 victory over Boston at Comiskey Park, where he held Babe Ruth hitless in four at-bats. Several newspapers stated that it was Faber's final game before reporting to the Navy, but apparently he received an extension. He started again on June 15, but his bid for a 5–0 record was spoiled by shaky defensive support, and Washington won 3–1. "He pitched as if he will be a welcome addition to any service baseball team," *The Washington Post*'s J.V. Fitz Gerald noted. "He allowed only six hits, and had great control, but Chicago errors were sandwiched in ... and they were enough to send him to navy with a defeat in his last major league game."[15] Faber's work in his 11 appearances left him atop the list of American League pitchers with an earned-run average of 1.22, slightly ahead of Walter Johnson, who averaged 1.28 over the entire season.[16]

Faber reported to Great Lakes Naval Training Station in suburban Chicago, but his absence from Comiskey Park was brief. Seven days after losing to the Nationals, he returned to the field — this time wearing a Navy uniform — to participate in the ceremonial raising of the pennant commemorating the White Sox championship of 1917. Faber told reporters that he hoped for an assignment on a submarine, apparently forgetting his legendary bouts with seasickness during the 1913–14 world tour. If he indeed desired combat duty — would it have appeared unpatriotic to admit otherwise? — he did not get his wish. His responsibilities included directing conditioning drills and pitching for the Great Lakes ball team. The naval squad, which at one point included 10 ex-major leaguers, took on teams from other military bases, semi-pro teams and, occasionally, the major leagues. (Meanwhile, the 1918 White Sox, deprived of many stars due to the war, already had come as close to first place as they would get that season.)

Less than a week after exchanging his White Sox uniform for that of the Great Lakes Naval Station team, Faber found himself on the disabled list briefly. A Camp Grant batter's line drive shot into his pitching hand.[17] By early August, he chalked up two victories in three days against the Atlantic fleet; the second contest occurred at Cubs Park — later known as Wrigley Field. "These games are of no small importance," Faber's hometown weekly reminded its readers, "as most of the men are former major leaguers, now enlisted men."[18] In late August, facing the eventual National League champs, the Chicago Cubs, Faber gave up 14 hits in a 5–0 loss.

The exhibition against the Cubs occurred just before the major leagues halted operations. Earlier that month, the U.S. War Department announced that, effective September 2, organized baseball would be classified nonessential to the war effort. The leagues prepared to abbreviate the season, and there was some doubt whether they could stage the World Series without violating the order. The government finally announced that players on the World Series teams (Red Sox and Cubs) would be temporarily exempt from the work-or-fight order — provided that the government received a cut of the World Series revenues. For the balance of the autumn, with their futures uncertain, many major leaguers caught on with semi-pro teams. In the Chicago area, a team called the All-Stars featured Faber's friend and batterymate Ray Schalk and pitcher Joe Benz. These exhibitions drew huge crowds. In late September, Faber and Benz battled each other in a contest that went into the 11th inning, when Benz gave up five runs and suffered the loss.[19] (This might have been the game in which Benz suffered a serious arm injury that effectively ended his career. In 1919, Benz had but one relief appearance before the White Sox released him.) "The Great Lakes naval training station, the largest in the world, is assured a strong ball club next season, even if half of those affiliated with its club last year depart for other scenes this fall and winter," *The Sporting News* reported at season's end.[20] By that time, of all Great Lakes' 1918 regulars, the only man still stationed at Great Lakes was Red Faber.[21] The Navy team's prospects for 1919 became a moot point by mid–November, when the armistice brought an end to the Great War. The government gave organized baseball, which only weeks earlier anticipated canceling the 1919 season, the go-ahead to set a schedule. Teams happily prepared to restock their rosters with military veterans as well as those men who, in the view of detractors, dodged the service by finding civilian jobs. White Sox owner Charles Comiskey was publicly outraged in June 1918 when pitching star Lefty Williams and backup catcher Byrd Lynn abandoned the White Sox to join hitting star Joe Jackson in shipyard jobs in Delaware. "There is no room on my ball club for players who wish to evade the Army draft by entering the employ of ship concerns," he fumed. Williams and Jackson were close friends on the White Sox, and the association of Williams and Lynn went back to their minor league days in Salt Lake City. Sportswriter George S. Robbins noted, "President Comiskey gave Red Faber a kit of valuables to take to the Great Lakes training station with him. Commy has a warm spot in his heart for his World's Series hero, also for Scotty [Jim Scott], who volunteered into the Army service." In contrast, Comiskey was galled that Williams and Lynn left the team even though they were not expected to receive a military call-up before the end of the baseball season.[22] However, when the war ended, the owner took them all back. (One can only speculate whether or to what degree Comiskey's indignant attitude toward these alleged slackers fueled players' betrayal in the 1919 World Series.) As the White Sox lost players during 1918 — no other team lost more starters — they faded deeper and deeper in the American League standings. When the abbreviated regular season ended September 2, they were in sixth place. Manager Clarence Rowland, celebrated as a genius after Chicago's World Series title in 1917, was fired and replaced by coach Kid Gleason. That the White Sox lost so many players during the troubled season was outside Rowland's control, but Comiskey decided that Rowland had to go. The Dubuquer was a war casualty of a different sort. However, Rowland remained in baseball for decades in a variety of roles. He served as an owner-manager, a scout, an umpire, president of the Pacific Coast League and executive vice president of the Chicago Cubs. A baseball man all his life, he died in 1969 at age 90.

After 6½ months in the Navy, Faber received his release from active duty on January 4, 1919, and four days later returned to Cascade.[23] Though his military career was not long, rigorous or dangerous, he re-entered civilian life ill, out of condition and underweight. Worse, he had a bum pitching arm.

14

Black Sox

Faber, who went 4–1 for the 1918 White Sox before his naval enlistment, was the first White Sox star to sign his contract for 1919. Matt Foley of the *Chicago Herald and Examiner* gave a rosy assessment of Faber's prospects. He reported that the pitcher still showed the "beneficial effects" of his Navy stint, had spent most of the off-season outdoors and appeared "set for the gateway gong any time it is sounded."[1] Added the *Chicago Tribune*: "Yeoman Red Faber reported [to Sox headquarters] from Cascade, Iowa, where he has been wintering since his discharge from Great Lakes Naval Training station and announced himself ready for mound service immediately, in spite of the fact the hunting has been negligible in Iowa all winter."[2] One had to wonder whether the sportswriters had actually seen Faber. As spring training opened in Mineral Wells, Texas, Faber obviously was not in shape for major league competition. Wrote the *Tribune*'s I.E. Sanborn: "Faber's condition is giving the boss and some of the players a bit of worry. Although the former Great Lakes yeoman, the hero of the 1917 World Series, declares he feels well, he doesn't look it."[3]

Faber was struggling to recover from influenza. He was not alone, and he was relatively fortunate: as much as 40 percent of the world's population became ill during the Spanish Flu pandemic, which killed an estimated 20 million people worldwide. Between September 1918 and April 1919, it killed a half-million Americans.[4] People could feel fine in the morning, take ill at noon and be dead that night.

Throughout the 1919 season, Faber was at least 15 pounds underweight.[5] Years later, he told an interviewer that he was as many as 30 pounds below his usual 190 pounds.[6] Faber was weak and sore-armed, so his pitches lacked their usual zip and movement. Everyone in the Sox training camp searched for hopeful signs. In early April, Sanborn reported, "For the first time this spring Faber was able to get some steam on the ball without breaking his arm.

He could stick to it only a short while, however, before tiring, but everybody was encouraged."[7] The optimism was short-lived. About three weeks later, in his season preview, Sanborn didn't mince words: "Faber, who combines both youth and experience in ideal quantities, was expected to have his best year this season, but for some reason which neither he nor any one else can understand he cannot deliver the goods. It may be a month or two before he will be available for regular work."[8] Even team owner Charles A. Comiskey added a pinch of realism to his usual optimistic message on the eve of its season opener: "We could use another good pitcher, and may get him. But even if we don't, we'll get along. Faber will come through with warm weather, then we will be all set. We'll be in the pennant fight right from the start."[9]

Though his plan was to work Faber into the season gradually, Manager Kid Gleason had little choice in the fourth game of the year, in St. Louis, where the Browns shelled starter Frank Shellenback. "With the regular pitchers already used up, Gleason had to take a chance and send Red Faber to the mound," the *Tribune* reported. Faber responded by holding the Browns to four hits over the final 6⅔ innings while his teammates rallied for a 9–4 victory. Faber made his first start in the team's 11th game, on May 7, scattering nine hits in a 9–3 win over Detroit. Despite that promising debut, and despite playing for a team that won 63 percent of its games while claiming the American League pennant, 1919 was a disappointment for Faber. He barely posted a winning record.

His frustrations were not limited to the pitching mound. On May 24, en route to a 2–1 loss to the Yankees, the weak-hitting Faber lined an apparent single to right field. However, outfielder Sammy Vick, playing shallow, scooped up the ball and threw out Faber at first base. Later in the season, on June 8, Faber secured some measure of revenge against the Yankees. It was not viewed as particularly significant in the third inning when Faber singled. However, that wound up being the only hit Bob Shawkey surrendered all afternoon. "If it had been anyone else but Faber who got the single hit, the fans wouldn't have been so disappointed," *The New York Times* observed, "but Faber's batting average at best is about the same figure as the size of his shoes." Faber was a better hitter than pitcher that day; he did not last four innings and suffered the loss.[10]

Faber's best day of 1919 was July 9 in Chicago. In the first game of a doubleheader against Philadelphia, he pitched two innings of relief, stroked a bases-loaded single in the eighth and received credit for the 8–7 victory. After the intermission, Faber kept pitching. He started the second game and mowed down the Athletics for a 6–2, complete-game victory.[11] The next day, after another victory, the White Sox regained first place — a position they did not relinquish the rest of the season.[12]

The 1919 White Sox faced adversity and dissension on all fronts. In opposition stadiums, fans constantly derided and ridiculed the White Sox as unpatriotic slackers because several of them — including stars Joe Jackson and Lefty Williams — opted for essential civilian jobs instead of entering the military during the Great War. Internally, the team was wrought with being deepseated dissension. The cliques barely spoke to each other; communication was essentially limited to the playing field and then only when necessary. Pinpointing the reasons and genesis for the feuding factions is problematic. In his book on the Black Sox scandal, Eliot Asinof identified several possibilities. Start with jealousy: An easy target was Eddie Collins, the best-educated and highest-paid player; his salary was more than twice that of any teammate. The team captain and its future manager, Collins headed the faction of players who had more schooling and less bravado. Collins, Faber, catcher Ray Schalk and rookie pitcher Dickie Kerr were constant companions. The other group, which looked toward Arnold "Chick" Gandil for leadership, was generally unschooled, rowdy and coarse. This group had a history of heavy drinking and raucous behavior. In 1919, a Boston hotel invited the White Sox to find other accommodations after some intoxicated players wrecked furniture and dropped furnishings — even beds — out the windows into the hotel courtyard. The roster of Gandil's clique matched that of the Black Sox.[13]

Despite their internal friction and Faber's lackluster performance, the 1919 White Sox topped the American League standings a team-record 134 days. Yet, dogged by Cleveland, New York and Detroit, the White Sox did not dash Cleveland's hopes for the pennant until four days remained in the season. The first-place White Sox recognized pitching as their liability. The bullpen roster changed abruptly in mid-season when Grover Lowdermilk quit the team. His place was taken by a local semi-pro, John "Lefty" Sullivan, who had tried out for the team during spring training. In his major league debut, Sullivan, a spitballer, drew as his mound opponent the legendary Walter Johnson. The Senators knocked around the nervous rookie, but Sullivan took a no-decision when Chicago rallied to beat Johnson in 11 innings.[14] (Lowdermilk had a change of heart almost immediately; Sullivan stayed on the roster but saw little action.) About this time, Faber continued to struggle; he missed a couple of weeks in late June and early July. Comiskey pursued a trade for a quality hurler. Carl Mays, of the Boston Red Sox, was the Old Roman's objective. "The chances are that, in addition to coin, [Red Sox owner Harry] Frazee will want a player or two, and, in that event, a club other than the White Sox will stand a better show of landing the underhand twirler," analyzed the *Tribune*. "What men the Sox now have they cannot part with. However, Gleason is hoping that 'Red' Faber will swing into his old stride one of these days. If he does then it will not make much difference who lands Mays. Cicotte, Williams and Faber, with a little help in the shape of runs, could keep the Sox up there."[15] (Mays went to the Yankees, and the next season one of his underhand pitches beaned and killed Ray Chapman of Cleveland.) The July 26 game in Comiskey Park pitted two spitballers named Urban — Faber of Chicago and Shocker of St. Louis. "Both of them get their hands up to their mouths and do funny things before they deliver the ball," sportswriter James Crusinberry noted. "Apparently that is done for the benefit of the grandstand. Anyway, their bluffing doesn't seem to have much effect upon the boys who are in the game." Urban Shocker and the Browns easily defeated Urban Faber and the White Sox 5–2.[16] By the second week of August, Faber was out of the rotation again — a spectator for most of the pennant drive — and nursing a gimpy ankle. After five weeks of inaction, Faber gave it another try September 15 in Philadelphia. He managed to receive credit for the win — barely. The lowly Athletics' ninth-inning rally ended just a few feet of the home-run wall, and the White Sox survived 11–10.[17] Nonetheless, Faber's performance made it evident that he was not in condition for the postseason. "White Sox partisans who rather fancied that Urban Faber was being kept under cover may change their minds after the poor showing he made against Connie Mack's rookies," *The Sporting News* noted. "If Faber is fit for another World's Series he certainly was doing a good job of camouflaging."[18]

The White Sox clinched the 1919 American League title September 24 in Comiskey Park. The Browns knocked starter Eddie Cicotte out of the box in the seventh, first baseman Gandil was too ill to play and a temperamental umpire tossed an argumentative Eddie Collins. Still, the White Sox rallied with two runs in the bottom of the ninth inning to beat St. Louis 6–5.[19] Immediately afterward, Comiskey, other team officials and players headed toward the bleachers, where they participated in the ceremonial raising of the pennant.[20]

Faber's name appeared on the Chicago roster for the best-of-nine World Series, but he was not expected to be a factor.[21] "If Faber was right, Gleason wouldn't have a thing to worry about [in the World Series]," wrote American League umpire Billy Evans. (That Evans was assigned to umpire the series apparently was of little ethical concern.) "I have worked a number of games back of Faber this year, and in most of the games he lacked his old time stuff. In perhaps two games he looked to be his real self. But it is not impossible that he might come through with one of his good games, and if he should, the Reds would find him most troublesome."[22] However, that was a remote possibility. Even the boosters back in Cascade, so proud of their native son's heroics two years earlier, anticipated a benchwarmer role for their hometown boy. "On account of 'Red' Faber's bad luck in not getting off right this season the World Series fame will probably be monopolized by some other hero. However, Cascade is a fair-guyed burg and we are willing to give some other town in the U.S.A. a chance once in awhile to make a little history for itself."[23] Decades later, Faber said, "My arm was all right, but I could only go four innings."[24] That was not exactly the case; he completed nine of his 20 starts.

But Faber was neither dominating nor the Iron Man of old. His earned-run average ballooned to 3.83, and his 3–0 record in relief allowed him to eke out a winning record (11–9).

The story of the Black Sox scandal is familiar to students of sports history. Eight White Sox players — Gandil's clique — were accused of conspiring with gamblers to lose the 1919 World Series. The investigation and legal proceedings, which were filled with as much intrigue as the fix itself, included confessions exacted by questionable methods, purloined legal documents and jurors who celebrated with the very defendants they exonerated earlier that day. Despite the not guilty verdict, the new commissioner of baseball, Judge Kenesaw Mountain Landis, banned the defendants from ever again playing in organized baseball.

Faber, frustrated and angry, watched the 1919 World Series from the White Sox bench. Faber's closest friends on the team, Schalk and Kerr, already sensed a fix. In *Eight Men Out*, Asinof recounted how, after the Game 2 loss to the Reds, an incensed Schalk physically attacked pitcher Lefty Williams under the Cincinnati stands after Williams repeatedly crossed-up the catcher and refused to throw curveballs.[25] (Publicly at least, Schalk later denied that any confrontation occurred.) In that bitter atmosphere — and spending hours with their friends in clubhouse, hotels, restaurants and rail cars — Schalk, Kerr, Collins and Faber must have discussed their suspicions and their frustrations. Asinof and other researchers revealed that Comiskey soon knew about the fix — perhaps as early as before the first pitch of Game 1. After being rebuffed by the American League president, his enemy Ban Johnson, when trying to report his concerns, Comiskey gathered information on his crooked players but tried to keep a lid on the scandal, lest his team be decimated. Before Game 8, when Kid Gleason suspected Williams of "laying down," he considered benching him in favor of Faber. However, Gleason concluded that he had no choice; Faber simply was in no shape to pitch, so he'd have to go with Williams.[26] Mary Ione Theisen, who was born the day between the fourth and fifth games of the Series, years later heard her Uncle Urban discuss the travesty. "He said he just felt them losing that game," she said, and he asked to relieve. "They wouldn't put him in to save his soul. He just never got over that."[27]

The 1919 World Series was not the first occasion when players and gamblers fixed games, and it was not the last. Before and after the Black Sox scandal, a handful of players were banished from baseball, while others accused of corruption — stars Tris Speaker and Ty Cobb were notable examples — escaped with little or no punishment. Asinof and others have documented decades of corruption.[28] In the years immediately preceding the revelation of the Black Sox, gamblers became more brazen. Newspaper accounts of the day, including those detailing the 1917 World Series, matter-of-factly referred to gamblers' presence in the stands.

In the sportswriting fraternity, the *Chicago Herald and Examiner*'s Hugh
Fullerton was virtually alone in publicly contending that the 1919 World Series
was not "on the square." Another, the *Tribune*'s Jim Crusinberry, filed a story
about the fix; his editor killed it. Subsequent Crusinberry articles followed the
company line. The first published report that the Series was not on the square
appeared a few days after the final out — not in a metropolitan newspaper but
the sports and gambling tabloid *Collyer's Eye*.[29] In mid–December, as Fullerton finally got a watered-down but nonetheless sensational story into the *New
York Evening World*, Comiskey, Johnson and other baseball brass worked on
spin control.[30] The White Sox owner, who knew the situation, nonetheless
claimed that his internal investigation showed the allegations were groundless
"rumors." Nearly all the newspapers went along. "There never has been any
secret made of the rumor nor any attempt to suppress it by Comiskey, Gleason or the newspapers," explained the *Tribune*'s I.E. Sanborn. "Merely as a
rumor, without including the names of the players said to be implicated, it
was not a newspaper story. To name the players meant irreparable injury to
men who could not then and have not been proven guilty." Sanborn also
reminded his readers that in his Series preview he advised them to not wager
better than even money on the White Sox because they were overconfident,
out of shape and still feeling the effects of their American League pennant celebration.[31] Several years after the scandal and Comiskey's death, Fullerton
revealed that Comiskey told him he already knew about the fix and that Johnson scoffed at the report.[32] Nearly six months before the Black Sox indictments, Oscar Reichow in *The Sporting News* called for honest players to tell
what they knew.[33] None, including Faber, came forward before the indictments.

For years afterward, Schalk said that had Faber been healthy and able to
pitch in the World Series of 1919, there would not have been a Black Sox scandal. The conspirators did not dare solicit any teammates from outside their
clique, and Faber was not part of it. A healthy Faber might have started at
least three games in the best-of-nine series. But that is only conjecture. This
is fact: Faber and the other Clean Sox would never again compete in a pennant race, let alone a World Series. The longest-active member of the Clean
Sox, Faber was a major victim of the scandal. In the short term, the Black
Sox denied him an honest shot at the 1919 championship as well as a strong
opportunity to play in the 1920 Fall Classic. They also cheated him out of *at
least* two more victories (and two fewer losses) in his career statistics. Worst
of all, the Black Sox scandal sentenced Faber to servitude on mediocre teams
the rest of his career.

However, the recuperating athlete was unaware of all that in the days
following the 1919 World Series. Faber returned to Cascade and soon afterward departed for a month-long hunting trip in Helix, Oregon, home of boy-
hood friend Fritz Moes.[34]

15

A Team Divided

Back in Cascade, Faber used the winter of 1919–20 to regain his health and reflect on what he had witnessed during the World Series. During an unusually snowy winter in Iowa, *Chicago Tribune* sportswriter James Crusinberry, who hailed from Faber's hometown, offered a somewhat embellished account: "Having nothing else to do, 'Red' and a couple of other fellows of Cascade who own cars and like to drive into Dubuque to see a movie, attempted to shovel a path on the highway. It's only *twenty-six miles* from Cascade to Dubuque. The path was completed after some days of strenuous bucking and shoveling, but that very night another storm came and filled it up." The unconventional exercise program and home cooking apparently agreed with Faber: Crusinberry reported that Faber had gained back 12 to 15 pounds and appeared in fine form.[1] The prospect of a healthy Faber had Chicago sportswriters predicting that the 1920 White Sox would be better than the previous season's pennant-winners. However, would Faber remain White Sox property?

Faber, who a year earlier had signed his one-season contract immediately, was more deliberate about terms for the 1920 campaign. In February the 31-year-old traveled to Chicago to meet with Comiskey regarding the team's proposal. (Comiskey, virtually certain that that several of his players threw the World Series, but hoping to keep a lid on it, lest his team collapse, had difficult contract discussions. Several players yet to be exposed as Black Sox defendants, including Joe Jackson, most likely aware of Comiskey's predicament, pressed the Old Roman for heftier contracts.) For his part, Faber, who had no role in the scandal, claimed no dissatisfaction with Comiskey's offer, but Crusinberry said the veteran "did remark that he might quit baseball for good. Also he remarked that it might be a good thing for him to try to pitch for some other club." Crusinberry's view was that Comiskey would not trade a pitcher so pivotal to his team's pennant hopes.[2] After all, it was the absence of a healthy Faber that cost the White Sox the World Series the previous fall.

Ultimately, Faber signed his contract and reported on time for spring training in Waco, Texas. In his first exhibition outing, he pitched four scoreless innings. "'Kid' Gleason feels certain the Cascader will come back with all the old pep," the hometown newspaper reported. Meanwhile, back in the Midwest, Faber's mother, Margaret, underwent surgery for an undisclosed malady. She spent more than a month at the Mayo Clinic but returned home "in good health and finely improved."[3] The same could be said for her older son, whose seventh major league season was shaping up to be a comeback year — and perhaps his best ever.

However, would 1920 be the last season in which Faber and other pitchers could hurl the spitball? During the winter of 1919–20, the Joint Rules Committee outlawed pitchers' use of all foreign substances — including saliva, resin, talcum powder and paraffin. Also banned were the emery ball and shine ball, in which pitchers scuffed the surface of the baseball. The National League voted to prohibit the spitball among new pitchers, and the American League decided that each team could designate two pitchers who could throw the spitter one final season (1920). Faber and Eddie Cicotte were the White Sox designees. The decision was controversial. Said Washington star Walter Johnson, "I believe all the fans and most of the pitchers will be glad to see trick pitching discarded." Pitcher-turned-outfielder Babe Ruth saw it differently. "What does it matter if a guy wets the ball?" the Bambino said. "Gosh, Red Faber is the nicest man in the world"[4] Veteran umpire Billy Evans offered that, of all the American League's spitball practitioners, those who would be hurt the *least* by a ban on the pitch were Faber and Urban Shocker of St. Louis, who could compete effectively with the other pitches in their repertoires.[5] "Every once in a while I hear about a pitcher who 'has everything,'" Sox catcher Schalk said years into retirement. "Yet the only pitchers I ever saw who had everything were Faber and Cicotte — fast ball, curve ball, three-and-two, and spitter, three-and-two. There have been a lot of names for different pitches, but Faber and Cicotte could throw 'em all, whether you called 'em fadeaways or sliders or screwballs or knucklers or forkballs."[6]

Aware of the previous season's struggles of Faber, a notoriously slow starter, sportswriters as early as spring training marveled at the pitcher's "startling comeback" in 1920. During an exhibition game in Houston, Faber fanned 10 Texas minor-leaguers. If not for an overmatched local umpire, the strikeout total would have been higher. Said the *Tribune*: "The arbiter was puzzled by the queer way the baseball tended to deviate from a straight line."[7]

Faber kept it going when the regular season began, spoiling Detroit's home opener with a seven-hit, 8–2 victory. "Red seemed to have all the stuff that made him a terror to foreign batters back in 1917," reported the *Tribune's* Irving Vaughan. "He eased over fast ones, curves and even spitters, the latter variety being especially effective. Toward the close Faber appeared to tire a bit and his control went on the fritz. Despite this he managed to get by because his co-workers were able to take care of numerous line drives and healthy flies."[8] Those apparently steady fielders let Faber down less than a week later, when the Chicagoans traveled to Cleveland with victories in their first six games of the season. Battling another spitballer and future Hall-of-Famer, Stan Coveleski, Faber took a 2–1 lead into the bottom of the eighth, when he retired the first two hitters. Then a long drive by Larry Gardner sailed over Joe Jackson's head for an apparent triple. Shortstop Swede Risberg caught Jackson's relay throw but heaved wildly toward third base. Risberg's throw eluded Buck Weaver as well as Faber, who was backing up the play. Gardner completed his circuit of the bases to knot the game 2–2. Vaughan observed, "Risberg never should have made the peg, as there was no chance to beat the runner to the far bag."[9] In his book about the Black Sox scandal, Eliot Asinof cited that particular game — and that particular play — as evidence that the Black Sox continued to throw games after the 1919 World Series. They might have done it for money, but it is more likely that the gamblers were blackmailing them.[10] Despite pitching a masterful game, Faber took the loss in the bottom of the ninth. The Indians rapped a single, slapped a hit-and-run single through the vacated spot on the infield and then ended the game on a sacrifice fly. Little more than a week later, Faber again lost 3–2 to Cleveland and Coveleski, and again defensive miscues were a factor. Center fielder Oscar "Happy" Felsch, later exposed as a member of the Black Sox, misplayed a clean single into a three-bagger to give the Indians their final run. However, Faber, who allowed Cleveland six hits, contributed to the gift-giving with a run-scoring error of his own. With opponents on first and second, Faber hurriedly fielded a sacrifice bunt but fell as he turned to throw to third base. He regained his feet and, forsaking the force-out, threw to first base but his peg was so wild that the lead base runner came around to score.[11] Nonetheless, Sox rooters were confident that Faber had regained his championship form of 1917. So confident — or desperate? — was manager Kid Gleason that he started Faber on just two days' rest. However, the Indians knocked out Faber in the sixth inning.[12] That loss was the second straight during a 1–7 stretch for the White Sox, who, despite the likely thrown game, opened the season 10–2. With his usual rest before his next start, Faber pitched another masterpiece, winning 2–1 over Boston's Herb Pennock on May 15. The Red Sox starter lost some effectiveness after a half-hour rain delay between the seventh and eighth innings of the scoreless game. The weak-hitting Faber opened the top of the eighth with a double and scored the game's first run. Faber also struggled somewhat after the delay and gave up the tying run. But the White

Sox pushed across the go-ahead run in the top of the ninth, and Faber closed out the Red Sox for the victory.[13] His next time out, the Iowa native further proved that he was totally recovered from his maladies of 1919, pitching all 16 innings of an unusual contest in Washington. Nationals pitching legend Walter Johnson entered the 3–3 battle in the 11th, and he and Faber shut out their respective opponents through the 14th inning. The White Sox scored twice against Johnson in the top of the 15th, and Faber retired the first two Nats in the bottom of the inning. Though Washington then singled twice, it appeared that the Chicagoans would collect the victory when an easy bouncer headed toward second baseman Eddie Collins. However, after handling 13 chances successfully that afternoon, the future Hall-of-Famer booted the 14th, allowing Washington to pull within a run. Faber then gave up a game-tying single to Bucky Harris. Nationals left fielder Braggo Roth dropped an easy fly ball to open Chicago's half of the 16th inning and, *The Washington Post*'s J.V. Fitz Gerald reported, "The Sox landed on Walter with everything but their spikes and the Nationals did about everything but try to swallow the ball."[14] Before it was over, Chicago had scored eight times. The Nationals (Senators) went down quietly in the bottom of the 16th, and Faber earned a hard-fought victory. The 16-inning battle was the longest American League game of 1920, and Faber pitched every inning of it.[15]

Such was Faber's battle with Walter Johnson, a charter member of the National Baseball Hall of Fame. The spitballer also had many head-to-head contests with another charter inductee, Babe Ruth. There might have been more of those battles, but Chicago managers regularly ordered their pitchers to walk the Bambino. Spectators, even White Sox fans, hated the tactic. Many would have rather witnessed a Ruthian clout than a Sox victory. Faber himself followed orders under protest; he wanted to challenge the slugger. However, Chicago management was not of a similar mind, and fans roared their disapproval whenever the Sox did not force Ruth, now a Yankee, to remove the bat from his shoulder. In August 1920, most of the 25,000 fans in Comiskey Park booed Faber when he walked Ruth three times. "The multitude was deeply peeved and many of the fans yelled at Red and told him his nickname ought to be 'Yellow' Faber instead of Red," *The New York Times* noted.[16] The hometown customers were hardly placated in the third inning, when, with two out and the bases empty, Ruth nicked Faber's 2–0 pitch for a scratch single. Several fans expressed their protests to the *Chicago Tribune*. One wrote, "When the Sox pitchers here deliberately refused to give Ruth a chance to make a hit by passing him I felt that my admission money had been obtained by false pretenses." Said another, "If the Old Roman had advertised that Ruth was going to be passed would he have had the crowd? I thought so." A Detroit cor-respondent indicated that he would rather see Chicago victories than Ruth blasts: "What a pity! The Yanks lost three of four to the Sox, so little [manager] Miller Huggins cries, 'Don't be so hard on us. We have Babe Ruth. Please groove the ball to him so he can hit more home runs and give the fans a run for their money while we win the games.'"[17] The *Tribune's* Harvey T. Woodruff made sure his readers knew that the passes were not the Sox hurler's idea. "Red Faber did not relish the booing from the fans in Tuesday's game when, under orders, he issued three bases on balls to Babe Ruth. Faber wanted to take a chance, and it required imperative orders, cajolery, and finally threats from Manager Gleason to force Red to carry out instructions, but the Sox won a game (3–1) which they might not have won if Ruth had clouted another homer."[18]

Despite being in a pennant race from the start of the season, Faber did enjoy brief moments away. In June, between complete-game victories in Chicago, he made an extremely brief visit to Cascade. In the few hours he spent at home, he no doubt visited family — his sister-in-law and brother, Al, were expecting their third child — but the primary purpose of the trip was to retrieve his formerly snowbound automobile and drive it back to Chicago.[19] No doubt, he made good use of the vehicle over the next several weeks. The White Sox played 29 of their next 32 games at home.

In 1920, Faber pitched 319 innings — at that point a career high and nearly double what he worked the previous season. His 23–13 record represented his highest victory total since 1915, his sophomore season, when he went 24–14. The Chicago pitching staff had four 20-game winners — Eddie Cicotte (21–10), Dickie Kerr (21–9), Lefty Williams (22–14) and Faber. The latter three defeated every American League team at least once.[20] On August 20, Faber notched his 100th career victory, breezing past the Athletics in Philadelphia 7–4. Chicago's four-run first inning gave him plenty of breathing room.[21]

Still, Faber's statistics could have been better with honest ballplayers behind him. Despite whispers about a corrupted 1919 World Series, gamblers operated brazenly in 1920. The seven remaining Chicago players involved in the 1919 fix — Gandil retired from the major leagues after 1919 — were in no position to refuse the demands of the gamblers, who occasionally ordered games thrown. The April 27 game in which Faber was saddled with the loss probably was one such contest. On a road trip later during the pennant drive, the White Sox kicked away several games with curious plays. On August 28 in New York, Faber suffered the loss after errors by Risberg and Weaver allowed all the Yankees' runs in a 3–0 decision. "Risberg and Weaver were the best players New York had today," the *Tribune* seethed.[22] The loss was the second of seven straight, and the Sox's uncharacteristic slump, which dropped them out of the league lead, carried the aroma of gamblers' influence.

The Black Sox indictments arrived with just three games left in their season and with the Sox still hoping to catch Cleveland. The defendants were pitchers Cicotte and Williams; infielders Weaver, Risberg and Fred McMullin; outfielders Felsch and "Shoeless" Joe Jackson and the retired Gandil. Trailing Cleveland by a half-game (two games in the loss column) and losing the seven active suspects to suspension, the White Sox cobbled together a lineup. After three days off, they sent Faber to the mound in St. Louis on October 1. However, the Browns battered him for seven hits and three runs in three innings en route to an 8–6 victory, effectively killing Chicago's pennant hopes. (It was probably just as well, for the short-handed White Sox — had they been allowed to play in the World Series at all — would have been an easy mark for Brooklyn.) In any case, Chicago split the remaining two games and staggered to a runner-up finish, two games behind the Indians.

After the indictments, White Sox captain Eddie Collins described the tension on the 1920 team: "Even during batting practice our gang stood in one group waiting our turn to hit and the other gang had their own group. We went along and gritted our teeth and played ball. We had to trail along with those fellows all summer, and all the time felt that they had thrown us down."[23] Some questioned why the honest players — a group that included Faber — appeared to keep silent all that time. *The Sporting News* complained, "The odd thing is that the honest ball players now admit that was the system

Up to 4,000 fans ring the Cascade baseball field for Red Faber Day in October 1920. The exhibition game in the pitcher's hometown occurred less than two weeks after the Black Sox indictments. (Courtesy of the Tri-County Historical Society, Cascade, Iowa.)

Top: National Street, the main thoroughfare of Cascade, Iowa, is abuzz the day of Red Faber Day in October 1920. The Hotel Faber is in the left foreground. (Courtesy of the Tri-County Historical Society, Cascade, Iowa.) *Bottom:* Red Faber bats during the Faber Day exhibition against the Dubuque White Sox in October 1920 in Cascade, Iowa. Though a notoriously weak hitter, Faber later slammed a pitch past the autos parked in right field and, mistaken about the ground rules, went into a home-run trot. However, the ball remained in play and Faber had to settle for a triple. He scored on a squeeze bunt when an infielder's throw hit him in the back. (Courtesy of the Tri-County Historical Society, Cascade, Iowa.)

The guest of honor delivers a pitch during the Red Faber Day exhibition against
the Dubuque White Sox semi-pro team in Cascade in October 1920. Umpire
Forrest Plass, standing behind the pitcher, was Faber's manager when he entered
professional baseball in 1909. (Courtesy of the Tri-County Historical Society, Cascade, Iowa.)

[to lose certain games during 1920]. But it took grand jury disclosures to
force them to admit."[24] However, it was also revealed that several people —
players, sportswriters and even Comiskey — at one point or another were
stymied when they attempted to share their facts and suspicions.

Faber's outstanding year and his affirmation as one of the Clean Sox
heightened interest in a post-season "Faber Day" exhibition in Cascade, his
hometown. Though hastily arranged — Red accepted his brother Al's invitation less than two weeks earlier — the game attracted a huge crowd on a sun-
drenched autumn Sunday. Crowd estimates ranged from 2,500 to 4,000
fans — two to three times Cascade's 1920 Census population of 1,249.[25] It is
likely that the spectators included Cascade farmer Matthias Faber, Red's uncle
and the Iowa Farmer-Labor party's gubernatorial nominee.[26] He garnered
barely 1 percent of the vote.[27] The turnout far exceeded what Al Faber and
other organizers anticipated, and spectators ringed the field. Their automobiles were parked "hub to hub" beyond the outfield.[28] In a ceremony, Cascade officials presented Faber with an "automobile robe," and players for both
teams posed for pictures with the major league star. The exhibition's umpire
was Forrest Plass, who was Faber's first manager on the professional level
(Dubuque, 1909).

Faber pitched for Cascade against Dubuque's top semi-pro team; coincidentally, it was named the White Sox. He struck out 14 Dubuquers but gave up a run in the top of the ninth inning and fell behind 2–1. Leading off the bottom of the ninth, Faber, a weak hitter against major leaguers, teed off against his semi-pro counterpart. His smash soared beyond the outfield and into the parking area. "Red evidently figured it would be allowed for a homer so he just about walked around the bases," the *Dubuque Times-Journal* reported, "but by the time he reached third the Sox fielder threw the ball in and Faber didn't get home." The Cascade newspaper noted that Faber, unfamiliar with the local ground rule, could have easily raced for a home run had he been aware.[29] One out later, Faber scored the tying run on a bunt; the third baseman's throw to the plate hit the major leaguer. After a single, Al Faber won the game with a hit to left. The exhibition was such a success that Cascade and Dubuque representatives arranged a rematch for the following Sunday afternoon in Dubuque. Red Faber pitched again — he struck out 11— and the score was again 3–2. But this time it was the Dubuque team that prevailed. The Cascade newspaper attributed at least part of the loss on the umpire. "First off, the umpires were not in the class of baseball that was being played. Cretzmeyer was decidedly off-color on balls and strikes. Faber's twisters were too complicated and fast for his proper judgment."[30]

About the time Faber came to Cascade for the exhibitions, he brought along a special guest: Irene Margaret Walsh, a Milwaukee native who resided in Chicago. They met by accident — literally. The 22-year-old woman was injured in a traffic accident in Chicago, and the 32-year-old baseball star came upon the scene to provide assistance. He followed up with visits to Irene in the hospital, and the couple hit it off. To the surprise of many folks in Cascade, Faber married the girl. The ceremony took place in a Catholic church on Chicago's South Side on November 10, 1920.[31] Only a few friends were invited.[32] The marriage was surprising and unpopular among the Fabers, who came to consider Irene opportunistic, aloof and troublesome.[33] Nonetheless, the newlyweds took up winter residence at the family's hotel in Cascade.

16

A Pitching Staff Named "Red"

The 1921 season represented major changes for Faber. Newly married at age 32, he and Irene took up residence in a Chicago hotel. In a career-extending development, the ban against the spitball, which was to have been effective after 1920, was amended. Seventeen spitball pitchers — eight in the National League and nine in the American, including Faber — were permitted to continue to throw the wet pitch for the balance of their careers.[1] Another significant change involved the White Sox: The team was decimated by the suspension of seven players in the Black Sox indictments at the end of the 1920 season. (An eighth suspect retired after 1919.)

The White Sox had only a half-dozen other reliable returnees, including pitcher Dickie Kerr and three future Hall of Famers: infielder Eddie Collins, catcher Ray Schalk and Faber. Team officials spent the winter scouring minor league rosters for prospects. Some 50 hopefuls poured into Waxahachie (Texas) Jungle Park for tryouts during spring training. Faber, Kerr and Schalk reported to training camp a week early to help Manager Kid Gleason evaluate pitching prospects.[2] Days before the opening of camp, owner Charles Comiskey gave the White Sox a boost by trading outfielders John Collins and Harry Leibold to the Red Sox for veteran outfielder Harry Hooper, another future Hall of Famer.[3]

In addition to the uncertainty of their roster, the White Sox could not be sure how fans would respond to them. The Black Sox indictments broke after the team's final home game of 1920. What would be the reception for the reconstructed team? Those worries were eased when the team assembled in Comiskey Park for their final workout before opening the regular season in Detroit. Some 500 fans showed up to watch practice and try to figure out the identities of the many new players.[4] There was even a mood of tempered optimism. *Chicago Tribune* sports editor Harvey T. Woodruff predicted that the White Sox would be "fighters" who would escape the American League cellar but finish in the second division. Woodruff's "greatest fear" involved the pitching staff: Kerr (21–9 in 1920) and Faber (23–13) were all the Sox had.

Despite not being in top condition and chilly and damp conditions in Detroit, Faber, never considered a cold-weather pitcher, edged the Tigers 3–2 in their second game of the regular season. Hooper's timely hitting keyed the offense. "Faber was so good that the Tigers should have had no more than one tally," Irving Vaughan reported. The second run was attributed to shaky defense — a situation with which Faber was quite accustomed. The game was briefly halted for a presentation to Ty Cobb, who received two huge floral pieces and a life membership in the Elks Club. In his second outing, Faber and the Sox were unimpressive in a 4–1 loss at St. Louis.[5]

More than 25,000 supportive fans filled Comiskey Park for the home opener against the Tigers. The new commissioner of baseball, Judge Kenesaw Mountain Landis, watched from behind the Detroit bench. Kerr and the White Sox collected an 8–3 victory in a game cut short when rain and hail pelted the field in the top of the eighth inning. The next afternoon, Faber pitched well but trailed 2–1 when he was pulled for a pinch hitter in the eighth inning. The White Sox tied it in the bottom of the ninth and pulled out the win in the 11th inning 3–2. The victory pushed their season record to 3–3.[6] After that, the 1921 White Sox never had more wins than losses.

Despite their team's ineptitude, Faber and Kerr turned in sterling pitching performances. In his next start, Faber dominated the defending World Series champion Indians to win a 1–0 pitching duel with Jim Bagby. Faber gave up only two singles — an infield smash by Jack Graney in the second inning and a clean hit to center by Charlie Jamieson with two out in the ninth. "Throughout the afternoon Faber seemed to have everything," Vaughan wrote. "He employed spitters, curves and fast ones in about equal quantities. One was as successful as the other." Faber kept the ball in play all afternoon: he walked no one and struck out only two. Bagby was the hard-luck loser, allowing the Sox only five hits.[7]

Faber's brilliance did not carry over to his next start, in chilly Detroit, where he lasted but one inning. He allowed only two hits, but a walk and two Sox errors resulted in four unearned runs. The Tigers and Dutch Leonard cruised 13–1. Faber again gave up two hits in his next outing — but this time it was in a complete-game shutout over Cleveland. In just a six-day span, Faber had two-hit the defending world champions twice. He had a no-hitter going until player-manager Tris Speaker ripped a double with one out in the seventh inning. As was the case in his previous outing against Cleveland, the Indians did not register their second hit until the ninth inning — again by

Charlie Jamieson, this time on an umpire's disputed decision on an infield roller.[8]

Faber was pitching the best baseball of his life. Unfortunately, he was backed by one of the worst teams in the majors. The White Sox lost three straight until Faber returned to the mound and beat Boston 4–1.[9] He followed that with a 3–1 win over Philadelphia in which he limited the Athletics to six hits. Two days later, manager Kid Gleason, starved for pitching help, called on Faber to rescue Kerr, who had a case of the "wilds." Faber delivered. He allowed Philadelphia just one hit over the final 2⅔ innings while the White Sox pushed across the winning run in the eighth inning.[10] Just two days after that, Faber held the Yankees to five hits en route to a 12–2 victory. Babe Ruth went hitless in five plate appearances. (Before his second time up, the game in Chicago was halted for a presentation. "Two youngsters, hardly 5 years old, marched to the plate, beating a march on two tiny drums." Ruth accepted a floral tribute in the shape of a bat from Chicago's St. Mary's School. "After the presentation they shook hands with Babe, and expressed the hope that he would hit a home run." Faber did not cooperate, inducing Ruth to hit a comebacker to the mound.[11]) "Faber used a daring system to baffle Bambino. He pitched him groove balls most of the time, but with everything he could put on them, and the Cascade hero never had more on his fast one than he did yesterday," wrote the *Tribune*'s I.E. Sanborn. "In fact he had a hard time taming it, as four bases on balls and two batsmen hit indicates." The result left the Comiskey Park crowd of more than 18,000 divided: "It was disappointed in not seeing Ruth pole his thirteenth home run, but was elated at the Sox triumph."[12] Faber extended his winning streak to five in Chicago a few days later when Bib Falk blasted a grand slam homer to break open a pitchers' duel with Washington's Harry Courtney. The final was 6–2.

Faber's winning streak ended with a thud in Detroit. The Cascade native failed to retire a single Tiger, giving up five runs on six consecutive hits. The next day, Gleason decided to give another start to Faber, who exacted his revenge. He limited the Tigers to one run over 10 innings. The White Sox scored once in the eighth to tie and twice in the 10th to win 3–1. "Faber ought to have had a nine-inning shutout," the *Tribune*'s Sanborn said, "for the lone tally scored on him was an accident, and the Gleasons ought to have had an easy victory without going into overtime, for Mrs. Fate scowled on the visitors all the way to the tenth, then smiled broadly."[13] Faber was fortunate in his next outing, despite serving the Nationals (Senators) three runs on eight hits in the first three innings. He allowed only one hit the rest of the way, and another rare Sox rally gave him his 11th victory of the season 8–3.[14] His league-leading 12th win was another overtime victory: Faber pitched 10 innings as the Sox defeated host Philadelphia in a 9–7 slugfest.[15]

Pitching for a team that had won only 19 games all year, Faber had a league-leading 12 victories (against three losses).[16] A fan reflected the nature of the White Sox pitching in verse:

> *"Pray, tell me of your pitching staff,"*
> *The eager stranger said.*
> *The rooter, with a bitter laugh,*
> *Replied, "We call him 'Red.'"*[17]

The league's two winningest pitchers, Faber and Sam Jones (10–3), squared off June 13 in Boston. Jones' experience was similar to Faber's nightmare earlier in Detroit. He did not complete the first inning. "For five minutes the hits went whistling around Sam like bullets," the *Tribune* said of the White Sox's five-run opening frame. Faber had his own problems in the first inning, but a double play limited the damage to a single run. Faber weakened in the bottom of the ninth, allowing three more runs but holding off the Red Sox 6–4 to claim his 13th win.[18] Faber had to survive another ninth-inning jam to claim victory No. 14 in New York. Trailing Faber by a 4–3 margin, the Yankees had a runner on third with one out. With the White Sox infield playing in, Wally Schang worked Faber — or was it the other way around?— to a full count. On 3–2, Faber threw a low curveball to Schang, who swung and missed for the second out. The next batter was relief pitcher Carl Mays, who would hit .343 that season. Faber struck out Mays, too, with catcher Ray Schalk "gleefully" clutching a foul tip on the game's final pitch.[19] Faber continued to pitch well, but occasionally his teammates let him down. "Not Cleveland, but his own pals kept U. Red Faber from winning his seventh straight game yesterday and his fifteenth for the year," the *Tribune* reported. Sox outfielders dropped two fly balls, and a questionable umpiring decision stifled a Sox comeback. Despite teammate Happy Hooper's two solo home runs, Faber, who allowed eight hits, took the 3–2 loss.[20] Faber took a second consecutive one-run loss when Detroit prevailed 7–6 in a game marked by "rotten play" by the Sox. His third straight one-run defeat came in St. Louis, where the White Sox took a one-run lead in the top of the 10th inning. Chicago errors allowed the Browns to rally for two runs against Faber and claim a 4–3 victory.[21]

Though his teammates played some "frightful baseball" behind him, Faber finally collected his 15th victory at the end of the St. Louis series. He stifled the Browns on five hits — only one was of the "clean" variety — and coasted 5–1.[22] While his teammates departed for a short series in Cleveland, Faber returned to Chicago to rest in anticipation of meeting Ty Cobb's Tigers.[23] Faber and Detroit's George Dauss, backed by flawless fielding, allowed only four hits each. The game was stopped briefly in the fifth inning, when umpire George Hildebrand ejected player-manager Cobb, who was not in that day's lineup. "The Tyger pilot crabbed considerably about it, then hopped over the concrete barrier and sat in a box about three feet from where he had been planted," the *Tribune* reported. "As he was in citizen's rainment, it went." In the next inning, with Cobb watching from the stands, the White Sox put across two runs and Faber made it stand up for a 2–0 victory. It was his 16th win of the year.[24]

The Iowa native continued to overwhelm opposing batsmen. Some 30,000 fans packed Comiskey Park July 10 for a Sunday afternoon battle pitting Faber against Babe Ruth and the Yankees. On many occasions when Ruth came to town, White Sox fans' loyalty was put to the test. Many came to the ballpark preferring to see a Ruth home run over a Sox victory. Faber provided them the latter with a 4–1 decision. He allowed the Yankees just five hits, including a Ruth single, while striking out eight and walking three. Ruth also reached base in the eighth inning after lofting a fly ball too high for center fielder Johnny Mostil to handle. "It was just like trying to catch a ball dropped off three Washington Monuments piled on each other," wrote Sanborn, who claimed that "not a soul" rooted for Ruth that day.[25]

Sanborn did not mention the sartorial appearance of the Chicago team that afternoon, but Sox fans received some insight into why their favorites often took the field in soiled uniforms. It was a financial decision. During jury selection in the Black Sox trial, defense attorney Henry A. Berger revealed that Comiskey charged his players 50 cents a uniform per washing. Some players balked at the assessment, so they frequently wore uniforms bearing the dirt and grass stains from previous contests. When the team left for a road trip, Berger continued, White Sox management went into the players' lockers, cleaned the dirty home uniforms and withheld the cleaning charge from the players' paychecks. The morning of that revelation, Faber and six other members of the 1919 White Sox (including manager Kid Gleason) appeared in court under a subpoena from the Black Sox defendants. There was no sign of the rift or discord that supposedly so divided the team through 1920. The Clean Sox and Black Sox kibitzed, shook hands and slapped each other on the back. Manager Kid Gleason's conversation with ex-infielder Buck Weaver was interrupted when Faber and Kerr, aware of Weaver's ticklish nature, playfully went after their ex-third baseman's ribs.[26] "The only mention of the baseball scandal was when some of the men now on the team wished the others good luck in their trial," *The New York Times* reported.[27] The show of friendliness so shocked and outraged the country that Comiskey sent out Manager Kid Gleason to attempt spin control, trying to explain to reporters how people did not really see what they saw.[28] Judge Hugo Friend, who at first ordered the Clean Sox to stay in Chicago to be available for the trial, subsequently amended the ruling to state that witnesses could travel but had to return to the courtroom when called. His order raised the possibility that the White Sox, already a terrible team, might have to play league games without most of their veterans.[29] Until then, the White Sox had baseball games to play. They played them poorly, losing three straight. In his next start, Faber found himself locked in a pitching duel with Washington's George Mogridge. In the top of the fourth, Edmund Miller drove a Faber offering over the left-field fence. Through six innings, Mogridge gave up only two hits — both to Eddie Collins. In the bottom of the seventh, the Sox rallied for three runs, and that was enough for Faber to win 3–1 on a three-hitter.[30] It was Faber's 18th victory but only the 34th win for the entire team all year. Three days later, in another Sunday afternoon feature, Faber matched pitches with Boston's Elmer Myers. Helped by his defense, Faber held the Red Sox scoreless through 10 innings. In the bottom of the 10th, Chicago outfielder Bib Falk rapped a run-scoring single, sending the Comiskey Park crowd home happy and giving Faber his 19th win.[31] And it was only mid–July!

Falk helped Faber again four days later, when he homered in the bottom of the 14th to beat Philadelphia. Although the Athletics amassed 16 hits, they could push across only one run against Faber, who collected a 2–1 victory.[32] Faber's 20th victory was the 40th win for the White Sox. The *Tribune*'s Woodruff reminded Chicago fans that, going into this season, there were doubts about Faber. "The [Sox] management is fortunate that Faber was held in the hope of a 'comeback' when he seemed to have lost his effectiveness following his success of 1917. We shudder to think of the Sox this season minus Faber."[33] Fans had not forgotten. "Hero Worship Not Dead in Windy City," reported *The Sporting News*, noting the success of popularity of injured Cubs star Grover Cleveland Alexander and of Faber, already a 20-game winner. "Six defeats are charged to Faber, but he should have had only three. He has had to extend himself at all times, because the opposition usually sends against him its foremost pitcher. This, however, does not disturb Faber, as he has more stuff than any White Sox pitcher ever revealed, not barring Ed Walsh. Faber's spitball is not his only asset. He is using a puzzling curve ball, along with his speed, that keeps the batters guessing all the time and accounts for the steadiness with which he has been winning."[34]

As the White Sox boarded their train for Washington, they anticipated that several members of their delegation would be summoned back to Chicago for the Black Sox trial. The uncertainty was whether the rest of the team would be expected to continue playing during their absence. On July 26, Faber pitched well in Griffith Stadium, allowing the Nationals just five hits, but his luck ran out. Washington scratched together two runs in the sixth inning and John Thomas Zachary shut out the Sox for a 2–0 decision.[35] The next evening, after the Nats beat the White Sox again, Faber and the other subpoenaed witnesses rode the rails back to Chicago for the trial. Faber's travel companions included Gleason, trainer H.W. Stephenson and teammates Eddie Collins, Ray Schalk, Harvey McClellan, Dickie Kerr and Roy Wilkinson. Ernie Johnson, a shortstop with minor-league managing experience, was placed in charge of the remaining players in Washington. Meanwhile, officials of both the White Sox and Nationals asked American League president Ban Johnson to permit postponement of the balance of their series. No fan of Comiskey, Johnson, possibly recognizing an opportunity to add to the misfortunes of the White Sox, turned down the request. Of the Chicago players remaining in Washington, a *Chicago Evening Post* sportswriter quipped, "Even their best friends would scarcely recognize the White Sox this afternoon."[36] Acting manager Johnson moved center fielder Johnny Mostil to second base, penciled in a handful of reserves and tried to make the best of it. They lost two games, and a third contest was rained out with the Nats leading 5–1 in the second inning. The *Tribune's* James Crusinberry was bitterly critical of Washington manager Clark Griffith for trying to complete the final game despite rainy conditions and a turnout of just 300 fans: "It takes a cloudburst to stop Griff when there is a 'set up' game for him. Sometimes it looks as if there's no sportsmanship in baseball.[37]

Faber did not miss a start because of his summons to the trial. But it was a wasted trip. He did not testify. In a court session conducted at night to accommodate the players' schedule, Gleason and Schalk, called as defense witnesses to refute the chronology described by gamblers, spent the most time on the stand. They primarily answered questions about what time the players left for practice and whom they did and not see in the team's hotel. Collins, Wilkinson and Kerr appeared only long enough to give similar testimony. The brevity of his time on the stand clearly disgusted Kerr. Leaving the courtroom, he snarled, "I came 900 miles to tell this!"[38]

Their obligations to the court satisfied, Kerr and Faber apparently took out their frustrations on the Athletics, winning both ends of a doubleheader in Philadelphia. The twin bill was a battle between teams trying to put the other in the American League cellar. Kerr needed a ninth-inning rescue from Wilkinson to preserve a 9–7 win. In the second game, Faber's dominance over the Athletics irritated the Shibe Park crowd of some 15,000. The "fans" started jeering, and two or three fights erupted in the stands. Police arrived belatedly to disperse the combatants. Meanwhile, Faber cruised along and his teammates roughed up Philadelphia starter Bob Hasty. Before Faber served up a home-run pitch to Tilly Walker in the bottom of the ninth inning, he had allowed only three hits and held a 9–0 lead. As Faber closed out the host Athletics 9–1 and earned his 21st win, the irritated fans still around littered the field with their seat cushions; several people — but apparently no players — suffered minor injuries.[39]

August 1921 was not Faber's happiest month. The Red Sox beat him in Boston 3–2. "A half-dozen or more sparkling plays by Boston prevented the [White] Sox from scoring a lot of runs, while three or four dinky and fluky base hits beat Faber," reported Crusinberry. "Elmer Myers opposed Faber and gained as lucky a victory as he ever won in his life. Somebody always was turning out a miracle and getting him out of trouble."[40]

Historians who say that Faber pitched his entire major league career in a White Sox uniform are wrong — but only on a technicality. In early August, the Chicagoans arrived in New York, but their uniforms did not. Somehow, trunks containing the White Sox garb were not loaded on their train in Boston. The Chicago players wound up borrowing their hosts' road uniforms, down to the Yankees caps and blue socks. "The Sox were an odd looking lot in the strange regalia. Some of the uniforms made good fits, but several of the visiting players simply dangled in Yankee livery," *The New York Times* noted. "[Ray] Schalk's head was half hidden under a blue cap that completed an almost perfect disguise for the Chicago backstop." Faber, dressed in Yankees grays, suffered the 2–0 loss in the Polo Grounds. Rain ended the game with two out in the bottom of the fifth inning. "Getting a decision over Faber was something new in the campaign of 1921 Yankees," the *Times* noted, "and they were perfectly satisfied to pass out of the picture without playing any more innings and endangering the rather scanty lead which they had picked up."[41] No one argued the decision to end the contest early. "A crowd of at least 28,000 was on hand and it was at least 6 o'clock before all of them got away from the ground," Crusinberry reported. "The field was a regular lake and the streets were like rivers."[42]

Stan Coveleski was Faber's mound opponent when the White Sox moved on to Cleveland, and the match between future Hall-of-Famers was far from an epic battle. The Indians rocked Faber for five runs in the first four innings; he did not come out for the fifth inning. "Faber appeared to have all his speed as usual, but as in all of his starts of this trip, he had things break against him," Crusinberry told *Tribune* readers. "There were indications in the first inning that Faber wasn't just right, though he might have gotten away all right except for the trick right wall. Jamieson boosted a high fly that any one could have reached in an ordinary park, but it hit the short fence and caromed off for a double." The right-field foul pole at Dunn Field (known before and after as League Park) was just 290 feet from home plate. Meanwhile, Coveleski scattered seven hits in the 6–1 victory, which, combined with a Yankees loss, put Cleveland back atop the league standings.[43] The Indians' hold on first place did not last through the White Sox series. After his star pitcher's abbreviated outing, Gleason started Faber on just one day's rest. "Faber didn't pitch any better in winning this one than he did in losing two or three others on this trip," Crusinberry wrote, "but he got not only strong but sparkling support from the other boys." Faber allowed the Indians five hits in his 4–1 win for his 22nd victory of the season.

Faber's 23rd win occurred August 18 in what Crusinberry described as the most exciting game in Comiskey Park since the Great War. The White

Sox edged the Yankees, despite Babe Ruth's 46th homer of the campaign. The Bambino's blast, a three-run shot in the seventh inning, curved inside the left-field foul pole, 363 feet away. Rookie umpire Frank Wilson ruled it a homer, and a row ensued. Manager Gleason and third baseman Eddie Mulligan joined catcher Ray Schalk in surrounding Wilson to argue that the ball was foul. Several bat-wielding Yankees came out to commend Wilson on his eyesight. Mulligan and first baseman Wally Pipp nearly came to blows. When the game finally resumed — minus Schalk, whom Wilson had excused for the duration — the Yankees had moved into the lead 6–4. The Sox's fiery catcher missed quite a finish. In the bottom of the eighth, Chicago rallied for three runs and took over the lead for good 7–6. Faber was removed for a pinch hitter during the rally, and Shovel Hodge pitched a scoreless ninth inning to preserve the win.[44]

Faber was not his best in his next start, facing lowly Philadelphia in Comiskey. The Sox jumped to a 4–0 lead after two innings, but gave it back by the seventh, when the Athletics tied the contest 5–5. Faber hurt his cause with a wild pitch at a critical juncture. The game extended into the 10th inning, when the Athletics pushed across the final run against Faber, who went the distance.[45] He squandered another early 4–0 lead, and the visiting Red Sox posted three-run innings in the fourth and seventh to prevail 6–5. Boston received a gift during their seventh-inning rally. The Red Sox had runners on first and third with nobody out. Outfielder Bib Falk caught a fly ball in short left field. The runner on third, Everett Scott, decided against trying to score on Falk's arm. However, Falk decided to try a trick. He bluffed a throw to home plate and immediately fired toward second base, hoping to nail the other base runner. Unfortunately, Falk's heave sailed over first base and Scott trotted across the plate.[46]

Despite losing five of his previous seven decisions, Faber was still a subject of great interest back home in Dubuque County. Boosters in Dubuque and Cascade booked a special excursion aboard the Chicago, Milwaukee and St. Paul Railroad to see Faber pitch against the St. Louis Browns in Comiskey Park. The train was to leave Dubuque at 4:30 A.M. September 3 and start the trip back at 10 P.M. The round-trip fare was $4.15.[47] However, the excursion was scuttled after the featured attraction wrenched his knee on August 31. Trailing 6–0 in the seventh inning in the first game of a doubleheader, the Browns had a runner on first with nobody out. Faber caught up with a bouncer on the first-base side, and a teammate shouted for him to throw to second base. With his momentum taking him toward the foul line, Faber turned and attempted the force-out. He completed the throw, but twisted his knee and wound up flat on his back. The star pitcher limped to the clubhouse. Relievers Doug McWeeney and Roy Wilkinson nearly blew Faber's six-run lead, but managed to hold on 6–5 and qualify Faber for his 24th victory.[48]

Thus ended Faber's hopes of winning 30 games in 1921. He missed three weeks of action. Though sidelined, Faber traveled with the team to New York. (This time, the Sox had their uniforms.) On September 14, a Rip Collins fastball struck Chicago batter Amos Strunk in the head, knocking him unconscious. With the aid of a doctor summoned from the stands, Strunk came to after three or four minutes and walked to the bench under his own power. During the stoppage, Faber and Babe Ruth, playing right field, sized up each other for a fight. "What the Faber-Ruth argument was all about was not entirely clear," *The New York Times* reported. "Other players rushed to right field, where Babe and Red were closing in on each other, and there wasn't as much as a swing."[49] It was an uncharacteristic confrontation, as Faber and Ruth were usually on respectful terms. In 1920, Ruth described Faber as "the nicest man in the world."[50] Eight years after their standoff, at the Red Faber Day ceremony, Ruth posed for pictures and shook hands with the honoree.

Faber returned to action as a reliever late in the September 19 game in Boston, but the Red Sox blasted him for six hits and three runs.[51] It appeared he would be in for more of the same two days later in Washington, where he gave up three runs in the first inning. He settled down and pitched shutout ball after that, but the Nationals already had all the runs they needed for a 3–2 victory.[52] Faber did not need his best stuff in Philadelphia, where, in the second game of a September 24 doubleheader, the White Sox exploded for 10 runs in the first two innings. The Chicago hitters kept piling it on while Faber kept the Athletics in check. He lost his shutout in the ninth inning on a wild pitch, allowing Philadelphia to close the gap to 18–1. Faber's career-high 25th win of the year was also his easiest. Reflecting the team's vulnerability with Faber out of the lineup, the win also ended the White Sox's 11-game losing streak.[53]

Starting the Sox's regular-season finale against Stan Coveleski and the Indians, who needed a win to retain any hope of winning the pennant, Faber pitched well but was nicked for three runs in the fifth inning. Though he allowed just three hits outside of the fifth, he was tagged with the 3–2 loss.[54]

Despite fading and missing starts in the final couple of months, Faber (25–15) was responsible for 40 percent of the White Sox's 62 victories. Faber and Kerr (19–17) accounted for 71 percent of the wins for Chicago, which finished seventh among the eight American League teams. Meanwhile, Faber, with his earned-run average of 2.48, was hailed as the league's best pitcher of 1921.[55]

However, the White Sox still had more baseball to play. The City Series with the Cubs had baseball fans in Chicago buzzing. The prospect of a pitching duel between Faber and the Cubs' Grover Cleveland Alexander was particularly appealing. It inspired one fan to submit this verse:

Of ball games I have seen but few
Since gambling roused my dander;
But I shall watch Kid Gleason's crew
Hook up with Alexander.
I'd leave my home, I'd leave my friends
I'd leave my daily labor,
To see the Cubs combat the bends
Served up by Urban Faber.[56]

In Game 2 at Wrigley Field, Faber gave up a lead-off homer to Max Flack. However, he held the Cubs in check. The White Sox led 7–4 lead in the eighth inning when Turner Barber hit a high bouncer along the first base line. Faber bounded from the mound to field the ball and lunged to tag out Barber. Faber recorded the putout but in the process re-injured his right knee. He required assistance to get off the field. "Faber's injury is one that may give him a lot of trouble and that is likely to affect his work in the future to the extent that he may not be the marvelous hurler he was with the White Sox this season," wrote Oscar C. Reichow in *The Sporting News*. "It would be a severe blow to the White Sox to lose Faber."[57] Faber's knee locked so badly that he spent a week in the hospital before he could straighten the leg. He limped out of the hospital, but expressed hope that the knee would recover with rest.[58]

The injury also was a blow for Cascade. "Owing to the second injury to his knee in a city series game at Chicago last Friday, Urban Faber telephoned yesterday that he would be unable to pitch any more games this season," the *Cascade Pioneer* reported. "Therefore the proposed 'Red Faber Day' ball game here is regretfully called off for this year."[59] Shortly afterward, Red and Irene Faber drove into Cascade in his brand-new Essex sedan. They stayed in Cascade several weeks.[60] It is likely that residing in the Hotel Faber was not Irene's idea; she was a city girl who expressed little affection for the tiny Iowa community.

Faber's knee required more than just rest. He returned to Chicago, where, on the last day of November, Dr. Phillip Kreuscher removed floating cartilage from the knee. "A loose right knee is a bad thing for a right-handed pitcher, by the way," *The Sporting News* explained. "He pivots on the right foot and the knee is under a strain — anything out of kilter with that knee is bad business."[61] Dr. Kreuscher said that there was every indication that the surgery was successful, but everyone knew that the result would not be known with certainty until spring training 1922.

17

Best in the American League (Again)

During the off-season of 1921–22, Urban and Irene Faber vacated their Chicago hotel, resided briefly in Cascade and then took an apartment on the South Side of Chicago. The change in domiciles allowed Red to be closer to follow-up treatments with Dr. Kreuscher, who regularly subjected the joint to "electrical baths" intended to speed healing.[1] In mid–January, Faber was still using a cane but predicting a full recovery. The *Tribune's* Irving Vaughan not convinced. "While 'Red' is optimistic regarding his prospects for the coming race, it does not follow he will be the great pitcher he was in 1921. To him the knee may appear to be coming along in great style, but there is always that possibility of it bothering him considerably once he gets down to work in earnest. Only a tryout in spring camp will settle this point."[2]

One competing organization apparently believed that right-hander would return to his dominant ways. The Yankees, using an intermediary, contacted Faber about the possibility of his moving to New York. Tampering with another team's player was always prohibited, but under the commission structure preceding Judge Kenesaw Mountain Landis' arrival as baseball czar, not much was ever done about it. Tampering was discussed at the major leagues' joint meeting in December 1921, and it was on the baseball advisory council's agenda a few weeks later. Landis planned to raise the penalty for tampering from a mere fine to expulsion from organized baseball. To work around the reserve clause — free agency was a half-century in the future — a tampered player would hold out for a huge salary increase from his current owner. Rather than give in to the demand, the owner would sell or trade the player's contract — and typically it was the tampering party that stepped forward to express interest in the disgruntled player. Vaughan revealed that Faber showed little interest in the Yankees' overtures. The pitcher reportedly told the emissary, "Go and talk to the man I am working for."[3]

Under the supervision of Manager "Kid" Gleason, White Sox pitchers and catchers got an early start on spring training in Texas. The battery members spent one week in Marlin, which was noted for its hot-spring baths, before moving to regular camp in Seguin, 35 miles northeast of San Antonio. One of their first workouts was cut short by a dust storm — but not before Faber tested his arm and surgically repaired right knee. "Faber cut loose for the first time and showed some speed," the *Tribune* reported. "He even threw curves until Gleason cautioned him about doing too much so early."[4] However, the pitcher was not yet 100 percent. When the others moved on to Seguin, he and Irene stayed in Marlin an additional week, during which time he made use of the baths and received more electrical treatments on his knee.[5] A few days after rejoining the team in Seguin, Faber demonstrated that his knee was recovering rapidly. A sportswriter stated: "Just to give an idea of Faber's condition is the fact that he spent three hours on the hotel dance floor the other night and executed some fancy steps which none suspected were in his repertoire. The incident is related merely to show that the Sox pitchers are coming along."[6]

The New York Giants, winners of the 1921 World Series, and the White Sox arranged a series of a dozen exhibition games. Financially and competitively, the contests were superior to the usual fare of games against college and minor-league squads. The Giants might have mistaken Faber for a collegiate pitcher, however, when they met in rainy Forth Worth on March 27 and blasted him for 17 hits in six innings. Despite the shellacking, Faber at times appeared on his game. "The mauling of Faber was most peculiar," the *Tribune* reported. "He appeared to have a world of stuff, and in spots the Giants were helpless. On three occasions, however, they broke loose without caution, starting with six runs in the first inning, and adding three in the fourth and two in the sixth."[7] The Sox had a visitor in the Dallas area: erstwhile teammate Dickie Kerr, who was locked in a contract dispute with Comiskey. A winner of 40 games over the previous two seasons and considered a hero for nearly overcoming his corrupt teammates' plans in the 1919 World Series, Kerr asked Comiskey for a raise of $500. The Old Roman refused.[8] (Insulted, Kerr eventually played "outlaw" ball in Chicago and served a suspension for doing so. He finally rejoined the White Sox late in the 1925 season, but by then he had lost his edge.)[9] Kerr's departure left the team with only one reliable pitcher: Faber.

Only a week after the Giants hammered him in Texas, Faber rebounded in Knoxville, going the distance in a 6–2 victory. "Faber pitched a midseason performance," Vaughan reported. "He had more foolers than he knew what to do with."[10] *The New York Times* agreed: "Faber held the Giants under his spell practically through the game after the first inning," when he gave up a run. The Chicago pitcher rounded out his performance with two hits and two runs batted in.[11]

Chicago sportswriters, usually optimistic during the preseason, could find little to encourage them about the 1922 White Sox. "One man — Urban (Red) Faber — is all that separates the one time powerful white legged crew from an ironclad lease on the cellar position," Vaughan wrote.[12] "Red Faber is the White Sox ace. What a shame it is that he is not surrounded with Kerr and two or three more efficient pitchers," wrote Oscar C. Reichow. "Aside from the pitching staff the White Sox team is shaping up well, but no team has ever been known to finish anywhere in the race without a first-class hurling staff."[13] The Giants' John McGraw, whose world champs lost the preseason series to the Sox, was more positive on the Chicagoans' prospects. "Red Faber, of course, is a great pitcher, and he will win a lot of games this year ... but he may get some help from Wilkinson, Hodge, Acosta and one or two others. There's a lot of fight in that ball club, too."[14] In advance of Opening Day, White Sox officials applied a new coat of green paint to Comiskey Park, but they could not gloss over the deficiencies on the field.

The season-opener could have been described as "Urban warfare." It pitted the only two major leaguers with the first name Urban — Faber of Chicago and Shocker of the St. Louis Browns — against each other. More than 20,000 fans crowded into Comiskey Park. Faber, who had a history of rough first innings, gave up two runs on two hits in the opening frame. He allowed only one more hit the rest of the way — a bad-hop single in the seventh. However, every one of Faber's three walks factored in the scoring, and the Browns and Shocker, who allowed nine hits, earned a 3–2 victory.[15] Faber returned the favor in the Browns' home opener the next week, defeating Shocker 4–2. "Faber was so good that he didn't have much to contend with after the initial inning," reported Vaughan.[16] Faber and the Sox got a scare a few days later in Cleveland. The Chicago hurler put his pitching hand in the way of a hit by Larry Gardner. Faber, who midway in the contest enjoyed a 4–0 lead, stayed in the game, but he gave up a run in the bottom of the ninth and another in the 10th to lose 6–5; his record fell to 2–2.[17] He then dominated the Tigers in Detroit. "The deceptive manner in which Mr. Urban Faber throws the pill stopped the Tygers so abruptly today that they hardly knew what it was all about," said Vaughan of the six-hit, 4–0 victory. (Some newspapers called them the "Tygers," in homage to their player-manager Ty Cobb.) "To appreciate Faber's work one had to be a ringside witness. He had everything, in fact, so much that even the umpire behind the plate missed a few good strikes." The Tigers tried to mount a ninth-inning rally, loading the bases with two outs. However, pinch hitter Bob Fothergill topped a pitch back to Faber, whose throw to catcher Ray Schalk forced out Cobb on the game's final play.[18] After a three-game homestand, the White Sox returned to Detroit, where a pitchers' duel turned into a slugfest. Some 20,000 spectators jammed Navin Field for the Sunday contest; the crowd was nearly twice the team's season average. Thousands overflowed onto the field. Mounted police and ropes were used to keep the fans confined to the margins of the playing surface, and special ground rules were enacted. The extra company in the outfield did not bother Chicago right fielder Harry Hooper, who in the second inning backed into hostile territory to snare Emory "Topper" Rigney's long drive. During his career, Faber often suffered losses despite giving up few hits; this game was not one of those occasions. By the time it ended, the Chicago hurler was blasted for 17 hits but still pitched a complete game. The White Sox broke open a 1–1 game in the top of the seventh inning with a six-run rally, which featured a rare single by Faber on a hit-and-run play. Later in the inning, Cobb, playing center field, threw out Faber as he tried to score on a single. In a frenetic bottom half of the seventh, the left-handed hitting Cobb smashed a Faber offering over the right field wall for a three-run homer. The excitement was too much for a fan seated behind the Tigers dugout, Alfred Kenning. The 65-year-old man rose to cheer Cobb's drive, but fell back in his seat. Kennig died on the spot. His body was carried from the grandstand, and the game continued. (Of Cobb's 117 career home runs, it was his only one against Faber.[19]) The Sox made it 9–4 with a two-run ninth and then held off yet another Tiger rally to survive with a 9–7 victory. Cobb went five-for-five, collecting three doubles and a single to go with his homer.[20]

Throughout his professional career, Faber seemed plagued by teammates' miscues in the field and ineptitude at the plate. This misfortune was not limited to his time in the majors. Before Faber joined the White Sox, a Des Moines newspaper noted his calm acceptance of his hard-luck status. Newspaper archives are replete with accounts of Faber being charged with the loss after dropped flies, kicked grounders or errant throws. Bad luck hit Faber several times in 1922. On May 11 in New York, he allowed no earned runs but the Sox committed five errors and gave the Yankees a 4–1 victory. (For the record, Faber committed one of the errors.)[21] On June 18, Faber and Nationals great Walter Johnson battled each other through eight scoreless innings. In the ninth, Washington's Sam Rice was on second with two out when Frank Brower lifted an easy pop-up between home and first base. However, Chicago first baseman Earl Sheely muffed the ball, and Rice scored all the way from second with the game's only run. Sheely was the goat, but Faber, who scattered seven hits, went into the books as the loser.[22] Just two days later, Faber was charged with the loss in relief in a 13-inning contest; the White Sox had a great opportunity to win it for Faber in the 11th, but, with runners on first and second with nobody out, Chicago's Eddie Mulligan was picked off second base.[23] On July 20 in Boston, Faber suffered a 3–2 loss. "It took 10 innings to reach a decision," Vaughan reported, "but with good support Faber would have won it in regulation time and one run would have been amply sufficient for him."[24]

Faber's professionalism despite his teammates' failures inspired one fan, using the pen name Hoosier Pat, to submit this poem to the *Chicago Tribune*:

To Red Faber

The whining pessimists would have us feel
That baseball and its sentiment is dead.
I think of you at times, and smile. Their spiel
Amuses me. For I believe, instead,
That while the mem'ry of your art shall live,
Emblazoned in the true fans' hall of fame,
Your record will an added glamour give.
I pity him who has not known the thrill
That rises, as our infield starts to crack,
When, undismayed, you calmly mount the hill
And turn the nation's mightiest sluggers back.
The game, too true, has many sordid features,
But while you've strength within your good right arm,
Despite the petty cant of morbid screechers
It will retain for me its old time charm.[25]

However, it would inaccurate to say that the breaks always went against Faber. In the first game May 27, he and St. Louis star Urban Shocker locked up for another epic battle. The Browns held a 1–0 lead — and Shocker had a perfect game until the bottom of the eighth inning, when the White Sox put together a double and a single to tie. Faber and Chicago won it in 10 innings, when the Sox followed a Browns error with a sacrifice and a single. Shocker, having given up just three hits, walked off the field a 2–1 loser.[26] Occasionally Faber's misfortune was of his own doing. Sometimes it was his pitching. Sometimes it was his own defense. In Philadelphia on May 17, he dueled rookie Fred Heimach into the 13th inning, recording 13 strikeouts in the battle. However, the 13th inning proved unlucky for Faber. With two out and a man on first, Clarence Walker blasted a two-run, walk-off homer.[27] Faber's wild pitch and throwing error contributed to his own undoing in a 6–2 loss to Washington on August 5. Little more than a week later, he botched a run-down play. After two Browns found themselves both occupying third base, they bolted — one for home and the other for second. Instead of throwing the ball, Faber, never fleet of foot and a .946 career fielder, chased one of the St. Louis base runners — and lost the race.[28]

However, there were many highlights for Faber in 1922. He got the start May 22 in the nation's capital, where the spectators included U.S. president Warren G. Harding. On hand to support a fund-raiser for a Washington children's hospital, Harding autographed two baseballs, which sold at auction for $200 each. Meanwhile, with the president looking on, Faber held off the Nationals for a 4–3 win.[29]

Baseball was not the only thing on Chicagoans' minds. Faber and the White Sox played during the Roaring Twenties, when Chicago was noted for its speakeasies, gambling dens and street-corner shootings. Noting the apparent decline of the city, a reader submitted this verse to the *Tribune*:

> *The busy holdup plies his trade,*
> *The gangster makes his kill,*
> *The wave of crime,*
> *Unchecked in time,*
> *Will make Chicago Ill.*[30]

Nearly two years after the Black Sox allegations came to light, the specter of other fixed games emerged. Oscar "Happy" Felsch, one of the banned players, charged that the collection taken up by the 1917 White Sox, then in a pennant battle with Boston, was a payoff to Detroit for purposely losing four games to the Chicagoans. Three members of the 1917 team — Eddie Collins, Schalk and Faber — issued a denial. "Sure, there was a pool, but there was nothing crooked about it," Schalk said. "I remember we contributed about $45 apiece for a pool to be offered as a bonus to the Detroit pitchers if they defeated Boston in a series toward the end of the season." The catcher added, "We thought nothing of it, as it was quite a usual thing. All organized baseball knows that is often done." However, Schalk said that he did not know what happened to the money after it was turned over to Chicago first baseman Arnold "Chick" Gandil, a future Black Sox defendant. (Five years later, Swede Risberg and Gandil renewed the allegations. After conducting a hearing in January 1927, Commissioner Landis cleared Faber, his "Clean Sox" teammates and the Detroit players — but made it clear that no such "reward" pools would be tolerated in the future.)

Faber posted his second three-hitter of 1922 on July 16, when he stymied the New York Yankees at the Polo Grounds 4–0. One of the singles went to Babe Ruth. Even three teammates' errors could not deny him a shutout. "The game was all Faber," *The New York Times* observed. "He dominated it from the time Umpire Bill Dineen sent the teams on their way until he struck out Aaron Ward for the final out in the ninth."[31] Added the *Chicago Tribune*, "Faber was never better than he was today. Everything in his extensive repertoire worked like a charm."[32]

The two most unusual White Sox games of 1922 both involved the Yankees. The weather was threatening on August 1 in Chicago; the White Sox held a 5–1 lead after Faber struck out the side in the top of the fourth. Storm clouds approached and a downpour appeared imminent. The White Sox needed only to hold their four-run lead and retire the Yankees in the top of the fifth to claim victory in a rain-shortened game. The Chicagoans attempted to put themselves out as quickly as possible in the bottom of the fourth, to hasten New York's turn in the fifth. The Yankees, meanwhile, tried to prolong the proceedings. The New Yorkers stalled by making wild throws, changing pitchers and arguing with the umpires. Batting with two out in the bottom of the fourth, Faber hit an easy grounder to shortstop Everett Scott, who deliberately eluded the ball. While the Yankees tossed the ball among themselves, Faber tried to put himself out by leisurely trotting from first base to third, where he was finally tagged out. The White Sox retired two Yankees in the top of the fifth when the skies opened. After the half-hour cloudburst, Comiskey did everything he could to make the field playable, dispatching "a gang of huskies with brooms" to work over the diamond. However, just as it appeared that the Yankees' stalling attempts had been thwarted and the game was to resume, Mother Nature decided there would be no more baseball at Comiskey Park that day. "Not fewer than four Yankees should have been put out of the game and it should have been forfeited on at least two charges to the Sox," complained Ed Sullivan of the *Chicago Herald-Examiner.* "What has become of the old-fashioned umpire with some nerve?"[33] The White Sox protested to the league office and appealed for a forfeit victory. Four weeks later, President Ban Johnson issued his decision. He fined Yankees manager Miller Huggins $100 and assessed $25 penalties against Scott, Bob Meusel, Waite Hoyt and Wally Schang for "the disgraceful exhibition of stalling." However, Johnson rejected Chicago's appeal to receive credit for a victory and ordered the game replayed from the start. The president noted that Faber, Ray Schalk and Bib Falk contributed to the farce by trying to put themselves out in the fourth inning. He fined each of them $25.[34]

Faber next encountered the Yankees and Babe Ruth on August 20, in New York. Ruth swatted a two-run homer in the first inning, but otherwise he was having his difficulties that afternoon, particularly in the middle innings. He made a two-run, four-base error in the top of the third. Faber struck out Ruth in the bottom of the third and picked him off first base — after a bunt (!) single — in the fifth. (This was not the only time Faber picked off Ruth. According to umpire Billy Evans, who was working the game in Chicago, Faber nailed a Bambino who was deep in thought after learning from the first base coach — a teammate — that his tip at the horse track had just earned him thousands.[35]) Ruth lined out to first in the seventh. In the bottom of the ninth, holding a 5–4 lead, Faber found himself in a jam. He gave up a bunt single and a walk and had to face Ruth with no one out. The Polo Grounds crowd howled as if it were a World Series contest. After taking two inside pitches, Ruth deposited Faber's next pitch into the right-field bleachers. As Faber walked off the field, fans poured onto it to congratulate the Yankees slugger as he tried to circle the bases and make the 7–5 victory official. "Ruth almost had to fight his way to the plate," Irving Vaughan told his *Tribune* readers. "The fans swarmed on him, pounded him on the back and attempted to carry him, but it was too much of a load. Babe couldn't get free, however, and just had to move with the mob toward the center field exit. It took him fully ten minutes to make the short journey."[36] Two of Ruth's nine career homers against Faber came in the same game. That loss apparently left no permanent scars, for Faber was back on track in his next start, shutting out Connie Mack's Athletics on six hits 8–0. Only three base runners got as far as second base, and the Sox defense committed no errors.[37]

Before their final weekend of the regular season, major league teams took a half-week break and played exhibition contests. The White Sox turned barnstormers. They rallied to beat a contingent of minor league all-stars in Galva, Illinois, on a Monday. The next day, in Battle Creek, Michigan, they crushed a semi-pro team. After a day off, on their way to an American League game in St. Louis, they defeated a semi-pro team in Litchfield, a downstate Illinois community in the stomping grounds of Ray Schalk. (The star catcher was born in Harvel, about 20 miles north of Litchfield. Many baseball references incorrectly list Schalk's birthplace as Harvey, the name of a Chicago suburb.) To honor his friend and batterymate, Faber pitched a few innings in Litchfield. Though Faber and Schalk remained friends long into their retirement years, they had their professional differences about calling pitches. In the 1960s, a sportswriter asked Faber about it. "Oh, sure. We'd disagree quite often. Sometimes we'd even have a little argument, but nothing serious," Faber said. "I'd usually get my way, but that doesn't mean I was right all the time. I guessed wrong quite a few times."[38] After the Schalk Day festivities — the honoree received a pearl necklace from his local admirers — the White Sox made the short jaunt to St. Louis, where the Browns needed three wins and some "help" to win the pennant.[39] They might have thought their prayers were answered when Johnny Tobin hit Faber's first pitch of the series' first game over the right-field fence of Sportsman's Park. Tobin smacked another homer in his next at-bat, and the Browns won, 3–2.[40] St. Louis won the next day, but it was not enough; the Yankees clinched the pennant by beating the Red Sox in Fenway.

The 1922 White Sox exceeded the prognosticators' gloomy predictions. Entering the final two months of the season, Gleason's charges were 53–46 in third place and only 4½ games off the lead. However, they faded, going 24–31 the rest of the way to finish in fifth place at an even 77–77. Still, it was a 15-game improvement over their 1921 mark.

For his part, Faber again led American League regulars for lowest earned-run average (2.81) while posting a 21–17 record. "The hardest worked pitchers, and we take it the worth-while pitcher is the one who can do a lot of work for his team, are not far up in the 'won and lost' column," *The Sporting News* editorialized that August. "Faber, Coveleskie and Shocker are the pitchers in the American who have pitched more than 200 innings, and one has to run through a lot of names to find theirs in the averages. Yet how many of those 'above' them excel them in real worth?"[41] The White Sox's lack of pitching depth is reflected in Faber's other rankings. He was first in the AL in complete games (31) for the second straight year. First in innings pitched (352), Faber was fifth in victories (21) while ranking third in losses (17). He was second in shutouts (4), strikeouts (148) and most hits allowed (334), but third in fewest hits allowed per nine innings (8.54).[42] Such is the lot of a star hurler on a mediocre, pitching-deficient team.

For the first time since Faber's rookie season of 1914, the 1922 Chicago Series against the Cubs went the full seven games. In the opener, Faber was knocked around but extracted himself from numerous tight spots to collect the win 6–2. It was his fourth consecutive win in the City Series (and the Sox's 14th straight). He took a no-decision in Game 3, which the Cubs won, 8–5. His next start came in a must-win situation in Game 6 at Comiskey Park. The Cubs held a 3–2 series lead. Faber held up his end, shutting out the North Siders through nine innings on three hits. However, the Sox had their hands full with Cubs pitcher Ernie Osborne, who threw shutout baseball through eight innings and allowed only four hits — one of them by Faber. The game remained scoreless in the bottom of the ninth, when the White Sox advanced Earl Sheely to third with only one out. Schalk then laid down a squeeze bunt. It worked, the Sox forced a Game 7 and Faber received credit for the victory. In the finale, however, the Cubs prevailed 2–0 behind the brilliant pitching of 35-year-old Grover Cleveland Alexander.

Though it was an exciting series and a stellar season, Faber was anxious for it to end. "Faber has his hunting paraphernalia all packed and as soon as the series closes is going to strike out for the Oregon timber country," the *Tribune* noted. "Later he will go to California."[43] The previous off-season, his knee injury and surgery precluded hunting excursions. No doubt, he wanted to make up for lost time. One can only hope, however, that, while tromping the hunting grounds, the 34-year-old Faber stopped to smell the roses. After nine years in the major leagues, all his 20-win campaigns, 151 of his 254 major league victories and his most successful seasons were behind him.

18

"A Puzzle"

Soon after his third straight season as one of baseball's elite pitchers, Red Faber returned to Oregon and Washington for another hunting expedition. Sox first baseman Earl Sheely accompanied him. The teammates lived in a small tent, cooked their own meals and walked several miles daily.[1] While in the Pacific Northwest, Faber bagged an antlered deer and shipped the head to Cascade, where his brother, Al, displayed it above the tobacco case in his billiards hall.[2] After the trip, Red and Irene Faber spent the winter near San Diego, where he was a regular on the golf courses. His conditioning might have been a concern of management, because he sent the White Sox front office a letter detailing his off-season activities and specifying that he "has kept in the open air as much as possible." An automobile enthusiast, Faber further explained that he was driving regularly because he preferred to carry a few extra pounds until time to start training.[3] At spring training, Faber told the *Chicago Herald and Examiner* that he had lost weight since the 1922 season and never felt better.[4]

The pitchers and catchers reported for early training in Marlin, Texas, near San Antonio. (Regular camp would follow in Seguin, about 150 miles north.) An emergency disrupted the White Sox in their first week in Marlin. Fire engulfed the upper floor of the Bule Sanitarium, the team's temporary headquarters. Players, team officials and sportswriters "fought their way into the smoke-ridden quarters and wheeled out trunks containing baseball paraphernalia." They saved everything.[5]

Faber and the other pitchers were under the direction of a new coach, former spitball ace Ed Walsh. His training regimen featured miles and miles of hikes. Some days, a long walk was the only work they could accomplish because the weather was too cold, wet and windy for baseball. On yet another rainy day in late March, an exasperated Manager Kid Gleason scouted around Seguin and arranged the use of a cotton warehouse; under cover, the pitchers threw for a half-hour. Afterwards, like children at play, they frolicked by climbing around on the mountain of cotton bales.[6] However, Faber got in enough training to develop a painful blister on his pitching hand; it prevented him from "cutting loose" for a while.[7]

As they had the previous spring, the White Sox and Giants booked a series of exhibition games, including a two-week barnstorming tour. In San Antonio on March 24, before the teams broke camp, the Giants pounded Stubby Mack and Faber to take a 9–4 lead into the bottom of the ninth. The White Sox managed to score five times and tie the game. The umpires cancelled extra innings because of darkness — a decision that caused such uproar among fans that it reminded one sportswriter of a World Series atmosphere. ""The populace stood up and howled for more baseball," *The New York Times* reported. "The only reason Judge Landis was not surrounded by an angry mob was that he was not there."[8]

In their prognostications for the 1923 season, several sportswriters saw the White Sox as a puzzle. Only three players remained from the 1917 champions — Faber, Schalk and Eddie Collins. The *Tribune*'s Hugh Fullerton wrote, "It is a team to which almost anything may happen, excepting finishing last or first." Fullerton noted that Faber was the pitcher slowest to round into shape.[9] His conditioning was not of great concern to Larry Woltz of the *Chicago Herald and Examiner*: "Faber is as good today as any time during his long and honorable career. He has trained carefully. He knows how to get ready, and Gleason has permitted him to take his time. For the past several days the big red-head has been popping the ball over the plate in midsummer form."[10]

Despite everyone's high expectations, Faber's regular season started slowly. Not fond of working Opening Day contests, Faber drew that assignment before 20,000 fans in Cleveland on April 18. Though he trailed the Indians 4–1 and was lifted for pinch hitter Amos Strunk in the eighth, Faber nearly received credit for a victory. Strunk sparked a four-run rally to give Chicago a 5–4 lead. However, reliever Mack allowed the Indians two runs in the ninth and lost it 6–5.[11] After that no-decision, Faber two days later suffered his own loss in relief.[12] Next, he took a no-decision in St. Louis, where he left a tie game after seven innings. Faber went into the records books for stealing home in the fourth, when he and Ernie Johnson engineered a double-steal. After 14 innings, however, the umpires ended the contest and declared it a tie because of darkness.[13] With only one win and a tie in seven games, the White Sox arrived in Chicago, where Faber received the opportunity to start *another* Opening Day. About 30,000 fans jammed Comiskey Park to see their team take on Cleveland. The pre-game entertainment featured a novelty — a "radio concert." The *Chicago Tribune* explained: "The tunes will be picked up by the huge receiving set in the club office and distributed to different parts of the grand stand by the electrical enunciator."[14] As the game

was about to begin, two men emerged from the stands and presented a bas-
ket of roses to the *umpire*. The recipient was none other than Clarence Rowland, the manager of the 1917 champions, who was carrying out his first
umpiring assignment in Chicago.[15] (Rowland proved to be one of the major
leagues' worst umpires; the league dropped him after five seasons.[16])

The concert and other Opening Day falderal concluded, the game began.
Faber had his typical first-inning struggles, giving up three hits and a walk
to fall behind 2–0. He allowed just three more hits and one run over the subsequent seven innings, until he was lifted for a pinch hitter. Meanwhile, Cleveland spitballer Stan Coveleski — other references spell it Covelskie — scattered
eight Sox hits and collected the 3–0 victory.[17] Later, pitted against the majors'
other Urban — Shocker of St. Louis — Faber suffered another loss. He lasted
just five innings and gave up six hits, but it was a critical error by his erstwhile hunting partner, Sheely, that broke open the contest.[18]

Faber finally earned his first win of 1923 in Chicago on May 4, shutting
out the Tigers on seven hits. His second victory came on May 10, the day
after a freak snowstorm blanketed Comiskey Park, when he outlasted the Red
Sox 9–7.[19] However, his winning streak was short-lived. Faber gave up five
fourth-inning runs and committed *three* throwing errors in a 9–0 loss to
Philadelphia. Next, despite striking out seven Yankees, he lost on Babe Ruth's
double in the eighth inning.[20] Five days afterward in Detroit, Faber had
another terrible first inning, allowing the Tigers three runs on three hits.
However, he permitted only two hits the rest of the way, and the White Sox
prevailed 5–3. "A man is pitching real baseball when he can choke off a gang
of sluggers such as Cobb boasts," the *Tribune*'s Vaughan wrote. "The day that
Faber put over this feat was fine and warm and the performance augurs well
for this success in the future." In his write-up Vaughan, perhaps for the first
time, used the adjective "old" in identifying Faber. The hurler was but 34
years old.[21]

Despite his early season struggles, Faber remained a favorite among
Chicago fans. The *Tribune*'s Sally Joy Brown conducted a letter-writing contest and offered free tickets to a Sox-Yankees for 100 South Side boys. One
entrant, Joe T., wrote: "I cannot go to see them play, for there's nobody to
take me. My hero of the game is Red Faber, not because he is a redhead as I
am, but because he can pitch so good. I hope Sally will give me the chance
to see Babe Ruth strike out."[22] If Joe T. was in attendance that day, he saw
Ruth strike out twice during his hitless afternoon. (Faber was between starts
and just watched.) The White Sox were just one out from a one-run victory
when the Yankees scored twice to take the lead. However, the Sox tied it in
the bottom of the ninth and won it in the 10th.[23]

Yankee Stadium, the so-called "House That Ruth Built," opened in
1923. The White Sox paid their first visit June 5, and the next afternoon Faber

registered a career highlight. In the seventh inning of a 1–1 game, Faber sent a pitch from lefty Herb Pennock into the left-field grandstand on one bounce for a home run.[24] (The rules at the time still awarded homers of the single-bounce variety.) Meanwhile, on the mound, he held the Yankees to five hits — two of them going to the first two batters he faced. But Faber also struck out seven — including Ruth — en route to a 4–1 victory. "Faber never pitched better than he did on this occasion," noted Vaughan, who described "the big sorrel top" as "invincible." Ruth received some criticism from *The New York Times* for eschewing the sacrifice bunt and attempting to hit a dramatic home run. "The Babe" hit no homers, but "The Fabe" did.[25] His first major-league homer came in his 10th season; it would be five more years until his second.

A young fan poses with Red Faber in the 1920s. (Courtesy of the Tri-County Historical Society, Cascade, Iowa.)

Faber's victory came in the first of his seven consecutive road starts. After his heroics in New York, he lasted only six innings in Boston. He gave up eight hits, walked three, uncorked a wild pitch and hit a batter. The 10–4 loss dropped the White Sox into the American League cellar.[26] He recovered nicely for a 4–3 win at Washington. The game might not have been that close but for a base running miscue by Faber, who could not avoid getting hit by a Harry Hooper drive.[27] In his next outing, leading by two runs and just two outs from victory in sweltering Philadelphia, Faber wilted and was pulled for a reliever — but not before the Athletics scored the tying run and won it in 11 innings.[28] His seventh straight start in a visitors' uniform came Independence Day morning at St. Louis, where Faber exited after just 5⅓ innings but received credit for a victory, 9–7.

As that road trip reflected, Faber's 1923 campaign was an up-and-down proposition, a mix of mediocrity and excellence. While Faber had his struggles, spotty support from his teammates certainly did not help. For example,

he was saddled with a 3–1 loss against Philadelphia after backup second baseman John Happenny's drop of a two-out pop fly allowed two runs to score.[29]
Happenny was on the field only because team captain Eddie Collins suffered
a knee injury in early July. The game in which future Hall-of-Famer Collins
departed with a twisted knee, another future Hall-of-Famer made his major
league debut. With no minor league experience — he came directly from Bay-
lor University — Ted Lyons pitched a perfect eighth inning in a 7–2 loss at
St. Louis.[30] (Faber became lifelong friends with Lyons, who broke most of his
team records.)

Until Collins went down, and despite Faber's inconsistency, the White
Sox were only a half-game out of second place. Six weeks later, however, they
were going through the motions on their way to a seventh-place finish. "There
is … a spirit of resignation among the men," Vaughan observed. "Let the
opposition hand out a wallop of two or three runs early in the game and the
Sox are through for the day. This is not always true of course, but it happens
often enough to be noticeable."[31] Faber apparently was one who maintained
his motivation. After experiencing a "twinge" in his pitching arm and missing two or three starts, he returned to the rotation in late July.[32] In his first
outing back, in New York, he gave up 10 hits; Ruth had a triple and two doubles. Yet, the Sox prevailed, 3–2. Had the rest done the trick for Faber's "salary
wing?" In his first start of August, Faber was cruising after five innings, enjoying a three-run lead, when he suddenly lost it. Before Gleason could warm
up a reliever, the Red Sox had erased Chicago's lead; Faber wound up with
a no-decision in a Chicago victory. Gleason gave his starting pitcher a couple of extra days of rest. Faber responded by posting four nine-inning outings in five starts — three complete-game wins and a tie.

Just when Faber appeared to be the Faber of old, he suffered another setback. On September 1, during an easy, rain-shortened victory over Cleveland,
Faber removed himself from the game when, as a sportswriter put it, his "aged
arm went dead after five rounds."[33] Ten days later, after a brief workout, Faber
reported persistent elbow pain and an arm so sore he could hardly twist it."[34]
Observers figured his season was over, and they speculated what the injury
meant for the veteran's career. However, after five-week layoff, he came back
to pitch during the regular season's final weekend. He was in trouble throughout his three innings of work but escaped with a no-decision.

In handicapping the annual City Series, the *Tribune*'s Vaughan and Hugh
Fullerton did not expect Faber to play.[35] Calling the right-hander a "puzzle,"
Fullerton added, "His arm has been so bad that … it seems impossible that
he should work at all."[36] Faber did not agree. On the eve of the series, he said
that he could be ready for Game 3 or 4. Vaughan remained skeptical: "After
his long layoff, however, it is doubtful whether he will be able to stand a full
nine rounds."[37]

Though contested by the seventh-place White Sox and fourth-place Cubs, Chicago's City Series of 1923 again captivated the Windy City. Meanwhile, New York had a series all its own — the 1923 World Series, pitting the Giants and Yankees against each other. In this era preceding radio broadcasts and decades before the invention of television, fans who couldn't get to the ballpark had few options. Some bought a ticket to theaters where the games were simulated on a large board depicting the playing field. Still others phoned newspapers to request updates. The *Chicago Tribune* reported that its 14 switchboard operators were kept busy providing pitching matchups and scores. During the City Series and World Series, the *Tribune* said, the operators fielded some 100,000 baseball-related inquiries.[38]

No doubt, some callers were surprised by the news about Faber. After the Cubs won the first two City Series contests, Faber took the mound for Game 3. Before more than 26,000 fans in Cubs Park, he allowed the hosts just six hits in a 4–2, complete-game victory. His performance seemed to inspire his teammates, who went on to win the next two games for a 3–2 lead. Faber started Game 6 at Comiskey Park. He surrendered only two runs on six hits in seven innings, but when he exited he was on the hook for the loss. However, errors in consecutive innings by Cubs second baseman George Grantham gave the White Sox an opening. Gleason's men scored twice in the ninth to force extra innings and tallied again in the 10th for the 4–3 victory and the city title. "Faber's appearance (in Game 3) seemed to turn the tide and the Sox breezed right through to four straight victories," Vaughan noted.[39] Faber's share of the series proceeds was $1,175.25.[40] White Sox fans were ecstatic: Not only had their team salvaged a dismal season by beating the Cubs, but their leading pitcher seemingly had recovered from his arm trouble. Little did they know. "He complained that it hurt something fierce every time he let go of the ball," Irwin M. Howe of *The Washington Post* reported later, "but being game, he didn't let anyone know about it at the time."[41] In the locker room, as his players wound down their celebration, Manager Bill "Kid" Gleason asked for quiet. He shocked everyone by announcing his plan to resign. His boss, Comiskey, was not present and learned of Gleason's plans only by reading the *Tribune* the next morning. The Old Roman accepted the Kid's resignation, reportedly with tears in his eyes. Gleason, who managed or coached the White Sox a dozen seasons, was distraught over the 1923 results and his inability to reconstruct the team into a contender after the Black Sox scandal.[42]

The 1923 campaign also was a disappointment for Faber. It was his worst season since 1919, when he was ill and injured most of the year. Faber in 1923 went just 14–11 with an earned-run average of 3.41. Off-season knee surgery and about six weeks of layoffs were factors. Soon after the City Series, Faber drove his "Hudson super-six" home, to Cascade. It was an opportunity to visit with friends and family — and to ponder his baseball future.[43]

19

Cellar Dwellers

Faber's off-season routine was interrupted in early February 1924, when he was summoned to Milwaukee to testify at the trial of "Shoeless" Joe Jackson's civil suit against the White Sox. Banished from baseball after the Black Sox scandal, Jackson sued for $18,500. Most of the sum represented the balance on his playing contract when he was suspended at the conclusion of the 1920 season. Jackson also alleged that Comiskey owed about $1,500 from a broken promise. Jackson claimed that in 1917 Comiskey pledged to cover the difference between the World Series winner's share and $5,000 if his team defeated the New York Giants. The Sox did win the series but Comiskey never made good, Jackson said. On the witness stand, Faber at first said he knew nothing of Comiskey's offer but during cross-examination he admitted overhearing two teammates discuss such a promise. However, Faber testified that he could not remember the players' identities.[1] The jury issued a verdict in Jackson's favor, but the judge overruled, stating that jurors' decision was based on Jackson's fraudulent testimony.

After resting his arm all winter, Faber was optimistic that his elbow pain from late 1923 was behind him. In late February, he and Irene traveled to Hot Springs, Arkansas, where he enjoyed the spa and worked out to prepare for training camp.[2] Catcher Ray Schalk and pitcher Leon Cadore joined him.[3] Later, they traveled to Winter Haven, Florida, the team's new site for training camp, to find the team hotel still under construction. The Fabers wound up in Lake Alfred, about five miles away. "It looks like poor quarters for the Sox around here this spring unless the hotel figured on gets in running order in about five more days," Faber wrote to Ed Hogan, his brother-in-law back in Iowa. "This is a little place, smaller than Cascade. No, we are not having much excitement. Caught a few fish yesterday and am going to try it again."[4] During training camp, Faber made the acquaintance of Floridian Ed Cornell, the nephew of a Cascade resident. Cornell owned two automobiles, and he loaned Faber one for the duration of his stay.[5]

Faber entrusted to Hogan, an attorney, the filing of his income tax return for 1923. From Florida, the ballplayer jotted out all the information required:

Salary	$10,000.00
City Series split	$1,179.25
Interest on loan	$600.00
Total	$11,790.25

Faber also claimed making $150 in donations to "church and charity." He enclosed a blank check for Hogan to complete and send to, as the pitcher put it, "the *Infernal* Revenue."

Their Florida accommodations turned out to be the least of the White Sox's concerns. Kid Gleason's successor as manager, retired Cubs great Frank Chance, missed all of training camp due to pneumonia. He managed the team in only one game — an April 12 exhibition against the New York Giants in damp and chilly Chicago.[6] The lousy weather did nothing for Chance's fragile health. Within a week, "The Peerless Leader" underwent emergency surgery. Within five months, he was dead. (Another ex–Cub, Johnny Evers, replaced Chance. However, Evers experienced health problems of his own and missed dozens of games; Eddie Collins ran the team in his absence.)

Another distraction during spring training was rumors that the White Sox might trade Faber to Washington. "At this distance it has not yet been possible to confirm it or to form a definite idea as to whether there is anything to it," stated a sportswriter. "It doesn't seem at all likely, in the face of it, that Chicago would let him go."[7] Faber was not traded.

Optimism, based on Faber's performance in training camp, turned to worry in early April, when the arm pain returned. When rest did not help, doctors took another look. They acknowledged that a half-year earlier, Faber's problem was misdiagnosed.[8] This time, an X-ray revealed bone chips in his elbow. Team physician Phillip H. Kreuscher performed surgery on April 21.[9] While removing the three or four bone chips, Kreuscher made a discovery: Faber was double-jointed.[10] (He didn't actually have an extra joint; the term refers to unusual flexibility. Subsequent research indicates that the condition helps ward off arthritis.[11] Whether that helped Faber's baseball longevity is not known; but it did not hurt it.)

The sportswriting fraternity, which just weeks earlier said that Faber would bring good value in a trade, now speculated that Faber's retirement was imminent. *The Washington Times'* Louis A. Dougher, citing reports "from out of the West," said that even if Faber managed to return later in the season, he likely would not come back for 1925.[12]

Initially, the team expected to lose Faber's services for only 10 days. He missed two months. His first regular-season appearance of 1924 came in relief June 18, when he allowed Washington only one hit from the fifth through eighth innings. The White Sox held a 4–3 lead in the ninth, and Faber was just one out from victory when his teammates failed to convert a fielder's choice. It was a close play, and the crowd in Comiskey Park howled. The usually quiet Eddie Collins protested the decision so vehemently that he was ejected by the umpire — his former manager, Clarence Rowland. The game continued. Perhaps rattled after the brouhaha, Faber fell behind Roger Peckinpaugh and then grooved a pitch. Peckinpaugh's two-run single put the Nationals (Senators) ahead to stay.[13] Five days later, in his first start of the regular season, he was the hard-luck loser to Cleveland 4–3. "The first two runs off him resulted from the flukiest kind of hits," the *Tribune*'s Irving Vaughan reported. "The two other Indian tallies were brewed from the garden variety of errors."[14] In his next start, Faber escaped a third straight loss after staking the Browns to six runs in his only two innings; the White Sox rallied to force extra innings but lost on a 14th-inning error. Faber finally recorded his first win of 1924 on the last day of June, a 14–4 cakewalk in Detroit, despite giving up 11 hits.[15] Though he was still rounding into form, Faber won his next four decisions. Before his third win in that streak, in mid–July, the White Sox found themselves in Boston on a Sunday, when local "blue laws" still prohibited baseball. "All the Sox had to do was to try to kill time, and that's a tough job in this town on the Sabbath," Vaughan reported. "Some of the boys went down to the beaches; others played pinochle or slept or just sat in front of the tavern and watched the flat-heeled crowd drift past."[16] The next afternoon, Faber stopped the Red Sox on four hits 6–2. "Unlike his other victories, Faber gave no signs of fading out at the finish today," Vaughan said. "He was going as strong then as in the earlier rounds, and the journey hadn't been an easy matter, as he was wild and continually in the hole, and in the first few rounds had to bear down with all he had because his defense gummed up the works by kicking the ball around. Only for that Faber might have escaped scoreless."[17] He then cooled off slightly, suffering two losses in late July. The Yankees tagged him with one of those defeats, but Babe Ruth did not beat him. "Ruth was considerably distressed by the pitching of Faber. The star swatsmith was up four times against the veteran spitballer and in the first three attempts he died swinging at a third strike. The fourth time he lifted a foul back of the plate." After Faber exited, Ruth broke through with a two-run single in the ninth inning off Ted Lyons.[18]

Faber reeled off three straight wins in early August, starting with a complete-game, 2–1 decision over Boston on August 1.[19] Faber's record stood at 8–4 after his August 9 victory over the visiting Nationals. Immediately afterward, however, Faber started losing — and so did the White Sox. In the final 48 games, the team went 15–33, during which time it lost a team-record 13 straight. The final loss in that streak was assessed to Faber, who, after pitching 11 innings, served up a home-run pitch to Philadelphia's Joe Hauser in the bottom of the 12th.[20] During his team's slide in those final 48 games, Faber went just 1–7. However, he was impressive in that lone victory, in the second game of a Labor Day doubleheader at Comiskey. Leading Detroit 10–0, Faber had the Tigers down to their final out when Johnny Bassler stroked a two-run double to spoil the shutout.[21] As goes Faber, so do the White Sox: the pitching star faded to a 9–11 record while the team was 66–87 and finished dead last in the American League.

At the end, the Sox appeared to be just going through the motions, waiting for the Chicago Cubs in the City Series. "If there were any Cub spies on the grounds they surely will go back and tell [manager] Bill Killefer that there is nothing for him to worry about," the *Tribune*'s James Crusinberry wrote after Detroit battered Faber and Lyons in the final weekend of the regular season. Crusinberry said Faber, who gave up six runs in five innings, "didn't look as if he was right. But just wait until next Wednesday or Thursday [in the City Series] and watch him go."[22]

The 1924 City Series between the last-place White Sox and fifth-place Cubs made broadcasting history: the *Chicago Tribune*'s newly acquired radio station, WGN, became the first to provide a play-by-play broadcast of a major league game in Chicago. A.W. "Sen" Kaney did the honors, describing the Game 2 action from a seat in the Comiskey Park grandstand.[23]

Crusinberry was right. Faber defeated the Cubs in Game 3, 6–3. He survived a shaky eighth inning, when the North Siders scored three times to cut his lead to 4–3. The Sox answered with two runs in the top of the ninth. Faber found himself in a bases-loaded, nobody-out jam in the bottom of the ninth. Some 15,000 spectators — a good-sized crowd for a Friday afternoon — hollered for their favorites. Faber needed a strikeout — and he got it, whiffing Denver Grigsby. Next, he induced Charlie Hollocher to hit a grounder to second baseman Eddie Collins, who tagged the base runner and threw to first to complete a game-ending double play.[24] The White Sox went on to claim another City Series title in six games.

Soon after the last out, Faber rushed home to Cascade for a one-day visit.[25] He did not stay long because he was scheduled to depart for a post-season exhibition tour of Europe featuring members of the White Sox and the National League champion New York Giants. Eleven years earlier, Comiskey and Giants manager John McGraw staged a successful around-the-world tour — Faber was belatedly included on that trip — and they hoped to strike gold again. Faber rode the rails to Canada, where the White Sox and Giants played a couple of games before steaming to Europe. Poor organization, a weak post-war economy and a largely indifferent citizenry doomed the European tour of 1924. The low point occurred in Dublin, where but 20 paying customers showed up.[26] The highlights for the players were the opportunity to make the acquaintance of dignitaries. England's King George V, Queen

Mary and the Prince of Wales attended a game in London. When it became time for the seventh inning stretch, everyone stood, including the king, who rose belatedly and appeared puzzled by the peculiar tradition. After an extended period, the fans remained standing and looking toward the royal box. Finally, the prince, who was familiar with baseball tradition, quietly explained to the king that the game could not resume until he took his seat. In Paris, where the locals expressed surprise that the "Giants" were so small, barely 1,000 spectators turned out. Comiskey and McGraw, suffering a financial beating, called off the series after six games overseas. As a result, the players, some of whom were accompanied by their wives, had more than a week of free time for touring on their own. Faber joined a group that visited Rome, where they were granted an audience with Pope Pius XI. Afterwards, Faber and most of the entourage — it included veteran Casey Stengel, then of the Boston Braves — regrouped in Paris and returned to the United States on board the steamship *Leviathan*, billed as the world's largest ocean liner.[27] Though the tour was abbreviated, it surely provided plenty of experiences for Faber to recount that holiday season.

20

"Old" No More

Urban and Irene Faber spent Christmas 1924 apart, visiting relatives in their respective hometowns, Cascade and Milwaukee. A few days later, Irene joined her husband in Cascade, where they stayed for five weeks, during which time he hunted in the woods and fields around Cascade and they visited his friends and family.[1] After just a week or so back home in Chicago, the couple traveled to Hot Springs, Arkansas, where he planned to get in three weeks of treatment and workouts before spring training.[2] *Tribune* sportswriter James Crusinberry reported the pitcher's commitment to conditioning: "It is the intention of Faber to take the course of twenty-one baths at the famous Arkansas health resort after which one is supposed to be fit to fight Jack Dempsey or something." *Tribune* colleague Irving Vaughan said that Faber reported his arm "felt strong and that the elbow was loose." Added Vaughan, "And you can always rely on what the old boy says."[3]

Faber was not given to boasts or bold pronouncements. He "is a man of few words and even those words are delivered cautiously," observed Vaughan.[4] However, perhaps goaded by Crusinberry, a fellow native of Cascade, Faber said that the White Sox, who finished last in 1924, would be better than the defending World Series champion Washington Nationals (Senators) in 1925. "We have a better license to win a pennant than that bunch, and I think we will prove it this year."[5] (Faber was a better pitcher than prognosticator. The White Sox would improve by 12½ games over the previous year but remained in the second division. Meanwhile, the Nationals would repeat as American League champions.)

The 1925 White Sox had a new spring training site — Shreveport, Louisiana — and a new manager — veteran infielder Eddie Collins. The 36-year-old Faber was fit and pitching well, thanks in part to cooperative weather. The team won every one of its 19 exhibition games, battering an assortment of college and minor-league squads.[6]

Faber's regular season had a promising start. He held the Tigers hitless for the first 5⅔ innings en route to a six-hit, 4–2 victory. "Old Red was breaking over his famous spitter and mixing it cunningly with his curve and fast one," Crusinberry reported. "Red had nice control too, for this time of the year, walking only three." Faber had a rare offensive contribution, too, smashing an RBI-single and drawing a key walk during a ninth-inning rally.[7] Afterward, Faber told sportswriters that, for the first time in many seasons, his arm "felt free."[8]

In the White Sox's first homestand of the season, Faber again mastered the Tigers by another 4–2 margin. It gave the team a perfect 4–0 record at home. The next day, on Sunday, April 26, a Chicago-record 44,000 fans jammed Comiskey Park; about 8,000 of them stood behind ropes on the perimeter of the outfield and near third base. The Sox trailed Cleveland 7–2 with two out in the ninth inning when Willie Kamm hit an easy grounder to Indians shortstop Joe Sewell. The infielder's throw to reserve first baseman Ray Knode arrived in plenty of time, and the cooped-up standees streamed across the field to the closest exits. Meanwhile, however, Knode inexplicably received the throw with his foot at least two feet off the bag. He stabbed at the base but failed to touch it in time. Umpire Billy Evans declared Kamm safe; the game was not over. But by then, thousands of fans engulfed the field. "Even the umps couldn't find each other in the throng for some minutes," Crusinberry observed. When it was clear that the game could not continue, Cleveland received credit for a victory by forfeit; the chief umpire making the declaration was former Sox manager Clarence "Pants" Rowland.[9]

Faber was streaky in 1925. Between mid–May and mid–July, he lost three straight decisions, won five straight and then lost four in a row. His performances ranged from complete-game gems to disasters when he could barely last the first inning. One such nightmare occurred in May, when Boston visited Chicago. The Red Sox blasted Faber for five runs on five hits in the first inning. A walk and a Collins error kept the Boston massacre alive. "It was awful," Crusinberry understated. "Red couldn't stop 'em, but he finally got the side out and then he went to the shower bath and decided to wait until some other day to exercise his arm." Staked to a five-run lead, Boston held on 9–7.[10]

Meanwhile, from mid–May to early September, the White Sox sat in third place. Faber, who had predicted great things for the team, in June contributed by sandwiching five wins between a loss and a no-decision. On a steamy afternoon in Detroit, Faber struggled but fought the Tigers into the ninth inning of a 6–6 game. The Tigers won it with one on and one out in the bottom of the ninth when Frank O'Rourke lofted a Faber into deep left at Navin Field. The ball came down atop the concrete wall and bounced into the street for a game-ending, two-run homer.[11] Faber started his winning streak June 7 in Washington, but the occasion was not without its drama. He had his spitter working and was leading the Nationals 4–2, in the bottom of the ninth inning. On the threshold of victory, standing on the Griffith Stadium mound, Faber suddenly stopped the game. "As a pitcher, the veteran looked good all the way," Crusinberry reported, "but in the ninth inning it was apparent that his elbow was not hinging properly." While a reliever hurriedly warmed up, Faber massaged his surgically repaired right elbow. He took a couple of practice tosses, decided to continue, and earned his complete-game victory.[12] However, were his determination and perseverance worth it? Faber's arm became so sore, Crusinberry said, that he "couldn't eat asparagus comfortably." Nonetheless, he stayed in the rotation and humbled the Athletics on six hits 15–1. Gushed Crusinberry: "Old Red was simply great. Never in the old days before they dragged his arm on the operating table was it working better than it did today."[13] Faber's third straight win came in Boston, where he out-dueled fellow spitballer Jack Quinn 5–3. He next took the mound against the struggling New York Yankees. "There was cause for rejoicing on the banks of the Maquoketa River, out in Cascade, Iowa, tonight when the word was radioed that Red Faber had beaten the Yankees (9–2)," wrote Crusinberry, who often worked in references to their mutual hometown.[14] (Barely one week earlier, the Maquoketa River to which Crusinberry referred ravaged Cascade, killing two residents, and damaging or destroying dozens of buildings. The Faber Hotel narrowly escaped. The star pitcher's brother, A.J., was in a search party looking for the body of flood victim Edward G. Bell.[15])

A couple of weeks before the White Sox visited New York, Yankees manager Miller Huggins shook up the team, which was languishing in seventh place. Huggins benched slumping veteran first baseman Wally Pipp. "In his place, Huggins inserted Buster Gehrig, the former Columbia University star, who responded nicely with some solid walloping," *The Sporting News* noted.[16] No one could have predicted that Gehrig would proceed to play in every Yankees contest after that until April 1939 — 2,130 consecutive games. It was a major-league record until 1995, when Cal Ripken passed Gehrig on his way to 2,632 games. However, Huggins' shakeup did not help much: the Yankees still finished seventh.

Faber went the distance in Chicago, beating Cleveland 3–1. "It's about time to quit referring to Mr. Urban Faber as 'Old Red,'" Crusinberry opened. "He stepped out yesterday as a man in his prime and won his fifth straight game...." The sportswriter added, "The hurling of Faber is most encouraging to the Sox. On the road trip just completed he won his game in each of the eastern cities and on each occasion he looked as great as in his best years."[17] Faber improved his season record to 8–4.

On the final day of June, Faber nearly made it six straight wins. He limited the St. Louis Browns to one run in 10 innings before giving way to a pinch hitter. To Faber's certain frustration, his teammates had stranded 14 runners in 11 innings. In the top of the 12th, the White Sox finally broke through with five runs. George Connally received credit for the victory with two innings of shutout relief. After that no-decision, Faber dropped an Independence Day game in Cleveland 5–4 by allowing three runs in the bottom of the ninth inning. After a loss to Washington and a win over New York, he pitched shutout ball for seven innings before the Athletics knocked him out of the game en route to an 8–1 win. A few days later, in the first inning at Detroit, Faber suffered a line drive to his shin and limped out of the contest.[18] The injury was not considered serious. Faber made a relief appearance three days later and resumed his place in the rotation. Whether the incident affected his performance cannot be proven, but it marked a cool-down in the veteran spitballer's 1925 season. Including the game in which he limped off, Faber finished 2–4, with six no-decisions. In that stretch — during which Collins also missed three weeks with a leg injury — the White Sox went 28–30 and slid from third to fifth place.

In late September in New York, Faber received another no-decision when victory was within his grasp. Batting during the White Sox's three-run rally in the top of the 10th inning, he took the direct hit of a Ben Shields pitch and had to leave the game. With Faber out of the way, the Yankees staged a rally of their own against Connally. They won it on a walk-off grand slam by Babe Ruth. Yankee fans poured onto the field and swarmed around the Bambino as he trotted around the bases. As *New York Times* sportswriter James B. Harrison began his account of the game, "Ruth is stranger than fiction."[19]

The Sox had more on their minds than wins and losses during the 1925 season. There was utility infielder Hervey (other sources list it as "Harvey") McClellan, a member of the White Sox since their pennant-winning 1919 campaign. "Little Mac" missed most of 1924 with stomach ulcers. However, he appeared fit during spring training 1925 before suffering another health setback. By mid–June, after two gallstone surgeries, McClellan was fighting for his life, and the Chicago papers reported, "There is now only slight hope of his recovery."[20] A month later, several players visited Chicago's Mercy Hospital to tell McClellan goodbye before he returned home to Cynthiana, Ky. In October, his former teammates voted him a full share from the City Series. Within a month, McClellan was dead. He was 30 years old.[21]

The mound pairing for the 1925 City Series opener at Comiskey Park featured youth against experience. Veteran Grover Alexander of the last-place Cubs battled 24-year-old White Sox right-hander Ted Blankenship pitch for pitch for 19 innings and a 2–2 tie. The 38-year-old Alexander gave up 20 hits, including a leadoff hit in each of the final *eight* innings, but no runs during the final 16 innings. In Game 2, the Cubs eked out a 2–1 win and then jumped all over Faber and his would-be rescuer, Hollis Thurston, for an 8–2 victory in Game 3. Faber and the Sox were in trouble from the start, handing the Cubs four runs on three hits and an error in the bottom of the first inning. Faber lasted long enough to retire one batter in the sixth inning. After the Sox lost Game 5 to fall behind the Cubs, 3–1-1, Collins took a chance: He started Faber on only two days' rest. The manager's gamble looked good midway through the contest; the Cubs held only a 1–0 lead. Then Faber faded in the sixth inning, adding to his own misery with a run-scoring throwing error. As he did in Game 3, Faber departed after 5⅓ innings. His reliever, Connally, could not stem the rally, and the Cubs forged ahead 4–0 and claimed the City Series with a 7–4 win.

The American League campaign and City Series were over, but Faber wanted more. The final day of the City Series, he agreed to join teammate Harry Hooper's barnstormers. The troupe, made up of Chicago and Boston players, staged a series against the American Association champion Louisville Colonels. Irene Faber accompanied her husband on the tour.[22] For Hooper, the post-season tour was his last competition involving major leaguers. He retired when Comiskey's contract offer for 1926 called for a salary cut. Instead of re-signing, Hooper looked after his real estate interests in the west, coached two seasons at Princeton University and served as postmaster in Capitola, California.[23] Hooper was credited with being one of the first outfielders to attempt sliding catches and also for trying to convince Red Sox management to convert a star pitcher into an outfielder. The player's name was George Herman "Babe" Ruth. For his 17 years of steady hitting and outstanding defense with the Sox — Red and then White — Hooper was inducted into the National Hall of Fame in 1971. Hooper died three years after Cooperstown, at age 87.

21

"Simply Too Much Red"

In the days and weeks before Christmas 1925, if any of the gentlemen of Cascade struggled to select gifts for their mothers, wives and girlfriends, they could stop by one of their favorite haunts, A.J. Faber's billiards hall. In addition to offering the usual array of cigars, cigarettes and chewing tobacco, the star pitcher's brother promoted his establishment as Cascade's exclusive vendor of "The Appreciated Candies," produced by Johnston's. "There is a Johnston's package and assortment suited to every taste that will warm the feminine heart," Faber's newspaper advertisement stated.[1] In other business notes involving the Fabers, Red's father, Nicholas, rented the Hotel Faber's lower floor, office, dining room and kitchen to restaurateurs John and Mary Durkin.[2]

As was their custom, Irene Faber accompanied her husband to White Sox training camp, which returned to Shreveport, Louisiana. At the time, few wives attended spring training. Their presence occasionally created unusual and uneasy situations — especially when other wives were around or when a wife was overtly supportive. Chicago sportswriter Westbrook Pegler examined those dynamics in an article for *The American Magazine*. "The managers of ball clubs learned a long time ago that a bevy of ball-players' wives and a lot of fiercely conflicting ambitions and careers under one roof were not the recipe for serenity." His anecdotes did not name names — with two exceptions. Irene Faber was one of them. "Mrs. Faber, by the way, takes the breaks of the game very seriously," Pegler wrote. Even a workout was an emotional experience. "One day in Shreveport, when the White Sox were training there and Old Red was serving the hitters in batting practice, Mrs. Faber was seen to be much disturbed because the ball-players were taking toe-holds and flogging Urban's rather idle and inviting service to the far corners of the campus. Not even in practice could she endure to see the hitters do him so."[3] Whether her reaction reflected a supportive enthusiasm or a controlling personality, Pegler did not speculate; however, comments decades later from the pitcher's godchild suggests that it was the latter. In any case, 1926 training camp was largely uneventful — especially when compared to what would transpire the following spring.

Chicago Tribune sportswriter James Crusinberry struggled to predict how the White Sox would finish, saying that Comiskey's men, with some good breaks, could win the pennant but with reversals could drop to sixth in the eight-team American League. Assessing the pitching and recognizing the aging Faber's diminishing role, Crusinberry wrote, "One feels safe in predicting another big year for both [Ted] Lyons and [Ted] Blankenship, and in saying that the veteran Red Faber will hurl about one good ball game a week."[4]

In his first outing of the regular season, Faber gave up just five hits in a complete-game victory over the visiting Browns 5–1.[5] His mound opponent was former teammate Charlie Robertson, who lasted only two innings in his Browns debut. St. Louis turned the tables on Faber and the visiting White Sox five days later in another 5–1 decision. Southpaw Tom Zachary allowed the Sox just four hits, and the home team was helped by an umpiring decision. With a Brown on base, William "Baby Doll" Jacobson smashed a Faber pitch a foot or two from the top of the left-field fence. Some young fans reached for the ball, which bounded back to outfielder Bib Falk, whose throw appeared to hold Jacobson to a run-scoring double. However, the umpires ruled that the drive had cleared the fence and ricocheted off the spectators. They awarded Jacobson a home run. "Falk ran in and barked like an Airedale," Crusinberry noted. "He was joined by Boss Collins and Everett Scott. The yelping was fierce." The play provided the Browns with all the runs they needed. The White Sox did not help themselves with defensive and base running miscues. With no one out in the sixth inning, Faber, who reached on a single, was on third base and Johnny Mostil was on second after a single and an error. The next hitter, Scott, smashed the ball to the mound. Pitcher Zachary snared the ball, looked Faber back to third and threw to first to retire the hitter. "Then it was discovered that Mostil had legged it to third for reasons unknown. He tried to get back, but there wasn't a chance," Crusinberry wrote. "Finally Faber led off third and was run down, letting Johnny have the old bag if he wanted it so badly." A fly ball then ended the potential rally, and Faber suffered his first loss of 1926.[6]

Though never considered a cold-weather pitcher, Faber accepted his turn on the mound despite wintry conditions April 25. "Detroit has a population of more than a million and a half claimed, and at least a million and a quarter real," Crusinberry noted, "but it is surprising there could be 9,000 insane persons among them. Nobody who was in his right mind would have attended a baseball game today. It was so cold a pair of fleece-lined mittens and red flannels had no effect whatever. But the White Sox, having trained in the winds of Texas, the squalls of Louisiana and the snowbound peaks of Indiana, were in shape for just such weather." Faber managed well through eight innings, allowing just five chilly hits and holding a 4–1 lead. But then came the ninth. "Red's arm froze stiff as a steel girder and he started to hand out passes to everybody in Detroit." Actually, Faber allowed one hit and walked four in the final inning. His final pass came with two out and the bases loaded. Hollis Thurston rushed in to relieve and coaxed an easy fly ball to save the 4–2 victory.[7]

A decade earlier, Faber filled an "iron man" role for the White Sox, capably enduring extra-inning contests and, when the situation warranted, accepting starts with less than his usual three days' rest. By the mid–1920s, however, Faber's managers tried to give their veteran extra rest. Sometimes even that was not enough. After four days' rest, he suffered a six-run shellacking, exited after just two innings but escaped with a no-decision when the Sox rallied for a 9–6 win.[8] A few days later, Faber confessed uncertainty about his availability; the cold weather had left him down and out, and he missed a couple of starts. On May 10, Faber, scheduled to pitch the next afternoon, and Ted Lyons, who had pitched the day before, were excused from the White Sox's game in Washington. The pitchers got a head start to the team's next stop, Philadelphia, by motoring to the City of Brotherly Love with the wife and two sons of manager Eddie Collins. While the future Hall-of-Fame pitchers traveled, their teammate Thurston shut out the Nationals 2–0. Meanwhile, off the field, Nats manager Bucky Harris barred Washington sportswriters from the clubhouse. The reporters gave Harris reason to ponder. "They informed him that he might have to read some mean cracks about his ball team as a consequence," *Tribune* writer Irving Vaughan noted, "so he canceled the order."[9]

Faber's early arrival in Philadelphia did not help him the following afternoon. The Athletics' Lefty Grove struck out 11 Sox hitters and cruised to a 6–2 win. Faber suffered some bad breaks, again in the first inning, and again it featured Mostil. The outfielder, as Vaughan put it, "stumbled over a dandelion or something and lost a fly that proved good for two runs." Faber again made an early exit — this time after four innings.[10] He didn't even last that long in his next outing, in New York. While Yankees pitcher Herb Pennock permitted the White Sox only three hits all afternoon, the hosts clubbed Faber, who retired no one in the third, and his successors for the 10–1 victory. The highlight for the estimated 35,000 fans was Babe Ruth's 12th home run of the year. It probably was small comfort to Faber that he was not the one who gave up Ruth's home run; that honor went to rookie reliever Alphonse "Tommy" Thomas in the eighth.[11]

Collins did not start Faber again for more than two weeks. On May 22 in Boston, Faber received the call to rescue Thurston. The Iowa native began well, but the Red Sox figured him out, collecting four hits and drawing two walks over 2⅓ innings. Faber departed after the sixth inning, and the Red Sox unleashed another onslaught. "The process of scoring Boston's five runs in the seventh was too complicated and painful to bear narrating," Vaughan explained in his *Tribune* article on Boston's 14–8 win.[12] It was not a pretty sight for Faber in his next start, on Memorial Day in Chicago, where the Tigers slapped him around for 14 hits. However, Detroit's defensive blunders and outstanding work by White Sox fielders allowed Faber, who issued no walks, to receive credit for a 6–3 win.

Faber's best game of 1926 came in his next start, on June 8 in Chicago, where he battled the Athletics' Lefty Grove, who allowed the White Sox just a single through seven innings. Likewise, Faber held Philadelphia scoreless through nine innings. In the bottom of the ninth, the White Sox opened against Grove with two singles and then Willie Kamm dropped a bunt in front of the plate. The pitcher and first baseman Jim Poole were closest to the ball. "Poole and Grove ran for it and then decided to hold a conference as to the best method of procedure," Vaughan quipped. "Meanwhile Kamm, not being interested in what Grove and Poole were thinking about, hustled to first for a single and the sacks were full." On Grove's next pitch, Schalk laid down a bases-loaded squeeze bunt so effectively that all third baseman Jimmy Dykes could do was pick up the ball and watch Bib Falk cross the plate with the winning run.[13]

After a week of rest, Faber collected another victory — this time thanks to his bat as much as his arm. "It is a matter of common knowledge that Urban 'Red' Faber is not much of a batter. He has been known to hit one here and there, but never so many that he isn't able to figure his batting average without resorting to pencil and paper," Vaughan observed. However, Faber resembled Cobb or Ruth when he stroked a bases-loaded double in the second inning. He then held the Nationals to five hits to earn a 4–1 victory. "This most famous of the present-day baseball redheads had one of his good days and the Nats never had a chance," wrote Frank H. Young of *The Washington Post*.[14]

Faber did not fare as well in his next start, on June 20, when the White Sox hosted Ruth and his Yankees in a matinee on a sultry Sunday. The feature attracted a crowd of 43,000 — many, no doubt, were Sox fans hoping to see a Ruthian wallop. Fans jammed the grandstand and bleachers and spilled into the outfield.[15] "There was a heavy fringe from foul line to foul line," described visiting sportswriter James R. Harrison, "and a hit into the crowd was limited to two bases."[16] The ground rule helped the White Sox forge a 3–1 lead. However, Faber faltered in the seventh, when he managed only one out, gave up four straight singles and allowed the Yankees to tie the game 3–3. He gave up nine hits, walked three and struck out five. Yankees hitters

realized no advantage from that afternoon's ground rule, but the White Sox
dropped three hits into the outfield standees — including the eventual game-
winner in the bottom of the eighth. Without the excess spectators, Harrison
noted, those ground-rule doubles would have been easy fly-outs. Reliever Ted
Blankenship held the New Yorkers hitless the rest of the way to earn the victory, and Urban Shocker suffered the loss.[17] The victory nudged the White
Sox (34–28) into a tie with the Indians for second place, 9½ games behind
the Yankees. Chicago stayed in second or third for another month before fading.

Collins said he had a hunch that Faber would do well in his next outing, so he penciled him into the lineup card June 25 against the Browns in
Chicago. "While the heart was willing, the aged arm was balky," Vaughan
wrote of Faber. The spitballer, backed by a defense that "resembled a Chi-
nese Army the morning after pay day," gave up two runs in the top of the
first. Things got worse. Faber failed to retire a single batter in the third inning,
when the Browns plated five men on their way to an 11–4 "comic opera" victory.[18] Though Faber pitched less than one-third of a game against St. Louis,
Collins extended his rest to nearly 10 days, holding out the 37-year-old until
the Independence Day contest in Detroit. Tigers player-manager Ty Cobb
kept himself out of the lineup. Cobb no doubt was frustrated to see Faber
wriggle out of jam after jam despite being hit with regularity. On one occasion, a Tiger shot a line drive directly at Faber, who stopped the bullet with
his gloved hand. Despite allowing a dozen hits and three walks, Faber earned
a complete-game victory 7–2.[19] A couple of days later his left hand still bothered him from the liner, and an X-ray revealed a slight fracture of the thumb.[20]
The injury was not expected to affect his pitching, but one had to wonder
after his relief appearance on July 10 in Philadelphia, where the mercury
reached 97 degrees. Most of the 30,000 fans shed their suit jackets in favor
of shirtsleeves.[21] Meanwhile, in what Crusinberry called "the wildest, weird-
est game of ball of the season," the White Sox and Athletics engaged in a
slugfest. Faber was summoned from the bullpen in the bottom of the eighth,
when he promptly surrendered Chicago's three-run lead. It could have been
worse: After Joe Hauser stroked a Faber pitch for a game-tying double, the
next hitter, Max Bishop, laced an apparent RBI-single to center field. However, home plate umpire William A. McGowan ruled that he had granted
Collins' request for time before Faber had released the pitch. Collins wanted
a halt in the proceedings so he could summon a replacement for Faber, who,
in two-thirds of an inning, gave up two hits and a walk. Despite that bad
break, the Athletics went on to post a 17–14 win and retain second place.[22]
The next day was a Sunday, when baseball in Philadelphia was still forbid-
den, and many of the White Sox spent their free day trying to escape the heat
by seeking out the seashore temperatures and entertainment of Atlantic City.

Player-manager Eddie Collins, a former Athletics star who retained his residence in the Philadelphia area, hosted his star catcher (and successor as manager) Ray Schalk, to lunch at the Aronimink Country Club.[23] Faber did none of the above, choosing to while away the day in the easy chairs of the team's hotel.[24]

The White Sox wrapped up their Philadelphia series and moved on to the nation's capital, where Faber beat the Nationals 10–2. "It was simply a case of too much Red Faber," conceded Frank H. Young in *The Washington Post*. The light-hitting pitcher contributed offensively with a couple of base hits and a run batted in. "Red hasn't done much but rest lately because of an injured thumb on his gloved hand, and when the old Cascade hero is well rested he regains all of his youthful vim, vigor and vitality," Crusinberry reminded his readers back in Chicago. "He had all those qualifications today, along with a lot of speed, a sharp curve, a breaking spitter, and excellent control."[25] The losing pitcher was another future Hall-of-Famer, Stan Coveleski, who exited after four innings.

On six days' rest, Faber recorded another lopsided win — a 13–2 decision in Boston. "Red Faber pitched all the way for the White Sox, allowing 10 hits and giving one base on balls," noted the *Tribune*'s Pegler, "but he was coasting in the latter stages of the game with a 12-run lead and was not wrenching any tendons to pitch the game of his life." Faber also recorded six strikeouts in the contest. The plate umpire, Clarence Rowland, had an easy balk call against Boston reliever Del Lundgren during Chicago's five-run outburst in the second inning. Lundgren, a little-used right-hander, became so wrapped up in his windup that he hit himself in the chin with the ball, which fell to the ground. The balk scored Eddie Collins.[26]

Throughout his career, Faber was known to accept bad breaks quietly and professionally. However, his even temperament was put to the test July 24 in New York. "The White Sox were generous to a fault — they handed the Yanks three runs in the third and one in the fourth, much to the consternation of Mr. Red Faber, their veteran spitball pitcher," *The New York Times'* Harrison observed. "The infield gymnastics of the Chicago team were horrible to behold." With Eddie Collins sidelined with a leg injury, "the infield looked like that of a minor league team having a bad day," Harrison added. The Yankees blended base hits and Sox blunders to score three runs in the third inning. During the rally, Babe Ruth rocketed a Faber offering back to the mound, missing the pitcher's left ear by an inch. "If Ruth's drive in the third had hit Faber it would have carried Red right out into center field," Harrison quipped. Pitching six innings, Faber allowed no earned runs but trailed 4–1. He received a no-decision when Chicago tied it in the seventh before losing 7–4.[27]

Faber experienced another close encounter with a line drive four days later in Chicago. In the fifth inning, future Hall-of-Famer Bucky Harris, the Washington player-manager, shot a pitch back at Faber, who knocked down the ball and threw out Harris. "His plea was self-defense," *The Washington Post* said, "for the ball would have hit him in the head had he failed to stop it."[28] Vaughan noted that after the putout Faber "remarked that the fellows who want to move the slab closer to the plate should be locked up."[29] Backed by errorless defense, Faber posted a complete-game victory 5–2 to snap the team's six-game losing streak, during which the White Sox fell to sixth place.

Next to visit Comiskey Park were the white-hot Yankees, who had won nine straight. They extended the streak to 11 before coming out on the short end of the duel between the Urban spitballers, Shocker and Faber. It was a close decision, 2–1, with all the runs coming in the fourth inning. The Yankees had several chances, "but in times of stress the large figure of Red Faber of Cascade, Iowa, bulked across their path like a Colossus," the *Times'* Harrison said. "To say, however, that Mr. Faber moved easily and triumphantly to victory, with little children throwing rosebuds in his path, would be stretching the truth. There is no royal road to triumph when the Yankees are the opposing parties. Mr. Faber got himself into a fine jam in the ninth and the high, massive brow of the redhead was corrugated with wrinkles of worry."[30] For good reason. With one out in the ninth, Lou Gehrig doubled, and Faber — probably reluctantly — walked Ruth to put the potential go-ahead run on base. A long flyout advanced Gehrig, and Faber walked Tony Lazzeri to fill the bases. Faber then put an end to the drama by inducing Joe Dugan to hit an easy ground ball. For his part, Shocker allowed Chicago a half-dozen hits in seven innings of work. "This sort of slabbing endeavor is entitled to a win nine times out of 10," Vaughan wrote of Shocker, "but this was the 10th time because Faber was every bit as good as his opponent." Everyone knew when Faber had his "stuff," because hitters beat the ball into the ground. Such was the case that afternoon, when 17 of the Yankees' 27 outs came on plays in the infield. Ruth was one of Faber's two strikeout victims.[31]

Facing the Athletics on the same homestand, Faber was good — but not good enough. He gave up only three runs, but that was sufficient for Philadelphia and Howard Ehmke to win 3–2.[32] Five days later, in Cleveland, he had another off day, giving up 10 hits over five innings and all but one of the Indians' runs in a 5–0 decision.[33]

After the Cleveland series, the White Sox dashed home for a two-game series against the Tigers. Detroit won the first game; the next day, the teams sloshed around Comiskey Park for five innings and settled for a scoreless (but official) tie. The teams immediately high-tailed it to Detroit, where the schedule-maker gave the Tigers a one-game "homestand." Even in dry weather, the White Sox and Tigers continued to be incapable of scoring. After

10 innings, and needing to catch trains for the East, the teams halted play content with another 0–0 tie.[34]

After giving Faber an extra day or two of rest, Collins planned to pitch him against the Yankees. An off-the-field mishap in New York City changed that when Faber stepped off a curbstone awkwardly and suffered a twisted ankle.[35] Still gimpy and also experiencing digestive problems, Faber nonetheless beat the host Red Sox 5–1 on August 20. He allowed seven hits and walked none.[36] While Faber was dominant, the next day his teammate Ted Lyons was masterful. He walked Boston leadoff hitter Jack Tobin, and in the seventh shortstop Bill Hunnefield bobbled a grounder for an error. They represented the only Red Sox base runners all afternoon. As the Chicago pitcher continued to mow down their favorites on that Saturday afternoon, the 10,000 Boston fans cheered on the opposing pitcher with increasing intensity. The *Tribune's* Crusinberry described the scene: "At the finish, when [Topper] Rigney, the last batter, cut a sharp grounder down to [first baseman Earl] Sheely, who knocked the ball down and then tossed it to Ted covering first base, thus completing the no-hit game, fans jumped out of the stand and ran after young Ted in an effort to slap him on the back."[37] The 25-year-old Lyons achieved history — the only no-hitter of his long career — after coming close at the end of the previous season, when Washington broke up his no-hit bid in the ninth inning.

Lyons and his senior teammate, Faber, suffered losses in their next outings, on August 26, 1926. The doubleheader in Washington represented a baseball rarity — all four starting pitchers were future Hall-of-Famers. The Nationals featured Walter Johnson and Stan Coveleski. In the opening contest, Faber allowed 13 hits over seven innings while Johnson tossed a four-hitter. In the nightcap, with darkness looming, Lyons walked in the game's only run in the bottom of the 10th.[38] After the Washington series, the White Sox rode the rails to Detroit. Also making the trip were umpires Richard Nallin and Clarence "Brick" Owens. Nallin entered a railcar and saw Owens engaged in a card game with five Chicago players. "You ought to be able to beat five of 'em," Nallin joshed his partner. "You've beaten nine of them lots of times."[39] In the opener of an August 31 doubleheader, Faber pitched steady ball while his teammates pounded Detroit pitching; Chicago scored 11 times in the final two innings to make it a cakewalk 19–2. The Tigers came back in the second game 7–6. The offensive hero was Sox reserve infielder Ray Morehart, who in one afternoon slapped out a record nine hits in 10 at-bats. Five days after their series in Detroit concluded, the teams reconvened in Chicago. Labor Day 1926 and Faber's 38th birthday were the same day, and on that Monday Faber won the morning game of a doubleheader 5–4. Only about 4,000 fans showed up, compared to some 22,000 for the matinee, won by Chicago's Hollis "Sloppy" Thurston. Faber helped himself with a single in

Red Faber warms up in Wrigley Field before Game 1 of the 1926 City Series against the Chicago Cubs. He lost this day but won Game 5, and the White Sox took the series in seven games. (Chicago Historical Society, Chicago Daily News collection SDN-066296.)

the seventh, and George Connally helped Faber when he relieved the birthday boy in the ninth.[40] Rested a week, Faber engaged the Athletics' Ed Rommel in a tight battle in the nightcap of a doubleheader at Comiskey Park. Faber had allowed just three hits over eight innings in a scoreless game. With two runners on and one out in the bottom of the eighth, Rommel intentionally walked pinch hitter Eddie Collins to fill the bases. Collins summoned a pinch runner for himself and sent up Harry McCurdy to pinch-hit for Faber.

McCurdy delivered, lacing a bases-clearing triple to left-center field. Reliever Tommy Thomas gave up two runs but preserved Faber's 200th career win.[41] The victory was the first of eight straight by the White Sox. Faber also won the seventh game in the streak, a 7–3 decision over the league-leading Yankees, who collected a half-dozen hits — including two by Babe Ruth. Faber also contributed offensively; his infield single turned out to be the game-winner.[42] It was Faber's last start of the regular season — he was 15–9 with an ERA of 3.56 — but there was more baseball to be played.

The 1926 Chicago City Series matched teams with nearly identical records The 81–72 White Sox and the 82–72 Cubs. Faber drew the opening-game assignment in Wrigley Field. On an overcast day in the 50s, Faber pitched effectively, allowing seven hits in seven innings and striking out five, but the Cubs' Charlie Root was better. Trailing 2–0, Faber was pulled for a pinch hitter in the eighth. In the bottom of the eighth, the Cubs pounded Sox relievers Connally and Thurston for four more runs to make it easy for Root, who allowed the South Siders only four hits.[43] Game 5, in Comiskey Park, featured a Faber-Root rematch, but neither hurler distinguished himself. Root pitched a complete game, but was continuously in trouble. "Faber's departure from the game was hurried," the *Tribune*'s Frank Schreiber reported. "Red eased along in fine shape for five rounds and was out in front by virtue of a Sox rally in each of the fourth and fifth sessions. Then he blew up." Faber might have been flustered seeing friend and batterymate Ray Schalk clobbered in a sixth-inning collision with Hack Wilson. "The shock evidently affected Umpire Ernie Quigley as well as Schalk, for he first ruled Wilson safe and then called him out," Schreiber wrote, "and it wasn't five minutes afterwards that the fans became sure of what the umpire's decision was and they razzed him long and loudly." Immediately after that episode, Faber issued a walk then turned to the Sox bench and signaled for help. Connally rushed to the mound and preserved Faber's victory 3–1.[44] Schalk, who stayed in the game after his close encounter with Wilson, backstopped the White Sox to another City Series title. That November, "Cracker" Schalk was named player-manager. The promotion was news to the incumbent. "I have not received any word from Comiskey and have not talked to him since the close of the baseball season," Eddie Collins said. "I have nothing to say and will not talk until I am officially notified by the club." Eventually, notice reached Collins, who left Chicago to rejoin the Athletics.[45]

22

"Not the Same Faber"

In the winter of 1926–27, Red and Irene Faber lived in Milwaukee, her hometown, and occasionally visited Cascade.[1] Controversy interrupted their holiday season. Swede Risberg, exiled as a Black Sox conspirator, resurfaced the allegation that the 1917 White Sox bribed members of the Detroit Tigers to "lay down" in their back-to-back doubleheaders during the pennant race. The four victories smoothed the way for Chicago to win the American League pennant and go on to claim the World Series. Nearly all the White Sox players contributed $45 each toward a gift to reward Detroit, but they said it was for Detroit defeating Boston, Chicago's closest challenger. Meeting with Commissioner Landis for two hours on New Year's Day 1927, Risberg implicated several men, including Faber and then-manager Clarence "Pants" Rowland. Contacted in Milwaukee, Rowland, an American League umpire since 1923, told a reporter: "If Risberg says I had anything to do with framing games he lies." Landis, whose current investigation of game-fixing allegations against Tris Speaker and Ty Cobb prompted Risberg to step forward, decided to look into the events of 1917 as well. Rowland and Faber were among the 38 men Landis summoned to Chicago. Not everyone sent a telegram showed up for the hearing. Some were excused because they were not members of the White Sox or Tigers in 1917. (The best excuse involved Jack Lapp, whose ninth-inning infield hit spoiled Faber's bid for a no-hitter in 1914. Not only was Lapp on neither team in 1917, the reserve catcher had been dead nearly seven years.)

Arriving in Chicago, Faber told a reporter, "I don't know what it is all about, but I'll be there to tell the world I had nothing to do with sloughing off ball games."[2] He did just that at Landis' hearing the next day. Faber and 25 others refuted the allegation of Risberg, who smoked cigarettes and grinned while listening to witness after witness call him a liar. The first up was Rowland. Landis asked, "What have you to say to Risberg's story?" Rowland did not hesitate: "It's a damned lie." Ty Cobb, already on the hot seat because of his link to Speaker, denied knowing anything about money from the White Sox — a statement confirmed by both sides. Later, Pittsburgh manager Donie Bush, a Tigers player in 1917, challenged Risberg to a fight. Eddie Collins, his voice breaking, echoed Rowland, shouting, "It's a God-damned lie!" Faber's interview was neither that emotional nor noteworthy. *Chicago Tribune* sports editor Don Maxwell mentioned Faber's appearance only at the end of his article and did not directly quote the spitballer.

Faber's connection with the games and the gift was part of the record. He started both ends of the second doubleheader, on Labor Day 1917 in Chicago. The Tigers roughed him up for 11 hits and four runs over 4⅔ innings in the morning game, but Rowland sent him back out for the afternoon contest. Faber lasted just 1⅓ innings, giving up four runs on four hits and issuing three walks. In each game, after Faber departed, the White Sox came back to win. According to testimony from both sides, when the assessments of $45 — worth about $685 in 2005 — were being collected, several teammates did not have the money at the time. Faber advanced them their shares, writing a $500 check that was cashed at the Ansonia Hotel in New York.[3] Gandil and Risberg later delivered $870 cash to then–Detroit pitcher Bill James, who told Landis that he and his teammates considered it a gift to the Tigers hurlers for beating Boston.[4]

The shady reputations of Risberg and Gandil, and the denials of some of the game's leading lights notwithstanding, was there something to the allegation?

Consider, first, that fixed games did not begin and end with the Black Sox scandal of the 1919 World Series. Many times, gamblers were believed to have influenced the odds — if not the outcomes — of major league games. Sports pages routinely referred to gamblers, their presence at games, and the betting line. Several other players — not just the Black Sox — were banned for gambling-related actions. Even before he was implicated in the Black Sox episode, first baseman Hal Chase threw games and wagered against his own team.[5]

Consider, too, that a couple of weeks before Detroit's three victories over Boston (September 19–20), a Chicago pennant was a virtual certainty. The White Sox clinched the American League by defeating Boston the next day. However, the Chicagoans explained that the gift was offered when they still believed they would need the Tigers' help against the Red Sox.

Finally, it cannot be disputed that the Tigers played poorly against the White Sox. In their two doubleheaders in Chicago, the Tigers allowed 21 walks, committed 11 errors and gave up 21 stolen bases. "No club has ever taken such liberties on the paths with our pitchers," E.A. Batchelor of the *Detroit Free Press* noted at the time. "The 'feline' catchers were not to blame, either. The Sox were beating perfect throws when receivers had them guessed and called for pitchouts." Batchelor blamed one loss on "hard hitting" by Chicago and "amateurish fielding" by Detroit.[6]

After the hearing, Commissioner Landis dropped the matter, claiming insufficient evidence and professing disinterest in events occurring before he took office in late 1920.[7] However, he made it clear that no longer would such gifts between teams be permitted. (Meanwhile, Cobb and Speaker wriggled off the hook and won free agency for the 1927 season.)

In mid–February, Urban and Irene Faber again traveled to Hot Springs, Arkansas, where he planned to work out and visit the spa to get ready for spring training. Schalk, in his first season as player-manager, suggested that two new members of the White Sox, veteran infielders Roger Peckinpaugh and Aaron Ward, join Faber in Hot Springs.[8] Despite his early workouts, Faber was not in tip-top shape when training camp opened in Shreveport, Louisiana. "Faber, slightly overweight, threw for a time and ended his exercise with a long hike around the place, wrapped in a leather jacket," the *Tribune* reported. "He was drenched when he went to the clubhouse and sat there an hour staring at the water cooler, but not daring to take a drink lest his weight increase." Between workouts, Faber, an avid outdoorsman, eyed the bass inhabiting a fountain in the Hotel Youree lobby. The *Tribune* described it as a "cynical fish that loafs behind a brick, evincing no emotion even when Red Faber, himself, pauses at the white tiled shore and remarks that there is a hell of a fine fish."[9] Such was the nature of dispatches from laid-back spring training camps. Within a few days, however, more dramatic—and tragic—news emerged from the Youree.

As soon as he arrived in Shreveport, Johnny Mostil, 30-year-old outfielder and team hypochondriac, begged to see a doctor. Team personnel and sportswriters no doubt rolled their eyes March 7 when, entering the field for his first workout, Mostil took a batting-practice line drive to the middle of his chest. "It is stated that if there is typhoid in Alaska or an epidemic of hang nail in the Dantzig corridor, Mr. Mostil will turn up with symptoms of his own," the *Tribune*'s Westbrook Pegler wrote, "and today's smack on the chest is expected to get him off with a rousing start."[10] Mostil told Schalk, "I'm sick and I'm worried and I'm boiling up inside." At Schalk's request, the hotel manager summoned a physician. A Dr. Slicer arrived to find Mostil nervous, complaining of a wisdom tooth and experiencing elevated blood pressure. "That boy is in bad shape," Slicer told Schalk. The next day, rain washed out practice. Most of the White Sox entourage, including Mostil, passed the time in the hotel. After a mid-afternoon nap, Mostil visited Faber's room. Later, about 5:30 p.m., team booster Pat Prunty returned to his hotel room to discover Mostil on the bathroom floor, unconscious and bleeding from deep slashes in his wrists. Hoping to avoid publicity, team personnel used the hotel's back door to deliver Mostil into an ambulance. At Schumpert Hospital, he received the Roman Catholic sacrament of Last Rites.

Meanwhile, team executive Lou Comiskey sent traveling secretary Lou Barber back to the hotel to try to dissuade the sportswriters from reporting Mostil's "little accident." Barber suggested that newspaper accounts would upset Mostil's family. Nothing doing: The next morning, the story topped the front pages of the Chicago papers. "Even if he should recover," the *Tribune*'s Pegler stated, "Mostil will have caught his last ball as a professional player. The injuries to his wrists are so deep that the use of his hands will be impaired."[11] Pegler's conclusion was premature and inaccurate. Not only did Mostil survive his close call, he played some late-season games.

Various rumors and theories surfaced regarding Mostil's motivation for his desperate act. Some said he was self-conscious, bothered and depressed about dental problems. A woman identified as his girlfriend — Margaret Carroll, of Hammond, Indiana — told The Associated Press that Mostil experienced nerve inflammation: "He had been suffering from neuritis in the face, but said he would beat it yet."[12] She said she had known Mostil for some time, "and although we were not engaged, we had considered getting married during the late summer." Miss Carroll added, "I cannot imagine what motive he could have had for attempting to take his own life." Less than two weeks after the incident, the *Tribune* reported that dentists would pull the two teeth "blamed for the physical disturbance which brought on Johnny's worry and temporary mental collapse."[13]

Others said that he didn't like his contract. A month after the incident, Chicago sportswriter Irving Vaughan reported, "One source claims the player became melancholy over salary differences with his employer."[14]

The sauciest theory was that his affair with Irene Faber was discovered, and that when Red found out about it, he threatened to kill Mostil, who proceeded to slash his wrists. Of all the rumors and stories, this one has the most visibility. It is detailed on a leading baseball Internet site, and in 2004 the *Chicago Tribune* referred to the rumor without naming the Fabers. No Faber relatives interviewed for this book acknowledged ever hearing the rumor. The pitcher's only son — his mother was Red's second wife — scoffed at the notion of Red Faber threatening Mostil over Irene. "My father didn't have a jealous bone in his body," Urban C. Faber II said.[15] Further evidence that Mostil's motivation did not include the Fabers: The couple remained married until Irene's death 16 years later, and in several newspaper reports over the years, Red volunteered positive references to Mostil's abilities as a player, and the men remained teammates for several seasons afterward.

Mostil might have worried about his teeth and his contract, but the most likely theory involved his love life: He became despondent when he learned that his girlfriend, the aforementioned Miss Carroll, had thrown him over. The "other man" was teammate Bill Barrett — his spring training roommate, no less. Sox catcher Bucky Crouse told an interviewer about it more than a quarter-century afterward.[16] Margaret E. Carroll, initially identified as Mostil's near-fiancée, later became Mrs. William Barrett.[17]

As Mostil recuperated, the White Sox returned to the diamond. Curiously, one of their exhibition victories was partially credited to a greyhound track's mechanical rabbit. The Sox were dubious when they arrived at the Texas League ballpark to hear that Shreveport star Dutch Hoffman was out of the lineup after a mishap with the rabbit during an exhibition race. "All the boys, with extreme skepticism, said they knew of many things that have happened to ball players, but none, it seemed, ever had heard of a playing being incapacitated by a mechanical rabbit," the *Tribune*'s Edward Burns reported. "But Hoffman actually did lose his match with the rabbit, investigation revealed." The Sox defeated Hoffman-less Shreveport 10–3.[18] (Two years later, Hoffman played his only major league season with the White Sox.)

In mid–March, the assessment of Faber's conditioning seemed to change by the day. Schalk left Faber in Shreveport while the White Sox embarked on a 10-day exhibition tour in Texas.[19] Faber's reaction to being dropped from the travel roster was not reported, but chances are that he concurred with Schalk. However, some players grated under their new player-manager. It appeared that Schalk, the fiery catcher, would be a fiery manager — in contrast to the laid-back style of predecessor Eddie Collins. Barrett and Schalk got into it on the diamond one day. "Schalk is supposed to have knocked Barrett's hat off with some hot and emphatic words while the Sox were struggling through the last few days of their tour," Vaughan reported. "Barrett, whose idea of life is to laugh it off, hadn't been playing in a manner indicating undivided attention to business on his part. He has done such things before, so it required no time for Schalk to observe the objectionable mental attitude." Barrett was not alone. "Schalk's 'ride' of Barrett bears out stories from the South that some of the players on the team were heated under the collar because of the new pilot's stern attitude. They are said to have complained lustily, but even though this may be true, it doesn't necessarily mean that any harm will result." Vaughan added, "When Collins was manager, he was inclined to be mild mannered in giving his orders. Some of the men took advantage of him and the team suffered accordingly. Hence nobody can blame Schalk if he gets a bit wrathy."[20] Later, however, Schalk softened.

As they worked their way north, the squabbling Sox stopped in Louisville for an exhibition game and to transact some business. The major leaguers visited Louisville's famous baseball-bat factory, where "nearly every player on the squad purchased six or more new war clubs." On the diamond, the White Sox and Louisville Colonels, defending champs of the American Association, tied 4–4 in a contest called after 10 innings to allow the Chicagoans to catch a train for Toledo.[21]

After opening the regular season in Cleveland and St. Louis, the White Sox arrived in Chicago for their home opener in a newly renovated and expanded Comiskey Park. Built in 1910 to accommodate 41,000 patrons — its largest crowd was 43,825 in the 1925 City Series — the enlarged stadium could seat 55,000, and team officials said as many as 60,000 could squeeze in.[22] After spending about $600,000 of his own money on the improvements, owner Charles Comiskey anticipated that all those seats would be required for the 1927 home opener. The day's agenda included a parade from Wacker Drive and Michigan Avenue to the ballpark; brass bands; welcoming ceremony and gifts for new manager Schalk; and the debut of a new fan club, the White Sox Rooters Association.[23] However, despite strong advance sales, only 30,000 customers arrived. Mother Nature did not cooperate, delivering a breezy day and temperatures in the low 40s. "The fans lustily cheered, the bands played until the musicians became numb with cold, and flowers were in abundance," the *Tribune* reported, but Cleveland defeated Ted Lyons 5–4.[24] Thousands of other fans listened to the contest: For the first time, radio station WGN, owned by the *Tribune*, planned play-by-play broadcasts of every home game of the Cubs and White Sox. In 1926, WGN aired Cubs' home contests on weekends. The 1927 arrangement was a first in the American League, which lifted its ban on such broadcasts.[25]

Faber did not start until the 12th game of the 1927 regular season. Leading Detroit 5–2, after five innings in Comiskey Park, Faber fell apart in the sixth. The Tigers rallied for a 6–5 lead, scoring four runs on five hits against Faber. George Connally rescued Faber, shut out the Tigers the rest of the way and won his own game with a run-scoring single in the bottom of the 10th.[26] The Tigers did it again in Faber's next start, in Detroit, where he barely lasted five innings and took the 5–1 loss. He was so unimpressive that the *Chicago Tribune* carried a headline, "THIS IS NOT THE SAME FABER WE USED TO KNOW." A subheadline referred to Faber as a *"former* Sox ace."[27] The *Tribune* had to reverse course six days later, when Faber held the defending American League champion Yankees to a single run over 10 innings as the White Sox won 2–1. "The triumph was doubly sweet, because it marked the return to form of Urban Faber, the old master, who had been praying for just such a warm day as yesterday to come along and soothe that historic right arm of his," wrote Edward Burns after Faber's seven-hit performance. After giving up a leadoff single in the top of the 10th, Faber struck a batter, threw out the next hitter pitcher-to-first and covered first base on a grounder to the first baseman. Meanwhile, Babe Ruth, who would slug a then-record 60 homers, failed to drive any of Faber's offerings out of the infield.[28]

However, Faber did not start for nearly two weeks after his victory over New York — and then suffered a shellacking against Philadelphia. The spitballer exited when the Athletics opened the fourth inning with back-to-back hits, their fifth and sixth of the contest.[29] Four days later, Faber accepted the starting assignment on a terrible day in Detroit. "It was bitter cold . . . a gale was sweeping over the field, and the game had to be suspended in the early stages to permit a combination of rain, snow, and sleet storm to subside," Burns reported. "Not a pleasant tableau in which to cast our Red, but the grand old man of Cascade insisted upon going, though his salivary glands were chilled and his famed spitball gathered ice." Despite being on the ropes from the seventh inning on, Faber finally iced the Tigers, pitching all 12 innings of a 4–3 victory.[30]

Faber's up-and-down performances took another downturn four days later, on Memorial Day, when he managed to retire only one St. Louis hitter in the second inning. After his loss, the White Sox went on a 12–2 run and sat just one game behind the Yankees as they arrived in New York for a four-game series. The Yankees prevailed in the series opener. Rested nine days, Faber started Game 2, a contest that turned out to be one of the White Sox's most discouraging losses ever. Tony Lazzeri homered against Faber twice; his second round-tripper, in the eighth inning, was of the inside-the-park variety. Nonetheless, Faber took an 11–6 lead into the bottom of the ninth. Then the Yankees rallied. After giving up three runs and putting a Yankee on first base while recording only one out, Faber left the game still holding an 11–9 lead. George Connally came in to face Lazzeri, who drilled a pitch barely inside the right-field foul pole, 295 feet away, and just over the 4-foot-high wall. The 20,000 fans in Yankee Stadium, already electrified by the rally, erupted, "screeching and screaming like so many maniacs." Lazzeri's third homer tied the contest, and the Yankees won it in the 11th inning 12–11.[31] The loss started a White Sox tailspin. "Schalk says that in his 16 years of big league baseball he never has seen a defeat that so cast down an aggregation supposed to be hard boiled in such matters," Burns reported. "He admits it has had him on the ropes."[32] Including the collapse in New York, the White Sox went 9–14 the rest of June, during which time Faber took two losses and a no-decision; each time out, he was rapped soundly. In some quarters, Schalk was blamed for working his pitchers too hard. *The Washington Post*'s Frank H. Young wrote, "At the beginning of this season the White Sox big four — Ted Lyons, Alphonse Thomas, Ted Blankenship and Red Faber — alone carried the Chicago club to victory. But Schalk frequently used his men for relief work between their regular assignments, and, as a result, the whole four are only ordinary pitchers now. And that Schalk has not learned a lesson yet is indicated by the fact that in the last series with the Nats, he called on Blankenship in two games and used Lyons as relief man one day and then started him the next."[33]

Several weeks before Young's analysis, however, Faber was out of the starting rotation — even on a once-a-week basis. One game out of the league lead in early June, the White Sox by mid–July resided in fifth place, some 15 games behind. "They realize that the lack of pitching talent is more of a handicap than they can hope to cope with," Irving Vaughan told readers of *The Sporting News*. "Faber, despite long rests, appears to be at the end of a notable career that stretches way back."[34] He handled three relief appearances — one lasted six innings — the first two weeks of July, but then his name disappeared from the box scores, apparently the result of a bum knee. By late July, Faber stayed in Chicago when the White Sox went on an eastern road trip.

More than a month later, Faber, his arm rested and his knee apparently healthy, returned to the starting rotation. By then, the White Sox were 29 games out of first place. On September 3, the day after the recuperated Johnny Mostil made his first appearance of the year (as a pinch runner), Faber turned in his best performance of the year, limiting Cleveland to five hits in a complete-game, 4–1 victory. His bid for a shutout evaporated in the ninth inning when second baseman Aaron Ward bobbled a grounder.[35] Eight days later, he pitched seven innings of shutout ball against the Nationals. The game had a couple of unusual features. One was light-hitting Faber's two doubles. The second came in the top of the eighth, and fatigue from his base running duties might have contributed to his problems in the bottom of the eighth, when he allowed the Nationals their first run on a hit batsman and consecutive singles. In the ninth, leading 5–1, Faber allowed the first two batters to reach base before giving way to Lyons. However, one future Hall of Famer could not save another. Lyons failed to stop the Nats, who pushed the game into extra innings. In the bottom of the 12th inning, the Nationals appeared to pull out a 6–5 victory when pinch runner Stuffy Stewart beat the throw home after a sacrifice fly. The hometown crowd celebrated and headed for the exits — some of them cutting across the field. However, Lyons had other plans. He hollered for the ball to be given to rookie shortstop Roy Flaskamper, who "threaded his way through the mob of fans and touched [third] base, whereupon Umpire [George] Hildebrand ruled that Washington had not yet won the game," Shirley L. Povich of *The Washington Post* reported. The field was cleared "with much difficulty," and the stunned Nats were summoned from the locker room. Now batting with two out and the bases empty, Washington won it fair and square by promptly slamming back-to-back doubles off Lyons.[36]

The loss was Chicago's second in what would be a dozen straight losses. Faber suffered two one-run defeats during the streak; the 12th straight loss was a 2–1 decision in Boston in which Faber pitched all 10 innings. "This was the third good game he pitched since leaving Chicago," the *Tribune* noted, "but he could not win without assistance."[37]

Faber experienced no late-inning collapse in his final start of 1927. In the nightcap of a September 30 doubleheader, umpires called the game because of darkness after six innings. Faber and the White Sox received credit for a 4–1 win. The victory improved Faber's record to 4–7, his worst mark ever. He appeared in only 18 games, including three relief assignments.

Excepting seasons when Chicago had an entry in the World Series, tradition dictated that the White Sox and Cubs meet in the City Series. Tradition also dictated that the loser of the previous City Series challenge the rival for the next. On September 19, however, the Cubs announced that they would not issue the challenge. "The season of 1927 contained so many splendid possibilities that any series other than a world's series would be an ill-fitting climax," explained William Veeck, Cubs president, who acknowledged that he also wanted an early start on a Wrigley Field expansion project. Comiskey went along, but not without a dig at the North Siders: "As far as we are concerned, nothing is to be gained by the Sox defeating the Cubs in another City Series."[38] Comiskey chose not to mention that his White Sox were limping to a 70–83 record, a mark inferior to the Cubs' 85–68. Denied a share of post-season gate receipts, Faber headed home after what was anything but a fulfilling year.

23

"Youth Must Be Served?"

After his worst season in his 14 major-league campaigns, 39-year-old Red Faber arrived in Shreveport for spring training 1928 claiming to be in better shape than at any time in the last four years.[1] Observers were skeptical. Writing in *The Sporting News*, Otis Harris told readers that Faber was "about through."[2] The *Chicago Tribune*, evaluating the White Sox pitching staff, admitted that, except for Ted Lyons and Tommy Thomas, "enthusiasm tapers off." The *Tribune* noted that Faber last season had won only four games and struggled with control; he recorded five hit batsmen, three wild pitches and 41 walks in 111 innings.[3] Prognosticators, calculating how the White Sox could make the first division, penciled in Faber for 10 victories.[4]

There was reason for lukewarm optimism after Faber's first start of spring training. After a decent exhibition opener against the Shreveport minor league club, Faber suffered some unlucky turns. He missed a couple of workouts with what the *Tribune* described as "new-fangled miseries in his tummy."[5] Though not fully recovered from the malady, Faber on March 31 rolled out of bed to throw batting practice. During the workout, a line drive broke the pinkie of his pitching hand. His spring training suddenly terminated, Faber returned to Chicago for recuperation.[6]

Three weeks later, while the White Sox were in Detroit beating the Tigers, Faber sat in the Wrigley Field press box to watch the Cubs host the Pirates. The Sunday afternoon game between two National League contenders was a hot ticket. Some 48,000 fans — a record for Wrigley and perhaps for all Chicago — jammed the ballpark. Outside, Chicago police nabbed 11 ticket scalpers — they commanded as much as $10 a ticket — and four men selling hot dogs without a license.[7]

A little more than a week later, Faber ended his stint as baseball spectator and resumed his role as player. Starting against the Tigers in Comiskey Park on April 30, he "showed plenty of stuff" for the first four innings. However, the Tigers caught up with him in the fifth, staging a four-run rally. Fortunately, his teammates had staked him to a 10–2 lead, and Tommy Thomas held the Tigers in check to preserve a 10–6 win.[8]

In the first three weeks, player-manager Ray Schalk's team was unimpressive. "There seems to be a unanimity of opinion regarding the White Sox," *Tribune* sports editor Don Maxwell stated. "The club that hasn't finished out of the second division for eight years is as poorly a balanced team as a management could provide. Everyone except Harry Grabiner, the hard working secretary, admits it. He continues to talk about Mr. Comiskey's 'fine club.'" Turning to the pitching, Maxwell said Schalk's "efforts to win ballgames on the days when Lyons and Thomas are resting arouse sympathy." Running down (literally) the roster, Maxwell bluntly stated, "Faber can't protect a ten-run lead." The sports editor concluded, "Schalk deserves less talk about a 'fine club' and more effort to find him some one who can pitch nine fairly creditable innings. Of course, the White Sox were hard hit by the scandal of 1919, but Chicago's fans rate more than an eighth-place team nine years afterward."[9]

The day after Maxwell's rebuke, Faber pitched eight innings in Yankee Stadium. He would have pitched the ninth, but the Yankees did not require it, having a 4–2 win in hand. Some 55,000 fans turned out to see the pitching battle of future Hall-of-Famers Faber and Stan Coveleski. Though Faber took the loss, he allowed the Yankees just six hits, struck out two and walked four. A couple of those walks were of a defensive nature — issued to slugger Babe Ruth. Thus, it fell to Lou Gehrig, with a home run and two defensive gems, to beat Faber and the White Sox. Describing Faber as "one of those veterans coasting down hill after a brilliant career," a surprised Irving Vaughan of the *Tribune* said the spitballer "came up out of nowhere ... to hurl the kind of ball that rolled the calendar back almost a dozen years."[10]

Still, the White Sox struggled. Faber's battle with the league-leading Yankees marked the team's fifth straight defeat — and they would lose two more before breaking the streak. By then, Chicago occupied the American League cellar (7–17) and was the subject of extensive criticism by sportswriters and fans alike. Under the heading, "WHAT'S THE MATTER WITH THE SOX," the *Chicago Tribune* printed letters from its readers. Chicagoan Larry Gee noted, "'Old Red Faber' should be good for an occasional victory, but he cannot take a regular turn on the slab and should never work oftener than once a week." The fan's harshest criticism of the White Sox was directed to the team's owner and secretary: "But what are Comiskey and Grabiner doing about it? Aye, there's the rub! The White Sox have not been able to pull off a trade since the days of the Black Sox. Why? League politics. The Peckinpaugh and Ward trades of last season were one huge joke."[11]

In a mid–May review of the White Sox's many travails, Vaughan also listed front-office interference. "The old and persistent idea that there is entirely too much commerce between the business office and the actual handling of the team on the playing field is held even by the players," Vaughan revealed. One of them claimed he saw a telegram from Chicago instructing Schalk to use a certain pitcher on just two days' rest — and the pitcher was pounded."[12] Vaughan did not name names, but the pitcher involved apparently was Tommy Thomas, who started May 4 and again May 7. At that point in the season, no other Sox pitcher had as little rest between starts.[13]

With a 1–2 record, after pitching shakily in victory and creditably in defeat, Faber took on the Tigers at Comiskey Park. "Old Red Faber, forty years come next September, rolled back the seasons yesterday and while so doing rolled up the Detroit Tigers in a whitewashed blanket that gave the White Sox the second of the series by 1 to 0," Vaughan reported. "Old Red pitched in a way that made you think of him as the man who won three games in the world series of 1917 — eleven years back — and when he had finished pitching the Tigers had only five singles to show for their efforts to make progress around the bases." Faber was never a strikeout artist. His forte was to induce ground balls. Evidence of Faber's effectiveness against the Tigers: he struck out no one but only three of Detroit's 27 outs came on outfield flies. However, Faber had to battle for the win, as Detroit starter Ken Holloway also held the White Sox to five hits; the Chicagoans bunched two of them in the seventh to score the game's only run.[14]

Five days later, in the opener of the Memorial Day 1928 doubleheader in St. Louis, Faber pitched well but was the victim of faulty defensive support. As Vaughan put it, "Faber's defeat in a fairly respectable duel with Jack Ogden ... was due to Bill Barrett's peculiar ideas of baseball mechanics." With two out in the seventh of a 1–1 game, the Browns had slow-footed Wally Schang on second and Ogden on first. Instead of letting a short fly fall in for a bases-filling single, Barrett tried to make a spectacular inning-ending catch. He missed the ball, failed to chase it down and allowed Schang and Ogden to score the winning runs.[15] Plays such as these bolstered Barrett's reputation as one of the game's worst defenders. Thomas' loss in the nightcap dropped the White Sox into a last-place tie with Washington.

In *The Sporting News*, Vaughan noted Faber's achievements but added, "The trouble is that [Faber] can't work regularly. If he could, Schalk would have some reason to boast about his staff because Thomas, Lyons and Blankenship are doing fairly well."[16] That analysis was borne out shortly afterward, on June 4, when Schalk started Faber on limited rest. An old rival, 41-year-old Ty Cobb, in his second (and final) season with Philadelphia after two decades with Detroit, contributed to Faber's demise. Cobb rapped a single and a triple as the Athletics scored all their runs in the first three innings of a 6–3 decision. Faber wasn't around to see the end of the Tigers' barrage, giving way to a reliever after just 2⅔ innings. "The big mistake proved the starting of Red Faber, another venerable, with only four days of rest," Vaughan wrote. "[The Athletics] simply crushed the old spitballer with a run in the first, two in the second and three more in the third."[17]

Working on five days' rest the next time out, Faber faced the Yankees in a jammed Comiskey Park. The Sunday date and the visit of Ruth and the first-place Yankees swelled the crowd to some 40,000. The crowd got what it wanted: the spectacle of a Ruth homer. It was a fifth-inning blast against the ledge of the right-field deck. Faber did not stick around much longer, departing in the sixth while trailing 5–3. The last-place White Sox then staged late-inning rallies, grabbing the lead with two runs in the seventh and three in the eighth. Lyons, in a rare relief appearance, recorded the final six outs to receive credit for the 8–6 win — despite giving up a ninth-inning homer to Ruth.[18]

Faber, the man who allegedly could not "protect a 10-run lead," then put together back-to-back complete-game victories. Attendance in Comiskey was only 1,500 on June 14, when second baseman Buck Redfern's two errors on a single play nearly cost Faber a victory. However, the White Sox held on for a 5–4 win over the Red Sox.[19] Faber next helped his team escape the AL cellar with a 6–4 victory in Detroit. He nearly let it slip away. Leading 6–1 entering the bottom of the eighth, Faber endured a three-run Tiger rally, fueled by Charlie Gehringer's second homer of the day. "But when [Faber's] lead had melted to the point where he couldn't spare any more of it," Vaughan reported, "he went back to work in earnest and breezed right through to the final out."[20]

Less than three months into the season, The Old Roman had seen enough. After the White Sox (32–42) split an Independence Day double-header against the Browns, he removed Schalk as manager. (He stayed on as backup catcher.) Fiery as a player, Schalk was not a good fit as manager. "He was inclined to be lenient with his players and they took advantage of it. Some of them talked back when he gave orders. Some openly ridiculed his efforts," Vaughan revealed. "Such conditions brought on the inevitable shattering of morale and the team fell to pieces, also to eighth place."[21] That atmosphere would change significantly — and immediately — under Schalk's successor, Russell "Lena" Blackburne. Faber and his new manager were once teammates. In 1914, it was infielder Blackburne's lackadaisical effort on a ninth-inning grounder that cost Faber, then a rookie, a no-hitter.

A former White Sox player and coach, the 41-year-old Blackburne enforced discipline through hard words, hard work and continual threats of $50 fines against transgressors. "Boys, from now on this here club is going to be a one-big-inning ball club or nothing," he said in his first clubhouse meeting. "The one-run idea is the bunk in this league. Three or no count is my slogan." The team initially responded, going 9–3 — all on the road — before cooling off. Nonetheless, the White Sox under Blackburne played .500 ball (40–40) and finished fifth in the American League. Blackburne's tenure would prove to be short-lived — largely because of a man yet to join the team — but his contribution to the game continues today.

Faber started the first game of Blackburne's managerial career, July 6 in Washington. The team apparently responded to his "big-inning" philosophy. With their manager working the third-base coaching line, the Sox sent 11 batters to the plate in the fifth inning and poured across seven runs. However, by then Faber was already out of the game. He departed in the third inning with a 4–0 deficit. He escaped with a no-decision when the Sox won their new manager's debut 9–8.[22]

Faber, working his curve ball in Philadelphia, narrowly missed a shutout in his next outing. Al Simmons of the Athletics had a great doubleheader that afternoon, collecting six hits in eight at-bats, including three home runs. His final round-tripper came against Faber with two out in the eighth inning of the nightcap, which the White Sox won 5–1. Ty Cobb went two-for-four in each game.[23] Though no one knew it at the time, the nightcap marked the final time Faber and Cobb faced each other on the ball field.[24]

Faber got his shutout in his next outing, defeating the Red Sox in the first game of a doubleheader 4–0 in Boston. However, that paled to what he accomplished the next week. In New York, Faber employed his arm and, in an unusual manner, his bat to defeat the powerhouse Yankees 6–4. After spotting New York three runs in the first inning, Faber buckled down. The Sox took a 4–3 lead into the bottom of the sixth, but the Yankees tied it and threatened to break the game open by loading the bases and sending Babe Ruth to the plate. Faber doused the threat by slipping three strikes by the home run king — Ruth watched a beautiful curveball for the final strike — and then inducing Lou Gehrig to ground out. With the game still tied in the top of the eighth, Chicago put runners on second and third with two out. Faber was due to bat. Blackburne summoned reserve catcher Harry McCurdy to pinch-hit for Faber, a career .134 hitter who struck out in nearly half of his at-bats in 1928. However, Faber put up such a fuss about the prospect of being yanked from the game that, somehow, Blackburne relented. The manager probably was second-guessing himself as he watched Faber, a switch-hitter, at the plate. Batting right-handed, Faber looked befuddled against righty Wilcy Moore. "Mr. Faber swung firmly but awkwardly at the ball and missed it by one and a half meters," *The New York Times'* James R. Harrison said of the first pitch. "Tightening his hold on the bat, Mr. Faber again indulged in a terrific swing and agitated nothing but the atmosphere."[25] What happened next bewildered and amused the occupants of Yankee Stadium. Before Moore delivered his next pitch, Faber stepped across the plate and took a left-handed batting stance. He proceeded to lace a clean single into center field, scoring two teammates. With the lead in hand, he shut out the Yankees in the eighth, thanks to left fielder Bib Falk, whose long running catch prevented two runs from scoring. In the ninth, Faber retained his composure even after catcher Bucky Crouse and third basemen Willie Kamm collided and missed an easy pop foul. Faber was too much for the Yankees, who saw their eight-game winning streak end with the 6–4 final.[26]

After a successful road trip to open the Blackburne administration, the White Sox returned to Chicago and proceeded to lose seven straight. The fifth "L" in the streak came in the first game of a doubleheader when Faber failed to protect a 5–2 lead against Washington; the Nationals rallied for five runs in the sixth inning en route to an 8–5 win.[27] Once they got that losing streak out of their system, the White Sox won six straight. Faber contributed with a 4–2 victory over the Red Sox.[28]

Facing the Yankees in Chicago, Faber lasted eight innings — but that turned out to be barely half the game. As Edward Burns of the *Tribune* put it: "If you're a real baseball bug and let some silly thing like business keep you from Comiskey Park yesterday afternoon, shed bitter tears, for you'll have to wait years for a chance to see another baseball spectacle like the great battle those Sox and those Yanks put up for three hours and thirty-four minutes." When Faber left after the eighth inning, the Yankees held a 4–3 lead. Chicago tied it in the eighth and, as dusk descended on Chicago, won it on Kamm's triple with two out in the bottom of the 15th inning. The loss was the New Yorkers' 11th in 17 games. "When this trip is over your correspondent is going off to cover a nice, quiet massacre or a jolly little war," sportswriter Harrison of *The New York Times* quipped.[29]

When the Yankees and White Sox met later in New York, Faber accomplished another offensive feat. This time, instead of hitting both right- and left-handed in the same at-bat, he homered against Hank Johnson for only the second round-tripper of his major-league career. And, for good measure, he also contributed a single while collecting a complete-game victory 8–4. (Faber's first career homer also occurred at Yankee Stadium, in 1923.) Another feature of the game was Babe Ruth's 45th round-tripper of the season.[30]

Still on their road trip, the White Sox welcomed a late-season addition to the roster, C. Arthur Shires, a fun-loving 21-year-old first baseman from Waco, Texas. His pitcher in his major league debut was a man nearly twice his age, Red Faber. Even before Faber took the mound, Shires made an impact, slamming the ball to Fenway Park's flagpole for a first-inning triple. He registered three more hits that afternoon while Faber went the distance for a 6–4 victory.[31] In many ways, Shires embodied the Roaring Twenties. He enjoyed a night on the town more than an afternoon at the ballpark. His hard-drinking, undisciplined manner so challenged authority that it contributed to Blackburne's undo-

Faber was popular and well-respected by teammates and opponents alike. (Courtesy of the Tri-County Historical Society, Cascade, Iowa.)

ing as manager; the worst was yet to come. But on this August day, members of the White Sox — with the likely exception of first baseman John "Bud" Clancy, who lost his starting role — were glad to have Art Shires around.

After two rough outings in which he did not get past the sixth inning and lost both decisions, Faber earned a complete-game win against the visiting Tigers 3–2 in the nightcap of a doubleheader. Chicago won the opener by the same 3–2 score; pinch hitter Bill Hunnefield came through in both battles, providing a game-tying single in the opener and a game-winning sacrifice fly in the ninth inning of the nightcap. For Faber, it was victory No. 11 — already one better than the optimistic prognostication made for him during spring training. Nearly a month of the regular season remained. The win also edged the White Sox, one-time cellar-dwellers, into a fourth-place tie in the eight-team American League. A fourth-place finish would mean a sliver from the World Series pie — about $400 a man.[32]

The White Sox and Tigers met again the next week — this time in

Detroit — and Faber, in his first appearance as a 40-year-old, earned his 12th victory. His teammates appeared to do their best to kick it away. Chicago errors contributed to three unearned runs, but Faber held the Tigers to eight hits in a complete-game win 6–4. Faber contributed offensively with a two-run double during a five-run sixth inning.[33]

Back in Chicago, with his team clinging onto fourth place, Faber took a 2–0 lead into the seventh inning against Red Ruffing and the Red Sox. However, Boston scored once in the seventh and twice in the eighth and Faber headed for the locker room. Rookie Shires' third hit of the afternoon sparked an eighth-inning comeback and Chicago claimed a 4–3 win.[34] Rookie reliever George Cox received credit for what turned out to be the only victory of his only season in the majors.

The Yankees arrived for their final visit to Chicago leading Philadelphia by just two games in the race for the AL pennant. The White Sox, meanwhile, still had their sights set on their first first-division finish since the Black Sox scandal broke in 1920. The weather was cool — not conducive to Faber's effectiveness — and Blackburne considered skipping his turn on the mound. Faber talked him out of it. "I heard them [Yankees] say I was an old bird," Faber reportedly told Blackburne. "All I ask is that if I can keep going you'll let me stay in. Don't yank me for a pinch hitter. Just let me stay in there and I'll show them the old man's not through." It is unknown whether the account is accurate or just a sportswriter's embellishment, but that is how the game played out. Both teams needed the victory — and they played like it, requiring a dozen innings to settle matters. "Neighbors, it was a beautiful contest," gushed the *Tribune*'s Burns. In an iron man exhibition reminiscent of his performance when he was in his 20s, the spitballer battled the New Yorkers into overtime. In the top of the 10th, Faber found himself in a jam. With two on and two out, Babe Ruth stepped to the plate. Burns described the scene: "A lot of folks though that was the end of Faber. It might have been the end for some of those young pitchers who begin shaking whenever the Bambino walks to the plate. But old Red has courage. He just kept huddling with that ball and until the count was three balls and two strikes the Babe made terrible gestures with that bat. Everybody set up a little straighter and stopped talking. Would he walk him? Did he have nerve to put it over? Would the Babe knock it over the fence? Old Red was the only fellow in the park who wasn't just a trifle nervous. He just laid it over and the Babe nicked it and young [second baseman Karl] Swanson scooped it up and tossed him out." Faber pitched two more scoreless innings. With one out in the bottom of the 12th inning, White Sox rookie Carl Reynolds scored on rookie Swanson's sacrifice fly. Final score: White Sox 4, Yankees 3. In going the distance, Faber held the league leaders to eight hits over the 12 innings and prevailed over Waite Hoyt, who entered in the eighth inning.[35] Richards Vidmer, writing for *The*

New York Times, consoled Yankees fans: "The old man of the red thatch was almost invincible."[36]

The *Chicago Tribune*, whose sports editor earlier in the season characterized Faber as incapable of lasting nine innings or protecting a huge lead, the next morning published a feature under the headline, "Youth Must Be Served? Not in the Case of Mr. Faber." With occasional accuracy, the article opened by recounting Faber's career before he reached the majors. "Well, anyway, now you have an idea of how long Red Faber has been walking out to a baseball mound, hoisting the ball into a huddle until you can't see his face, and then hopping a spitter into the catcher's glove." The feature reviewed his containment of the Yankees the previous afternoon. "But the biggest kick of the whole affair was the way old Red Faber grinned and rubbed his arm and spat: 'Youth must be served. Blah.'"[37] The victory was Faber's 13th of the regular season.

The weather was again frigid for Faber's final start of the regular season, against the Nationals. "Football temperatures" hampered the entire series in Chicago, and Comiskey Park was virtually deserted. Only about 200 paying customers showed up, and they saw Washington nick Faber for two runs on nine hits before he was lifted for a pinch hitter in the bottom of the eighth. Meanwhile, Sad Sam Jones shut out the Sox to earn a 3–0 victory.[38] *The Washington Post* said the Nationals' share of the gate receipts was so measly that manager Bucky Harris held the cash instead of wiring it to Washington so he could buy his players breakfast the following morning. The loss ended Faber's regular season with a record of 13–7 — better than virtually anyone (but Faber?) could have expected for a 40-year-old pitcher on a second-division team. The White Sox (72–82) ended the season in fifth place — out of the money — and just one game better than their 1927 record.

After going on hiatus in 1927, the City Series of Chicago was back in business in 1928. While sportswriters were in the habit of characterizing the friendly rivalry as a grudge match, by 1928 there was substance to the reports of bad blood. "But let's get honest," Burns wrote in the *Tribune*. "For two years the Cubs have been sore at the Sox because they are accused of rooting against Cub success in pennant chases. And for the same two years the Sox have been ... jealous because the Cubs have been pets of the town." The Cubs were particularly irked when they were told that Sox personnel tossed their hats in celebration when they learned that the North Siders had lost a crucial series during the pennant race. "Comrades," Burns said, "it looks like a whale of a city series."[39]

In a feature article previewing the series, Burns compared and contrasted the possible Game 1 starters — Faber and 36-year-old Art Nehf, who, like Faber, collected 13 wins during the regular season. Burns noted that Nehf was a willing and popular after-dinner speaker. On the other hand, "Faber doesn't care so much for go-getter excitement, being passionately devoted to whittling. There's not a family within fifty miles of Cascade, Iowa, that hasn't got a fan whittled by Red out of a plain pine board. Red whittles for the love of it and never has accepted money for any of his ornaments."[40] When the City Series opened on a chilly Wednesday in Comiskey Park, Faber started but the Cubs went with 26-year-old Pat Malone instead of Nehf. Nearly 26,000 fans showed up. Faber did not last long. He struggled with his control, and the Cubs hit hard the pitches he managed to get over the plate. Faber retired only two North Siders before Blackburne called in Grady Adkins, a 31-year-old rookie. Adkins and George Connally shut out the Cubs for the final 8⅓ innings, but the damage had been done. Malone stifled the Sox on just five hits for the shutout. Final score: 3–0. The *Tribune*'s Harvey T. Woodruff, in a light-hearted column fashioned to be his first-person report to his editor, wrote: "In that first inning, the fellow next to me said, 'Faber ain't got nothing but his glove today.' That meant he didn't have any stuff. As far as the glove was concerned, I don't blame him for having it. If I had been Faber, I would have wanted another glove, a mask and a chest protector the way the Cubs were driving them past him."[41]

Faber received another start three days later, in Game 4 at Wrigley Field. He stuck around longer — through seven innings — but he again gave up three runs in a single inning and took the loss. "Outside of that one inning, Faber had the Cubs pretty well in hand, but Sheriff Blake was working along the same lines against the White Sox," *The Sporting News* noted.[42] Final score: Cubs 3, White Sox 2.

The series went the full seven games, with the North Siders taking the deciding contest in a romp. The Cubs earned about $1,200 a share. For their efforts, the White Sox were to receive about $850 each. "All jokes aside about eating acorns," Burns noted, "this is nice ham and egg money for the four-month winter faced by the ball players."[43] But the distribution among the White Sox became a matter of dispute. The team voted only a half-share for Art Shires, who joined the team in late August but contributed consistently for those 37 games and the City Series. The *Tribune* characterized the Sox as stingy: "It probably will be submitted that there is little justice in a plan which gives a ball player like Shires a half share, whereas such club liabilities as [Bill] Barrett, for instance, drew full shares. Barrett, incidentally, struck out in his one appearance in the city series, as he did in seven out of his eight last appearances as a pinch hitter in the American League."[44]

The White Sox were through for the winter, but Faber was not. He recruited batterymate Bucky Crouse and rookie pitcher Bob Weiland to accompany him to Iowa for a couple of games with Faber's hometown team, the Cascade Reds. (The team's nickname predated the ballplayer's fame.) The Saturday after the City Series, the major leaguers joined the Cascade team for a home-and-home series with the Giants of Decorah in Winneshiek County, Iowa. The Giants also received professional help: Ossie Orwoll, who starred at Luther College in Decorah and had just finished his rookie season with the Philadelphia Athletics. Faber pitched about two-thirds of the game before giving way to Weiland, a 6–4, 215-pound Chicago native with one game of major league experience (a 1–0 win over the Athletics). Orwoll almost single-handedly carried the Decorah team to victory 3–2. He pitched a complete game, allowed Cascade just four hits and starred at the plate — hitting a single, double and triple. Orwoll's offensive prowess was not particularly surprising — as an Athletics rookie he played some first base and hit .306.

The series moved to Cascade the next day, designated "Red Faber Day." Some 1,500 fans surrounded Legion Park to see Faber and Orwoll resume their duel. Cascade held a 2–0 lead after seven innings. In the top of the eighth, a two-out throwing error allowed an unearned run and put a runner on first. Orwoll then drove Faber's 3–2 pitch into a row of automobiles ringing the outfield, circled the bases and scored the winning run. "Cascade was not downhearted. They would have enjoyed a victory. However, they were satisfied," a Dubuque newspaper reported. "They saw 'Red' pitch. They saw him hurl victorious baseball. They saw a little error turn victory into defeat. But after all what cared they because they had 'Red' Faber home and they live and believe in their native son."[45] Cascade boosters had another reason to be happy: the huge turnout bolstered the team's treasury. As the Cascade paper noted, "This year was an expensive one, as the start of the season required $300 for uniforms and over $200 for diamond expense."[46] His civic duty completed, Faber probably stuck around Cascade for a while, visiting family and tromping some of his favorite hunting grounds.

24

"A Good and Deserving Fellow"

"Manager Blackburne held a short conference with Mr. Comiskey yesterday," the *Chicago Tribune* reported the day before the 1929 White Sox departed for spring training. "Afterwards he had no information to give out except the repeated assertion that he would be the big boss of the Hose this season."[1] Indeed, Blackburne carried himself as the "big boss," and his management style sparked team dissension, fueled on-field failure and provided a plot line for multiple incidents with young Art Shires, one of his most talented yet unstable players. Blackburne made it clear that few jobs were secure. Among the few exceptions were starting pitchers Faber, Ted Lyons and Al Thomas.

Just before heading to Dallas, the White Sox consummated a deal that had been the subject of negotiations for about three months, trading their malcontent outfielder Bib Falk to Cleveland for backup catcher Martin Autry.[2] The Sox moved another disgruntled veteran in late May when Bill Barrett, a liability in the outfield, went to Boston for outfielder Doug Taitt.[3]

At 11:30 the morning of February 28, a train carrying the main body of the team's spring training contingent pulled out of Union Station and headed for Dallas, their new site after four years in Shreveport.[4] Among them was William A. Buckner, long-timer trainer and equipment manager. Buckner, a lively and talkative character who joined the White Sox around 1910, liked to develop and test various lotions and liniments to use on the ball players. He was known to get so wrapped up in his storytelling that he would inadvertently massage the left arms of ailing right-handed pitchers.[5] By mid–February, Buckner had completed another duty — packing the team's trunks for shipment to training camp. However, once in the Lone Star State, Faber, Johnny Mostil, Lyons and Barrett had to watch the first workout because the trunks containing their uniforms could not be located. (What story Buckner told about the incident was not recorded.)

That tidbit was overshadowed by accounts of the fashionable arrival of Art Shires. Just 21 years old and boasting all of 33 games of major league experience, Shires received from Blackburne the title of team captain. (It was a decision the manager would regret and rescind almost immediately.) Shires, checking in from his home just 30 miles away, made headlines with his attire. "He came in as the last word in what the well-dressed men wear and the few cap-wearing old-timers in the party took one look and remarked that the game certainly is undergoing a change," the *Tribune*'s Irving Vaughan reported. "He was encased in a brown suit and a natty English overcoat of hue that would have made delightful camouflage for a tortoise shell cat. Gray spats hid his socks from view. Atop at a jaunty angle was a soft brown hat with the prevailing narrow brim. And on his left arm as he strolled about the hotel lobby shaking hands, was a heavy yellow cane that some of the athletes mistook for a bat that had warped at one end." After an extended period of gazing at Shires' attire, the players were "brought out of their trance by a remark from Blackburne that the purpose of coming was to labor."[6]

Even before spring training concluded, Blackburne suspended and fined Shires and Bill Cissell, a high-priced, second-year shortstop. The Associated Press said their offenses were "breaking training rules and 'raising whoopee.'" The dispatch also referred to dissatisfaction among the players. "I am going to weed out the bad element," Blackburne said, "Then we can make some progress."[7] Shires told reporters that if the White Sox did not want him he'd be perfectly happy to return to the Texas League.[8] Meanwhile, club secretary Harry Grabiner told the *Tribune* he knew of no dissension among the players but that Comiskey would support Blackburne in any disputes. However, Vaughan reported that many veterans were "peevish" over the amount of playing time given youngsters and the low quality of spring training competition. White Sox historian Richard Lindberg said that Shires convinced Cissell that Blackburne was showing favoritism toward Falk, Kamm and Faber.[9]

Faber did receive special consideration in preparing for his 16th major league season. Blackburne did not require the veteran to participate in any drills, and he allowed him to set his own conditioning program. Faber seemed to hold unofficial status as player-coach. In mid–March, Faber was left in charge of workouts with three teammates while the rest of the team went on an exhibition road trip.[10] Faber's training apparently went well: After his final exhibition tune-up, he reported that he had "cut loose" and his arm felt great.[11]

Speculative press reports listed a half-dozen players apparently on the "outs" with Blackburne; they were likely to be traded or waived. One, Shires, was reinstated when he signed a statement acknowledging that any future infraction would carry a $500 fine.[12] The only other positive news Shires experienced during this period came from a courtroom in Shreveport, where a Caddo Parish grand jury cleared him of any criminal charges. During a minor league game the previous summer, Shires threw a ball that struck the head of William Lawson, identified in the United Press dispatch as a "Negro spectator." Lawson, who had sued for damages, died several months after the beaning.[13]

For their last campaign of the 1920s, the White Sox donned new uniforms designed by Chicago merchant Harry Burton. In Comiskey Park, they wore "an elaborate uniform of white freely sprinkled with piping of scarlet and blue." The "Sox" monogram on the shirts was two-toned. The road uniforms were "of gray, with fancy decorations."[14]

The White Sox donned gray to open the regular season, and suffered three straight losses at St. Louis before Faber made his first start. He retired the first nine men he faced. "For a time he looked to be the Faber of palmier days," Vaughan observed. However, the Browns touched him for a run in the fourth and three in the fifth, when he "crumpled completely." He hung around seven innings but was losing 4–0 when he was lifted for a pinch hitter (Shires). Faber escaped with a no-decision when the Sox rallied for four runs in the eighth and one in the ninth to win 5–4; reliever Dan Dugan was credited with the win.[15] The principals met again a week later in Chicago. Again, Faber baffled the Browns for three innings, and he held a 3–2 lead entering the eighth inning. However, in that frame the Browns lit up Faber for five runs and claimed a 7–3 victory.[16]

Faber found his way into the record books in his next outing, on May 4, when the Yankees' Lou Gehrig launched one of his second-inning pitches onto the roof of Comiskey Park. It was the first of Gehrig's three round-trippers that afternoon — an American League record. Gehrig's other victims were Hal McCain, who took the loss, and Dugan.[17] McCain had the distinction of giving up homers to Babe Ruth and then Gehrig in the seventh inning. (In 1932, Gehrig hit four homers in one game to raise the American League record and tie the major league mark established in 1894.[18]) Four days later, Blackburne allowed Faber to overstay his welcome on the Comiskey Park mound; the Athletics nicked him for runs in the seventh and eighth innings to beat him 5–4. "In a way, old man Faber was entitled to something more than a beating," Vaughan observed. "He was unlucky enough to have his only two passes grow into runs. He was unlucky enough to have two tallies scored against him because Clarence Hoffman, fearing a collision with [Carl] Reynolds, didn't quite reach a fly ball that fell for a double in the fourth."[19] His luck turned in his next start, when the White Sox scored the tying and winning runs on Willie Kamm's one-out double in the bottom of the ninth. "The rousing conclusion was poetic or some kind of justice for Old Red Faber," Vaughan wrote. "Through nine rounds he hurled as beautifully as any

40-year-old gentleman ever hurled, but when he stepped aside in the home ninth to let a pinch hitter operate in his behalf, it looked much as if he was going to be beaten on a measly assortment of four hits."[20] Noted Frank H. Young of *The Washington Post*, "As a matter of fact, the Nationals did not deserve to win a game on but four hits."[21] The 3–2 final gave Faber his first win of the year.

During batting practice three days later, Shires, barely a month removed from suspension, stepped up to take his swings while wearing a red felt cap. The headwear was popular with young people of the day. Blackburne took exception to Shires' fashion statement, however, and ordered him to remove the cap and not "burlesque" the game. "Shires countered with a number of large words not suited to household purposes and added that before he finished he'd run Blackburne out of his job," Vaughan reported. Warm-ups stopped, and the players watched. Blackburne suspended the young player, fined him $100 and ordered him off the field. In the clubhouse after the White Sox beat Boston 8–4, Shires complained to Blackburne about his lack of playing time. The manager replied that that was Shires' own fault — he had broken team rules during spring training. Soon, Shires and Blackburne came to blows. "The ball players, many just out of the showers, watched," Vaughan wrote, "but none interfered." Blackburne's direct hit to the jaw sent Shires sprawling over a chair. Shires, barely half his manager's age, countered with blows below the eye and to the ear. The fisticuffs ended in a minute or so. Shires cleaned out his locker and tried to hold back sobs. "As he started for the door he is said to have turned to yell a 'good-bye' to everybody but he choked up. Tears rolled down his reddened face. Walking out of the park with a police escort, Shires cried as he told a sportswriter he didn't know where he was headed. Blackburne, meanwhile, walked about the clubhouse and joked about the skirmish, saying it was inevitable. It appeared that Shires' career with the White Sox was over, but subsequent events would prove the petulant player correct: Shires would rejoin the club and, by season's end, Blackburne would be gone.

As Shires departed, the Sox headed for Detroit, where Faber was scheduled to start the second game of the series. Before taking on the Tigers, Faber received bad news from Iowa: his father, Nicholas, was seriously ill. Nonetheless, Faber took his turn on the mound. He was a man in a hurry. After a shaky first inning in which he gave up two runs, Faber tamed the Tigers 6–2. His complete-game victory in the books, Faber rushed from Navin Field to the train station for an emergency trip to Cascade. He was too late. Seventy-one Nicholas Faber died at 8:30 the following morning — before his son reached his bedside. A stern hotelier and devout Roman Catholic, Nicholas made it known that, upon his passing, friends and relatives could honor him by having Masses celebrated in his memory instead of sending floral tributes.

The Hall-of-Famer's father, Nicholas Faber (1857–1929), was a successful hotelier and property owner in Cascade, Iowa. A family of Luxemburgian descent, the Fabers spoke German as well as English. A stern man and devout Roman Catholic, Nicholas was known to admonish his children for playing instead of praying. However, there is no evidence that he opposed the baseball pursuits of his sons, Urban and Alfred. (Courtesy of the Tri-County Historical Society, Cascade, Iowa.)

Nonetheless, "No one remembers more flowers at a funeral in Cascade," recalled granddaughter Mary Ione Theisen. The baseball community honored the father of one of the game's greats by sending dozens of floral tributes.[22] Comiskey himself sent a wreath of carnations, roses and sweet peas.[23]

Just two days after his father's funeral, Faber received no sympathy in St. Louis, where the Browns sent him to the showers in the third inning of the 7–3 decision.[24] That dismal showing made Faber's next outing all the more surprising. Back home in Comiskey Park, the 40-year-old threw a one-hitter against the Tigers. Spoiling Faber's 2–0 masterpiece was a clean single into center field by Charlie Gehringer with two out in the fourth inning. Only three other balls that reached the outfield all afternoon. "Faber's curve was so dazzling and his spitter so deceptive that the Tigers couldn't even get their bats squarely in the path of the pitches," Vaughan reported. Twenty-one of the outs came on ground balls; the others came on three strikeouts and three fly balls to Douglas Taitt, who was making his White Sox debut after being traded by the Red Sox in the Bill Barrett deal. Detroit had only one other base runner all afternoon — Eddie Phillips, who was nicked with a pitch in the fifth. The game lasted just 75 minutes.[25] (It was Faber's third one-hitter. His first came early in his rookie season, 1914, when infielder Lena Blackburne, his present manager, played a ninth-inning grounder lackadaisically. The second occurred on September 15, 1915, when Tris Speaker lashed a clean single.) Next, Faber again defied his advancing years by posting another complete-game victory, a 3–2 decision over visiting Cleveland. He improved his season record to 4–3 — not bad for a team that was 10 games below .500.[26]

The White Sox embarked on a road trip to New York. A stranger in their hotel lobby was overhead saying, "I was thinking of going out to see a ball game. Haven't seen one in a long while." A respondent said, "If I knew for certain I was going to play, I'd advise you to go out. It would be worth your while." The speaker was none other than Art Shires. Incredibly, the White Sox had removed him from the suspended list. Shires was not kidding; he believed he was just that talented — and important. "He was strolling down the aisle to his seat for the third act of a Broadway show a few nights ago when there was an outburst of applause from the orchestra seats," *New York Times* sportswriter John Kieran revealed. "He appreciated it very much. He bowed to the right. He bowed to the left. He turned around to bow and came face to face with Douglas Fairbanks Jr. and his bride, for whom the applause was intended. Then he sat down."[27] Shires returned to the Sox lineup in the final game of the series, which Faber started. Shires had two hits, but the Sox had only two others all afternoon, and the New Yorkers beat Faber 4–2. The Yankees did not require the services of Babe Ruth, who, it was reported, was nursing a wrist injury and a cold.[28] (Years later, sportswriter Red Smith, who covered Ruth, said it was common for reporters to dream up cover stories if the Bambino had overindulged in one vice or another, but it is unknown if this was one such occasion.[29])

After another loss and a no-decision in which he lost a four-run lead in the ninth, Faber squared off against the only other (legal) spitballer remaining in the American League, Jack Quinn, on a sweltering afternoon in Philadelphia. The Sox chased Quinn in the fifth inning, and Shires contributed two hits, including a two-run shot that left Shibe Park entirely, as Chicago won 6–4.[30] That performance did not diminish Shires' opinion of himself. In St. Louis, he intercepted a live radio microphone. "Without any advance notice he walked up to a microphone and talked for 10 minutes without a break," Vaughan reported. "He informed his listeners that there were only two stars in the game, the other being Babe Ruth." Speaking to a St. Louis audience, Shires said, "Come out to razz me. You'll go away cheering me when I slam 'em against those bleachers. I sure can hit that ball, and I'm not so bad around that first base, either." After he relinquished the microphone, Shires remarked, "Well, I guess I said enough to make 'em mad and they'll be there tomorrow calling me a lot of trick names."[31] The next day, Shires had a double in five at-bats while the Browns romped 11–3.[32] Shires' return to the team rarely resulted in team victories. Through June, the White Sox had lost two of every three games (23–46) and sat just one game out of the American League cellar. Despite losing two games late that month, Faber was the team's leading pitcher and starting with greater frequency than he had the previous season. In Detroit on June 24, Sox catcher Moe Berg opened the top of the fifth with a single, and Faber stepped to the plate. Already trailing 4–1, he did not sacrifice. Instead, he lofted an Emil Yde offering over the

After concealing the baseball close to his mouth, Faber entered his wind-up, which included raising ball and glove high above his head. Photograph taken in 1929. (Chicago Historical Society, *Chicago Daily News* collection SDN-068991.)

left field wall of Navin Field to cut Detroit's lead to 4–3. However, the Sox continued to commit errors — they had five — and Faber continued to give up hits — he allowed 11 in seven innings — and the Tigers romped 13–4.[33] The homer was the third — and last — of Faber's career.

After an Independence Day victory at Cleveland, Faber engaged Quinn in a rematch. Again, the Chicago spitballer prevailed as the lowly White Sox won their third out of four against the league-leading Athletics 6–4. The Yankees, pursuing the A's, then nicked Faber in the first game of a Comiskey Park doubleheader 4–2. Though the Sox continued to struggle, Faber distinguished himself as the team's leading pitcher (8–8) after beating the Red Sox 2–1. Faber's spitter was working well: Chicago outfielders recorded only five putouts all afternoon, while Faber struck out eight Boston batters.[34] The White Sox again rallied late in Faber's next outing, in Washington, where he trailed 2–1 after seven innings. He was lifted for a pinch hitter in the top of the eighth inning, when the Chicagoans scored twice and held on for a 3–2 win. Faber then received credit for his third straight win in Philadelphia. The heat wilted him after five innings, but he had built up a 6–1 lead. Handling the final four innings, Ted Lyons nearly let it get away, allowing four runs after one was out in the ninth, but preserved the victory 8–6.

The day was also marked by the unpredictable Art Shires' debut as a poet. Sportswriters often referred to him as "The Great Shires." While he didn't mind that, Shires said that he actually he preferred, "What-a-man." Shires decided that giving an autograph with only his signature was insufficient; he would include original verse composed daily. His first installment:

A phonograph and some dancing create a party atmosphere during a train trip. Among those pictured are manager Lena Blackburne (lower left), Ed Walsh Jr. (hand on phonograph), Alphonse "Tommy" Thomas (dancing), Red Faber (standing at right) and Irene Faber (lower right). This party probably ocurred in 1929, Blackburne's only full season as White Sox manager. (Courtesy of the Tri-County Historical Society, Cascade, Iowa.)

There is a ball player,
He is the Great Shires,
Which he can paste the old apple,
Whenever he tries."

That afternoon, Shires used other choice words after being called out for oversliding second base on a double. The *Chicago Tribune* reported, "The Great Shires kicked dirt and gloves all over the premises in a stirring temperamental outburst which caused him to be showered with straw hats and other missiles."[35]

The composition of the baseball changed in 1926 when the cork center was cushioned to make the ball more "lively." Baseball men in 1929 debated whether manufacturers had made the sphere even *livelier*.[36] Conspiracy theorists cited what they said was a higher number of line drives striking pitchers and increased distance off the fungo bat. Umpire George Moriarty stated that he had no doubt that the ball was livelier, citing run production and pitchers' close encounters with line drives. Moriarty suggested that the livelier ball might require baseball's powers to lift the ban on new spitball pitchers.[37] Faber, one of the last legal spitballers, said he believed that the ball was, indeed, livelier. He based that opinion not from pitching it but from hitting the ball for extra distance with a fungo bat.[38]

Certainly, Faber enjoyed some lucky breaks during his 25-year professional career. However, luck — or his defense — seemed to hurt him more than help him. Consider, for example, his experience August 2 in Boston. Battling the Red Sox into extra innings, Faber took the mound in the bottom of the 10th with a 2–1 lead thanks to Moe Berg's RBI single. After retiring the leadoff hitter, Faber appeared to strike out pinch hitter Johnnie Heving — but the third strike got away from his catcher, Berg, and Heving made first base. Instead of having two outs with the bases empty, Boston had one on and one out. Faber induced the next hitter, Russ Scarritt, to ground into a fielder's choice. But for Berg's error, the game would have been over and Berg would have provided a different sort of headline. However, the battle continued, and Faber faced former teammate Bill Barrett, who stroked a game-tying double. Bill Regan promptly singled, scoring Barrett and giving Boston a come-from-behind victory 3–2. Understated the *Tribune*'s Burns, "It was a tough one for Red Faber to lose."[39]

Though he came out on the losing end more frequently than during his prime, the success and competitive fire of the soon-to-be 41-year-old occasionally inspired verse:

Red Faber

A lot of water has passed the mill,
Since Faber, the Red, broke in;

But they shudder still when he mounts the hill,
And flashes his aging fin.
He was old when the Sox were at their best,
Ere the scandal laid them low,
And he yet shines, though the rest are gone
From the big-time diamond show.[40]

Faber did his fans proud in the second game of a Thursday afternoon doubleheader in Comiskey Park, scattering 11 hits in a 6–2 victory. However, he could not solve former AL batting champion Heinie Manush, who collected four hits, including two doubles, in four at-bats. (Manush, a lefty who hit .330 in his 17-year career, and Faber were elected into the National Baseball Hall of Fame by the Veterans Committee in 1964.) After losing two-thirds of their games from April through June, the White Sox got hot — relatively — in July and August. In those two months, the team went 27–28, and Faber, despite being sick for part of August, collected six of his 14 wins during that stretch. After missing at least one start due to "the grippe" ("the flu"), Faber tried his hand against the Nationals. Though he gave up 11 hits during that span, Faber's defense was unreliable. Things turned against Faber almost from the start. Shortstop Bill Cissell was tossed out of the game for vociferously arguing with umpire George Hildebrand, forcing a "drastic realignment" of the infield. Bud Clancy, summoned from the bench to play first (his usual position), rifled a throw to third base into the stands. An easy pop-up was allowed to fall behind second base while, as *The Washington Post* described it, "three Comiskey employees went into conference in the immediate vicinity." Later, Clancy nimbly fielded a bunt and turned to throw to first — only to find no teammate covering the bag. Meanwhile, the Nationals earned three other runs in Faber's last inning of work on Goose Goslin's 30th home run.[41] Of all the miscues, only Clancy's throwing error went into the books, but so did Faber's "L" in a 9–4 decision.[42]

In Dubuque, Iowa, on the early morning of August 20, 1929, about 100 baseball fans — Red Faber fans — boarded a special train bound for Chicago. (*The New York Times* gave the passenger count as 1,000.[43]) In any case, the fans, from Dubuque and Cascade, journeyed to Comiskey Park to celebrate Red Faber Day. In the entourage were two former Faber batterymates, Nick Steffen and Art Melchior. Steffen — later the Rev. Nicholas A. Steffen, dean at Columbia College — was Faber's catcher during the college's undefeated season of 1909. Melchior, a bank teller in Dubuque, was Faber's catcher on the semi-pro Dubuque Tigers.[44] Several of Faber's relatives made the trip from Cascade, including his recently widowed mother, Margaret. She posed for pictures with her son and his wife, Irene. Also present was the pitcher's nephew, Fred, who watched "Uncle Urban" deliver pitches that "sounded like a thou-

Faber poses with his mother, Margaret, and his first wife, Irene, before the Red
Faber Day ceremony in Comiskey Park on August 20, 1929. His father, Nicholas,
died just three months earlier. Irene, who experienced health problems throughout their 22 years of marriage, died in 1943 at age 44. Margaret Faber died in
1947. (Chicago Historical Society, *Chicago Daily News* collection SDN-069105.)

sand bees."[45] Around 20,000 fans — attendance estimates among the Chicago
newspapers ranged from 15,000 to 25,000 — turned out on Faber's day. The
gate was healthy for a Tuesday — and especially when the home team was 27
games under .500 and the cross-town Cubs were in a pennant race. No doubt
that the visitors were Babe Ruth, Lou Gehrig and the rest of the New York
Yankees bolstered the turnout. "There are 'days' and 'days' in baseball, but
most of them are hollow affairs schemed out to click clickless turnstiles," the
Tribune's Burns noted. "But this one was different." During a pre-game ceremony, Faber accepted $2,750 in cash, flowers, a diamond ring and a large
radio set inside fine cabinetry. The cash gift came from various donors, including Comiskey ($500), his fans back home in Iowa and current and former
teammates. Former captain and manager Eddie Collins enclosed a note with
his check: "Not much, but at least I wanted to be a contributor to a good

and deserving fellow."[46] Comiskey told the *Chicago Evening Post*, "Urban Faber is my ideal of all a baseball player should be. He is an example of all American youth to follow."[47] Most newspaper accounts of the event were brief, and none mentioned whether the Old Roman, whose health was fading, actually participated in the ceremony. "Fabe has spent sixteen years doing a very excellent job of tending to business, keeping his eyes open and his mouth shut," sportswriter and broadcaster Hal Totten wrote in the *Chicago Daily News*, "and today Chicago fans are giving him his 'Day,'" something he has long deserved but never enjoyed." Totten added, "There is no more lovable or more popular player in baseball today. To his teammates Red is the warmest, most likeable of friends. Never a hard word, always a phrase of encouragement is his characteristic. And around the circuit that same popularity holds forth on other clubs."[48] Evidence of that occurred during the

New York Yankees star Babe Ruth offers his congratulations during Red Faber Day ceremonies in Comiskey Park on August 20, 1929. Ruth once described Faber, his pitching adversary, as "the nicest man in the world." (Courtesy of the Chicago Historical Society, *Chicago Daily News* collection SDN-068994.)

ceremony. Babe Ruth, the biggest name in baseball and a Faber rival since they were both rookies in 1914, stepped forward to shake hands and pose for pictures with the White Sox star. Ruth once shared with Sam Rice his frustrations of trying to hit Faber. "Well, one day he [Ruth] turned to me and asked, 'Sam, how does that Faber pitch you in Chicago?' I said: 'He steps toward first base and breaks that spitter low and outside, and I can't lay off it. I just dribble balls to the infield.' And Babe boomed: 'Me too, Sam! Isn't it terrible?'" Three decades into retirement, Faber revealed, "I used to half-speed the Babe a lot and he'd always swing out ahead of the ball," adding, "No matter how bad he looked against a certain pitch, it was a bad mistake to throw him the same thing on the very next pitch. He'd always be ready.... And how he'd bellow if you made him look bad." [49]

Pitching on his special day, Faber held Ruth hitless — the Bambino struck out swinging in the seventh inning — but the Yankees claimed a 5–4 victory. The winning run crossed after first baseman Bud Clancy was too deliberate in making a throw after fielding an infield tap.[50] Though tagged with the loss, Faber pitched well and no doubt was in good spirits. There was a reception with the Iowa contingent immediately after game, and that evening he was honored at a banquet at the Southland Hotel.[51]

Faber Day festivities provided a respite from the unhappy lot of the 1929 White Sox, an American League doormat seething with dissension. The sources of their discontent were Blackburne, traveling secretary Lou Barbour and, indirectly, Comiskey. The players saw Blackburne as gruff and ineffective and, like Barbour, a spy for Comiskey. After yet another altercation with Blackburne, Shires claimed that everyone on the team hated that the manager and traveling secretary constantly wired Comiskey with reports about the players' performance in and out of uniform. The arrangement should not have been much of a surprise; the Old Roman had long required his management personnel to file reports and respond to his directives about managerial moves. Sportswriter Vaughan noted Shires' complaints but defended the arrangement: "Whatever report Barbour and Blackburne make to Comiskey is at the latter's orders. After each game Barbour must wire the score, batteries and attendance. Then he writes a long letter setting forth all details of the day's happenings both on and off the field. If Barbour hears some player has been drinking a bit he has to report it to save himself. Some self-elected spy will pass the information to Comiskey and Barbour then has to explain why he didn't know about it. The team is Comiskey's property and he is entitled to know what is taking place, but the players feel that they are also entitled to be resentful over the system."[52] Justified or not, the players responded poorly. After a 12–13 August, the White Sox were stuck in seventh place, 24 games under .500 and 35½ games behind the Athletics. After team unrest again flared before the public in mid–September, the *Tribune's* Burns, shared his candid observations: "One trip around the eastern circuit with the White Sox in early August this year convinced us the club is the most utterly disorganized and disgruntled group of employees we ever have encountered, in or out of baseball. We recall some of the grumblings of the Sox in 1927 and 1928. They pale into joyful gurgles as compared with complaints of this year's band of Comiskeyites."[53]

After a loss and a no-decision, Faber started on a warm afternoon in Washington. After seven innings, and holding a 4–3 lead thanks to two unearned runs, Faber revealed that he was too tired to continue. Ted Lyons held the Nationals scoreless the final two frames to preserve Faber's 12th win of the season.[54]

The afternoon of September 14, the first-place Athletics led Faber and the White Sox 2–0 when the news from New York reached Shibe Park: The Yankees lost to the Browns, giving the Athletics at least a tie for the pennant. The Philadelphia crowd went into "frenzy delight," William J. Chipman of The Associated Press reported, and the Athletics proceeded to go after Faber to win the title outright. Philadelphia piled on three runs in the bottom of the eighth to put the game out of reach.[55] Their 5–0 victory over Faber, who went the distance, punched their World Series ticket. Meanwhile, in the National League, the Cubs were a day or two from claiming their pennant.

The Cubs' berth in the World Series meant that there would be no 1929 City Series in Chicago, so the White Sox had nothing to look forward to but a merciful close to the season. However, the White Sox would not go quietly; Shires saw to that. Hours before the Athletics won the pennant by beating Faber, Shires again fought the team's manager — as well as Barbour, the traveling secretary. It was the temperamental infielder's third physical altercation with Blackburne in one season. The scene this time was the Benjamin Franklin Hotel room Shires shared with Doug Taitt. In the hallway leading to the players' room, Blackburne heard through the transom the makings of a party. He opened the door and peeked in the room. "The Great Shires was using empty bottles as Indian clubs and shouting for more liquor," one report stated. "When he caught Lena's amazed glance the Great Shires shied a bottle at his boss and invited him in." Blackburne confronted Shires — "Are you drunk again?" — and fists started flying. Hearing the commotion, Barbour entered the room and tried to rescue Blackburne, who was getting the worst of it. In the skirmish Barbour nearly lost the tip of an index finger to a bite. Shires was blamed, but the player claimed it was Blackburne, mistakenly thinking it was Shires' digit between his teeth. "Barbour's cries for help awoke most of the guests in the hotel," the *Tribune* reported, and 15 guests simultaneously phoned police. Blackburne and Barbour took refuge under a bed. When Philadelphia police arrived, however, the team officials declined to file charges. They allowed Shires to sober up under "house arrest" in another hotel. Noted the *Tribune*'s Burns, "We know there are several players who would have enjoyed blacking Mr. Blackburne's eyes were it not for the restraining power of discretion." Blackburne, nursing two shiners, composed himself and stated: "Shires is out, gone, through, busted forever. And I'm not kidding. He'll never get back into organized baseball after this." Shires responded, "I'm through with the White Sox forever, no matter what happens."[56] Both men were wrong.

The White Sox went 3–9 between the Shires altercation and announcement that Blackburne would not return in 1930. In each of their final three losses, the White Sox blew ninth-inning leads. In the third such defeat, the team rebounded after Faber managed to record just one out in the first inning in Detroit. However, after blowing a lead in the ninth inning, the White Sox blew another lead in the 11th inning and lost.[57] It might have been just coincidence, but after the announcement that Donie Bush would succeed Blackburne as manager, the White Sox, with the lame duck still at the helm, closed the season by winning three out of four. However, everyone — perhaps even including Blackburne — was glad to see the Blackburne era end. He never managed in the major leagues again — he was an Athletics coach in 1933 — but Blackburne remained involved in the game in an unusual way. He established a side business bottling and marketing the Delaware River mud that umpires use before games to remove the gloss from new baseballs.[58]

Faber, at 13–13, was the only pitcher on the 1929 White Sox (59–93) without a losing record. Ted Lyons, who would go on to break most of Faber's team records, was 14–20 and Tommy Thomas was 14–18. Could new manager Donie Bush turn things around?

25

In the Doghouse

Internal strife, accentuated by his battles with Art Shires, scuttled Lena Blackburne's regime as White Sox manager. He lasted only a season and a half, during which time the team went 99–133. Suspended again late in the 1929 season, Shires engaged in a couple of headline-grabbing boxing matches — he knocked out one opponent in 21 seconds — and toyed with the notion of playing professional football. However, after Blackburne exited, Shires received another chance from the White Sox, who quietly looked for a team willing to take "The Great Shires" in a trade.

The Comiskey administration replaced Blackburne with Owen Joseph "Donie" Bush. (A few hours after Bush accepted Chicago's offer, the Yankees made their own bid. Bush considered backing out on the White Sox, but American League president Ernest Barnard set him straight.[1]) After managing Pittsburgh to the 1927 National League pennant, Bush quit the Pirates in late August 1929 after a 5–12 road trip doomed the team's pennant hopes. Owner Barney Dreyfuss' interference in playing decisions was the final straw. Bush's playing career spanned 16 seasons, nearly all of it at shortstop for the Detroit Tigers. After being traded to Washington late in 1921, he played sparingly but served as Nationals (Senators) player-manager in 1923. Like Blackburne, Bush was known as a disciplinarian with a streak of vindictiveness.

In early February, 41-year-old Red Faber met up with teammates Bill Cissell and Bob Weiland at Comiskey Park, chatted with trainer and equipment manager William Buckner and posed for a *Chicago Daily News* photographer.[2] Fellow Cascade native James Crusinberry, an ex–*Tribune* sportswriter who had joined the *Daily News*, described Faber as "the coolest hurler ever seen" on the mound. "It's just impossible to get him fussed even in the most exciting and trying times of a ball game," he wrote. "He isn't the kind of ball player who yells and cheers and jumps around on the ball field." Crusinberry, who covered Faber's early career for the *Tribune*, recalled a tight game in which the White Sox were getting the "bad end" of some umpiring. Faber watched it all quietly from the bench. "The manager looked at Red and said: 'How the h___ can you sit there so quietly in a time like this?' Red answered: 'I may be quiet and not yelling, but I'm burning up inside.'"[3]

In addition to a new manager, the White Sox also had a new spring training site — San Antonio. Charles Comiskey's frugal franchise contracted, sight unseen, to use the new grounds at St. Mary's University for spring training. The *Tribune's* Edward Burns arrived in San Antonio a couple of days before the team and checked out what St. Mary's had to offer. "Our White Sox, who have spent the winter successfully building up morale and everything, are due, we fear, for an awful shock when they see the premises," Burns wrote. "The flat space which has been charted as the training ground is a quarter-mile from any structure whatsoever, the infield is rough and the splotches of grass make it less desirable than an old-fashioned skinned

In February 1930, shortly before starting spring training for his 17th major league season, Faber reflects in a snowy Comiskey Park. (Chicago Historical Society, *Chicago Daily News* collection SDN-066995.)

diamond. Unless the infield is corrected by some miracle not known to ball ground landscaping at present, it would be folly for Manager Bush to attempt an infield practice. The casualties in the form of broken noses from wild hopping baseballs and wrenched leg and ankle muscles would be appalling." White Sox officials, who still had not seen the field, complained that Burns' concerns were exaggerated. They said they had assurances from university officials that the field would be satisfactory.[4] (In contrast, the New York Giants, planning their second spring in San Antonio, sent their groundskeeper to the home of the local minor league team two weeks in advance to make sure their facility was ready.)

Bush arrived in San Antonio the day before the first scheduled workout and went to look over the grounds.[5] Burns was right. The facilities were impossible. Bush hastily accepted the Giants' offer to split time at their site. The cohabitation could last no more than a week, until the Giants' second team was due to arrive.[6] Team secretary Harry Grabiner, particularly stung by the snafu, donned Mexican garb and, accompanied by a translator, found an excellent field in San Antonio's "Little Mexico."[7]

Though their working conditions improved, the White Sox remained a struggling squad. Money the team saved on groundskeeping apparently was not directed to player salaries; the team had so many contract holdouts that Bush recruited three San Antonio locals to round out a second unit for an exhibition game. "Donie says they're pretty good," Burns wrote, "although he doesn't know their names. He addressed each of them at today's workout as 'Hey, you!' which is sufficient in so far as their association with the Sox is concerned."[8]

While his squad coasted through a rare light workout, Bush held court with reporters and — not surprisingly — gave an optimistic view of the upcoming season. "Old Red Faber, Donie thinks, will be ready to perform about Monday or Tuesday," Burns wrote. "With a hustling ball club back of him, Red ought to have a great year."[9] Faber gave evidence of that a couple of weeks later, when he allowed the Giants only a single and double over seven innings; rookie Pat Caraway held the New Yorkers hitless in the final two innings of an 8–1 exhibition win in Indianapolis, Bush's home town.[10] The next day, the teams removed to Fort Wayne, where a capacity crowd saw the White Sox outslug the Giants 14–8. The highlight of the contest was rookie Smead Jolley's monstrous home run, which cleared the center field wall, soared out of the ballpark and struck a lineman working on a telephone pole. "The workman whirled about his perch, but his life was saved by a safety strap," Burns reported. In the same game, a drive by Carl Reynolds struck a boy sitting atop the center field fence; despite Bush's protests, Reynolds was denied a home run when the ball bounced off the boy and onto the playing field.[11]

The White Sox opened the 1930 regular season respectably, winning seven of their first 11 games. After that, ineptitude and dissension took their toll. Losses came in bunches. Comiskey's crew appeared ticketed for the American League cellar. Faber performed erratically from game to game. On May 5 in New York, he faced a Yankee pitcher barely half his age — 21-year-old Vernon "Lefty" Gomez. Through the first six innings in New York, Faber had a shutout on three hits. "In the seventh, however, our patriarch engaged in a personally conducted flop that gave the Yanks three runs," Burns reported. That was plenty for Gomez, who held the Sox to five hits in a complete-game victory. Faber contributed to his own demise in the seventh by muffing a throw at first base, unleashing a wild pitch and allowing two hits. "The only thing that Red could salvage was the fact that he struck out Ruth three times and held Gehrig and Lazerri helpless."[12] In Faber's next start, in the nation's capital, his supporting cast let him down. The White Sox appeared lifeless in losing their seventh game in eight tries while handing 23-year-old Ad Liska his first major league complete game. Describing the team as "spiritless," Burns wrote, "Added to the startling continuance of batting inefficiency were amazing mental lapses. Cissell, one of the two or three Comiskey employees who has appeared to be awake during the last week, allowed a runner to steal home because he forgot there were two outs." Burns pointed out that it was the fourth game in which Faber pitched well but suffered the loss.[13] Faber, no doubt, had noticed that, too.

After more than a decade of pitching on losing ball clubs, the veteran pitcher was increasingly given to squawk about the shaky play of his teammates. (It is not a stretch to argue that, had Faber played on just average teams after 1921, he might have attained membership in the elite 300-victory club.) As the Sox suffered loss after frustrating loss, Faber's complaints became a growing irritation to Manager Bush and, most likely, many Chicago players. And yet, Faber had a legitimate case. In his account of the White Sox losing a late May doubleheader in Cleveland, Burns reported, "In the second inning the Sox made Faber feel quite natural by giving him the same kind of support they've been tendering him in many of the games he's pitched this year." The frame included two botched double-play opportunities and an easy grounder that escaped an infielder.[14] In his next outing, Faber pitched as well as he had in years. That made the manner in which he lost all the more frustrating. In St. Louis, he had allowed the Browns only three hits and held a 2–1 advantage entering the ninth inning. He started the inning by striking out Heinie Manush. However, Faber opened the door by issuing a walk to Red Kress, who raced to third on Fred Schulte's single. It appeared that Faber might still escape with the victory when Sox second baseman Bill Cissell fielded Oscar Melillo's grounder and threw out Kress at the plate. Just one out from victory, Faber gave up a game-tying double to light-hitting Earl McNeely, whose drive to left pushed Melillo to third. Rick Ferrell stepped into the batter's box with the chance to be a hero. As Faber wound up to deliver his second pitch to Ferrell, Melillo shocked the crowd — not to mention the veteran pitcher and rookie catcher Johnny Riddle — by racing down the third-base line. Burns summarized the result: "Luckless Red Faber this afternoon reached the heights of ill fortune when Oscar Melillo stole home with two out in the ninth to win, 3–2."[15] Bad luck or not, the losses piled up for Faber (1–7); meanwhile, the team wallowed in seventh place (15–23).

In mid–June, as the White Sox negotiated the trade that sent problem child Art Shires to Washington, Faber's record fell to 1–9. Speculation grew that 1930 would be his final year in professional baseball. Burns defended the struggling spitballer, saying he "deserves being with the nine next year and perhaps the remainder of this season as a coach."[16] Faber seemed to justify Burns' support in his next start, when he battled Lefty Grove of the defending champion Athletics but suffered a 2–1 loss. Six days later, Faber looked like a different pitcher, recording only four outs before the Red Sox sent him to the showers. After another six days of rest, the report was different: "Old Red Faber of the rapidly vanishing race of spitball hurlers is not through yet," wrote Irving Vaughan from Comiskey Park. "His aged arm came back yesterday with some of the glory that was his in his palmy days." Win No. 2 came at the expense of the also-struggling Browns, 8–1.[17] When the teams met again a week later in St. Louis, only 500 fans showed up. Faber himself didn't stay long — only three innings — but had a no-decision. In another no-decision against the Yankees four days later, Faber struggled so badly that Vaughan described his pitching as "atrocious."[18] Arch Ward, *Tribune* sports editor, weighed in on the spitballer's future: "It looks like Urban Faber is in his last year as a pitcher for the Sox."[19] However, those critiques coincided with the start of a Faber rally. After opening 2–10, he went 6–3 the rest of the season. That good news was not without controversy as Donie Bush's White Sox continued their slide.

On July 30, early in a Comiskey Park contest against the Browns, Faber's impatience with his teammates' fielding miscues collided with Bush's general frustration. In the first inning alone, the White Sox infield committed a pair of two-out errors that, sandwiched by a double and single, put the Chicagoans in a 2–0 hole. Back in the dugout, Faber fumed, stewed and squawked about the defensive lapses. Bush had heard enough. He benched Faber and sent in Ed Walsh Jr. to pitch the rest of the game. Despite continued defensive lapses, the Sox managed to send the contest into extra innings. They lost it in the 10th inning, thanks to Chicago's *seventh* error of the game. Bush kept Faber on the bench through his next scheduled start, opting to use Walsh on limited rest. "Faber should have cast yesterday but Donie Bush set him down last Tuesday because he had an attack of the grumbles," the *Chicago American* noted. "Seems that Mr. Bush is running this ball team."[20] The *Tribune* noted, "For years it has been Faber's custom to kick about errors behind him,

Donie Bush (left), the White Sox manager in 1930 and 1931, and Faber had an uneasy relationship. Bush benched Faber briefly in 1930 after hearing enough of Faber's dugout rants about teammates' defensive miscues. (Courtesy of the Tri-County Historical Society, Cascade, Iowa.)

but none of Bush's predecessors ever had the courage to accept the veteran hurler's challenge of authority." Interviewed a few days later, Faber confirmed that he complained because he was tired of losing due to teammates' errors.[21] Faber was in Bush's doghouse — but at least Bush brought him on the team's next road trip. The same could not be said for former captain Willie Kamm, who had been riding the pines for a couple of weeks due to indifferent play. Bush left Kamm behind in Chicago. The *Tribune* described the situation that prompted the decision: "A ball was batted almost directly at the third base-man [Kamm] and he not only let it escape him, but also moved so leisurely on its recovery that the batter made two bases." Bush's discipline of Kamm and Faber preceded his denials that the team was riddled with dissension. The manager claimed that the team was as close-knit as it had been in years, and offered as evidence the current upswing in its performance.[22] But it was not to last. Nonetheless, the discipline caused the Chicago papers to report with virtual certainty that when the 1931 season opened, the White Sox roster would not include those two veterans.[23] The sportswriters were wrong. Faber stayed, but by mid–May 1931, Kamm was wearing a Cleveland uniform. Kamm learned of his trade through a telephone operator and informant; no one in the White Sox management contacted him before the Chicago newspapers reported the deal.[24]

Faber, the hero of the 1917 World Series, returned to the team's good graces. After a week in Bush's doghouse, he took the mound in St. Louis, scattered 11 hits and posted a 5–2 victory. "The longer the Cascade Kid relaxes," the *Chicago American* noted after his complete-game win, "the better he seems to go."[25]

While the squad was in St. Louis, a criminal victimized White Sox secretary Harry S. Grabiner in his Chicago home. A bold robber entered the residence, confronted Grabiner, his wife and guest Mrs. Morton Hirsch, firmly but politely asked for their jewelry and money, and ran down Euclid Avenue with his loot.[26]

After Faber's victory over the Browns, the White Sox dropped doubleheaders on consecutive days in Philadelphia. At 44–67 and barely holding onto sixth place, the Chicagoans left their manager totally frustrated. "Sox Have Him Stopped, Donie Bush admits," stated a *Tribune* headline. In the story, Bush listed Faber among the few pitchers he would like to keep for the following season.[27] The day the article appeared in Chicago, Faber, in Philadelphia, broke the defending champion Athletics' winning streak with a seven-hitter.[28] After four more Sox losses, Faber posted another win when he beat New York 6–1 in Yankee Stadium. The game, the nightcap of a doubleheader, lasted only the minimum five innings, due to darkness.[29] Faber's win, his third straight, represented the only three victories for the White Sox in their previous 16 decisions.[30]

His streak ended a week later in Boston. "Under ordinary circumstances Faber's pitching effort in the first battle [of a doubleheader] would have resulted in a winning achievement," Vaughan reported after the 2–0 decision. "The trouble was that the attack behind the veteran was so meek as to provide him with no encouragement." The White Sox managed but three hits against Boston's Milt Gaston.[31] Despite those setbacks, Faber remained competitive, winning his final two starts of the regular season by holding the eventual AL champion Athletics to six hits (4–2) and then scattering a dozen Tigers hits (10–5).

Whether there would be a City Series in Chicago was an open question. There was no series in 1929, when the Cubs battled the Athletics in the World Series. The Cubs started September 1930 with a five-game lead, with the Brooklyn Robins, New York Giants and St. Louis Cardinals bunched in second through fourth. Within two weeks, St. Louis and Brooklyn shared first place, and the Cubs slipped to third. The Robins faded, but the Cubs could not catch the Cardinals. Their runner-up finish made the Cubs available, and there was Chicago's City Series after all.

The Cubs took out their pennant-race frustrations on the Sox, winning the series in six games. In a spirited series — during which patrons tossed lemons and other citrus items at opposing players — Faber lost Game 3 at Wrigley Field. Charlie Grimm, who homered in the second inning, and the Cubs drove him from the mound in the fifth inning en route to a 12–1 cakewalk.[32] The series had its frightening moments. In Game 5, with more than 45,000 patrons jammed into Wrigley, White Sox first baseman Johnny Watwood crumbled to the ground after a Pat Malone pitch struck him in the side of the head. Carried into the dugout by teammates, Watwood soon regained consciousness and, incredibly, was allowed to go directly to his residence in the Southmoor Hotel on the South Side. After a doctor examined him there, Watwood reported to a hospital, where an X-ray revealed a skull fracture. His season was over. His teammates' season ended the next afternoon, when the Cubs erased a 4–3 deficit with three runs in the top of the ninth and held on for the series clincher 6–4.

Formerly the American League's top pitcher, Faber in 1930 topped the league in another category — *worst* batting average. He scratched out two singles in 49 at-bats for a paltry .041 average. However, despite his dust-up with Bush, Faber's 6–3 record in his final nine decisions raised him to 8–13 and assured him a spot on the 1931 White Sox roster.

26

"Faber Luck"

The year 1931 brought change on and off the baseball field. The Great Depression worsened. Thousands of unemployed Americans marched on the White House, demanding a national jobs program and a minimum wage; the Hoover administration turned the marchers away. Further evidence that the Roaring Twenties were over: Chicago mobster Al Capone, who occasionally took in major league games, was convicted of federal income tax evasion, sentenced to 11 years behind bars — including time at Alcatraz — and fined $50,000.

Organized baseball felt the Depression. Major league attendance topped 10 million in 1930, but attendance fell 16 percent in 1931.[1] And it would get worse. Out-of-work Americans were in no position to buy tickets. Few of those lucky enough to hold jobs were in a position to take a weekday afternoon off to attend a game. Team owners cut many salaries, and one — Charles Comiskey of the White Sox — advocated reducing the major league rosters from 25 players to 20. Comiskey explained that it was unfair for each team to keep a handful of young athletes on the bench, since their prospects for playing time were limited.[2] That arrangement did not seem to bother the Chicago owner during the Roaring Twenties. To make games more accessible to fans and their scarce dollars, many teams — but not yet the major leagues — installed lights for night games. (The first professional baseball game under the lights was played in May 2, 1930, in Des Moines. The first night game in the majors was in Cincinnati on May 24, 1935.)

Another change involved the baseball itself: Its seams were raised slightly, and the cover of the National League ball was made slightly thicker. The idea was to help the pitchers. "The raised seam, a coarse thread and longer stitches of the new ball will afford the pitchers a better grip, enabling them to increase the spin of the ball and give it a better curve or break," stated Ernest S. Barnard, American League president. "The raised seams also will increase

197

wind and air resistance, thus making it seem reasonable that the new ball will not travel far when hit." Faber was an advocate: "They've been making it too tough for pitchers. This new ball will give us a break."[3] Following a trend, Comiskey's players started wearing numbers on their uniforms. Faber was issued Number 18.[4] However, it would require more than a new baseball and numbers on jerseys to change the White Sox's fortunes for 1931.

One significant event of the White Sox training camp of 1931 was the arrival in San Antonio of Comiskey himself. The owner, 71 years old and in failing health, last attended spring training in 1918, when the Sox worked out in Mineral Wells, Texas.[5] Starting after the wrenching experience of the Black Sox scandal, Comiskey rarely came to the ballpark and had decreasing involvement in his club's operations.[6] This visit was his last; Comiskey died the following October at age 72.

Bush, unpopular among players in his first season as Sox manager, was also back in camp. Players' grumbling started almost immediately. One late February afternoon, it was too rainy to play baseball — but not too wet to run laps on at their workout facility's cinder track. Or so Bush said. "The order wasn't acceptable to most of the fellows because of a fear that wet feet might do them more harm than the prescribed exercise could do them good," The *Tribune*'s Irving Vaughan reported. Bush ordered his pitchers to run one whole mile a day. "Red Faber doesn't favor it in the least. He has been using his legs for so long that he goes in for conversation in a big way."[7] Was Faber bucking for a return visit to Bush's doghouse? It appeared so. Bush left Faber behind instead of taking him on an exhibition trip to Houston and then postponed his starting assignment. Bush blamed it on the weather. "Red Faber is waiting for the warmer weather, and has not been held out of the White Sox exhibition games because of any tiff with the club," *The Sporting News* reported, citing the manager. In the final week of the exhibition season, the White Sox and New York Giants barnstormed their way north. In Charlotte, N.C., the Chicagoans grabbed a one-run lead in the top of the 11th, but Faber, working his fourth inning of relief, could not hold the advantage and suffered the loss.[8] The performance probably solidified Bush's plan to use the aged spitballer only as a reliever and spot-starter.

Assessing the White Sox's pitching prospects, Vaughan observed, "If both [Ted] Lyons and [Tommy] Thomas should be kept out for any length of time, the authorities might have to drag the river for Bush. It will be bad enough if only one of them can't function properly."[9] Lyons, who won 22 games the previous season, injured his shoulder three weeks before Opening Day. Faber did receive a start in Game 3 of the regular season, but he did not last beyond the third inning in a 7–0 shellacking at Cleveland. As a reliever, he lost to the Athletics on May 13 when he gave up two runs in the top of the 11th inning; the final run came when Jimmy Dykes swiped home on a double-steal. After that, it was nearly a month until Faber received his second starting assignment. That opportunity was forgettable: he lasted but five innings, and his teammates sealed his fate (and that of reliever Hal McKain) by committing eight errors in the 12–8 loss to Boston. It was the White Sox's seventh straight loss.[10] Eleven days later, Faber started again — and lost again after serving up a two-run homer to Detroit pitcher George Uhle.[11] He was even less impressive in his fourth start, failing to complete the second inning at Philadelphia but escaping with a no-decision.[12] That performance solidified Faber's status as a reliever only — at least for the next six weeks. However, Lyons continued to struggle, and Bush, concluding that the right-hander had a "dead arm," sent Lyons back to Chicago. In a public rebuke of Bush by the front office, Sox executive Harry Grabiner ordered Lyons to rejoin the team. "The implication, of course, is that Manager Bush, 23 years in the major leagues, does not know a dead arm pitcher when he sees one," quipped the *Tribune's* Edward Burns.[13] (Despite being countermanded, Bush did not start Lyons for six weeks. The future Hall-of-Famer completed the season 4–6 and pitched only 101 innings.)

By this time, Bush's frustration with Comiskey, who refused to acquire talent to replenish the depleted pitching corps, was an open secret. Speculation grew that Bush would depart when his two-year contract expired at season's end. Bush considered his pitching options so limited that three times in a week he refused to pull starter Pat Caraway even after he obviously lost his control. The shellacking he suffered in Boston July 23 was an especially painful scene. With American League president Will Harridge looking on, Bush did nothing while the Red Sox knocked Caraway's offerings at will. Burns of the *Tribune*, suggesting that Caraway had been dogging it after a good start to the season, said, "Manager Bush had his own theories about Caraway's reversals and elected today to let him take it." The manager ignored the 25-year-old Caraway's repeated signals that he wanted to be removed and, between the first and second innings he "could be seen shouting at Caraway with great gusto and many gestures." In the fifth inning, Bush finally excused Caraway, who was tagged for 11 runs. (The only highlight for the Chicagoans that day was their execution of a triple play when third baseman Billy Sullivan snared a line drive, stepped on third for the second out and threw to first to complete the gem.)[14] A couple of days later, Bush explained that he was not insensitive to Caraway's plight — just that he could not spare a rested pitcher with six games scheduled over the next four days. The national economy might have been a factor: in addition to not adding pitchers, the White Sox had dropped their scouting program.[15]

The team's pitching difficulties allowed Faber to return to the starting rotation. Starting every three or four days from mid–July through August, Faber showed some promise. His 1931 highlight came August 7, when he shut

Bill Cissell (left) and Red Faber flank Boston Red Sox manager Shano Collins in 1931 or 1932. Collins joined the White Sox in 1910, and he and Faber were teammates from 1914 through 1920. (Courtesy of the Tri-County Historical Society, Cascade, Iowa.)

out the St. Louis Browns 2–0 and helped his cause by rapping a double (only his second hit of the entire season) and scoring a run. Faber allowed the visitors only five singles all afternoon. "Old Red Faber yesterday showed the home folks what all the chroniclers were gurgling about during that last eastern trip," Burns wrote. "Only Red was even better than he was during his eastern brilliance...."[16]

Faber continued to earn respect from some of the game's top players. "He was a pitching star in the league back in 1921 when I broke in as a rookie, and he was as good last week as the first time I faced him," future Hall-of-Famer Leon "Goose" Goslin told an interviewer. "The old boy tied me into a knot swinging at this stuff. He'd slide a slow curve around my knees. He'd give me a fast one on the outside and then side-arm me with his spitter. A batter can't guess with Faber. His only chance is to close the eyes and hope the bat meets the ball."[17]

Faber pitched well but then suffered back-to-back shutout defeats. The second of those, on August 15 in Chicago, was particularly frustrating: The Red Sox scored the game's only run due to sloppy fielding. The White Sox offense was of no support to their veteran: to that point they had gone 23 innings without plating a single run for Faber. The *Tribune* described the spitballer's misfortune with the heading "Faber Luck" over the box score and, over a photograph, "When Faber Pitched Victory Ball — And Lost."[18] The offense's abandonment of Faber finally ended after 32 consecutive innings.[19]

On September 9, the White Sox and Cubs gave up an open date to stage a Depression-era charity game. The beneficiary was Illinois governor Louis Lincoln Emmerson's unemployment fund. The Sox hustled back to Chicago from Cleveland and, immediately after the exhibition, departed to New York to continue their American League season. Nearly 35,000 fans paid their way into Comiskey Park, raising just under $45,000 for the cause. Among the spectators was Chicago's No. 1 gangster, Al Capone. Under indictment on federal income tax charges, Capone sat in a box seat among the White Sox faithful. Years later, Faber told his family that he and other ballplayers would be Capone's guests for dinner, where the menu featured big steaks with plenty of bourbon and Scotch. "He [Capone] would take a lot of the baseball players out to the fights," said Faber's son, who recalled the stories. "My father said he was a nice guy. Unless you were in a gang that was against him, he was a pretty nice guy."[20] It is likely that this 1931 exhibition game was the last occasion Faber and the mobster might have exchanged greetings: five weeks later, a judge found Capone guilty and sentenced him to 11 years in prison.

Though Faber's best games were behind him, he remained popular with fans. The *Tribune* noted that Faber, who started, "received the biggest hand during the early stages of the game." However, the applause had nothing to do with Faber's base running abilities. In the third inning, he drew a walk off

Charley Root. One out later, Billy Sullivan ticketed a Root pitch for an apparent triple. However, the slow-footed Faber, who had turned 43 earlier that week, could only hobble from first to third, forcing Sullivan to pull up at second. Root recovered to strand the baserunners. Faber left after the sixth inning trailing 1–0; outfielder's Johnny Watwood's muff of a fly ball contributed to the deficit. Faber "had completed control of the situation so long as he had the American League ball, but he didn't like the National League product," the *Tribune* noted. "One ball seemed about as good as the other to Root," who pitched a complete game and drove in all three of the game's runs.[21]

After the exhibition, the White Sox returned to the road and staged a brief undefeated streak — three wins and two ties. From there, the Chicagoans lost 14 of their final 15 games to assume their place in the American League basement and virtually ensure Bush's exit. Before that parting, however, Bush and the White Sox had to take on the third-place Cubs in the City Series.

In a rematch of their exhibition earlier in the month, Faber faced Root at Wrigley Field. This time, Faber allowed the North Siders just five hits while the Sox exploded for seven runs in the seventh en route to a 9–0 victory. "The Cubs didn't try to alibi their failure to hit Red Faber in the opening game," the *Tribune* reported. "Most of them volunteered the information ... that the veteran had shown them about as deadly a spitball as they ever hope to see."[22] Bush described it as "one of the best games I ever saw."[23] Faber and Root tangled again in Game 5, before 41,523 fans at Comiskey, and again the White Sox delivered another offensive barrage — five runs in the fifth inning, three in the seventh and four in the eighth — en route to a 13–6 win and a 3–2 series lead. In Game 6, the Cubs staved off defeat with a ninth-inning, come-from-behind victory 3–2. Despite finishing dead last in the American League, the White Sox played like champions in Game 7, again using the Big Inning (a six-run fourth) and stellar pitching (a four-hitter from Tommy Thomas) to grab a 7–2 win and the city title. The victory energized Bush temporarily, but his resignation was announced three days later. "I feel there is no future for me with the White Sox," Bush said. "I don't mind losing ball games if there is a prospect of better days ahead, but I feel that whatever reputation I possess as a manager would be jeopardized by remaining another year."[24] Bush received another chance to manage in the major leagues in 1933, when he guided the Cincinnati Reds to a last-place finish.

Despite his age, his early-season struggles and spotty offensive support from a last-place team, Faber posted a 10–14 regular season record and secured two decisive victories in the City Series. His prospects for 1932 appeared solid. But would his next manager agree?

27

Two Wins

No one was surprised that, by the end of the 1931 season, the last-place White Sox and manager Donie Bush had had enough of each other. The next man to accept the challenge of leadership was a man already on the White Sox roster, 32-year-old Lewis Albert Fonseca. The 1929 American League batting champion came to Chicago from Cleveland in the Willie Kamm trade the previous May. Granted a two-year contract, Fonseca said he planned to be a player-manager and a dealmaker. Fonseca lamented the sensitivity of contemporary players. "Ball players today aren't the rough and ready type of old," he told the *Tribune*. "You must handle them to suit their natures. You can call some of them in public and they don't object. Some you must call in private. Others can't take a panning of any kind. Those are the ones you must slap on the back when they're down." Chicago was not his first opportunity to lead a ball club. When he was barely 20, Fonseca took over an outlaw league team in Smithfield, Utah. After losing his first three games, the investors informed Fonseca that a fourth straight loss would cost him his job. Smithfield won the next game — and the next 15.[1] Fonseca, occasionally called "Fractures" because of his numerous baseball injuries, possessed an operatic voice and for several years spent the off-season performing in West Coast music halls.[2] Fonseca became Faber's ninth manager — not including the short-lived stints of Frank Chance (no regular-season games) and Ed Walsh (three games).

When Fonseca signed on as manager, executive secretary Harry Grabiner was on hand to congratulate him. Team owner Charles A. Comiskey, suffering heart and kidney problems, was confined to his woodland home in Eagle River, Wisconsin. Less than two weeks later, on October 26, 1931, "The Old Roman," a founding owner of the American League, died at age 72. His wake was held in his South Side Chicago home, where "large throngs, representing every branch of life" came to pay their respects. President Herbert Hoover wired his condolences. The Comiskey family honored eight men with their selection as pallbearers. Only one was a ballplayer: Urban "Red" Faber.[3]

Comiskey, a widower and multi-millionaire, died without a will. The team owned the ballpark and other real estate worth about $2 million. The organization was debt-free and had "several hundred thousand dollars" in the bank, according to attorney A. S. Austrian. The team and personal estate went to his only son, 47-year-old J. Louis Comiskey, who was promptly elected team president and treasurer. Dispelling rumors that he might sell the franchise, Lou Comiskey vowed to rebuild it to championship form.[4] It was a promise broken. In Lou Comiskey's seven seasons as president — he died in July 1939 — the team showed occasional improvement but never finished higher than third in the American League.

In January 1932, Faber visited Dubuque and attended a basketball game at Columbia College. (He graduated from the institution's prep academy and pitched for the college varsity in 1909, when it was named St. Joseph's College.) The occasion gave local sportswriters the chance to reminisce about the early days of the player's storied career and to speculate on his future. "Faber, during his recent visit to Dubuque, seemed to be in the pink of condition," the *Telegraph-Herald* reported. "He says that he is feeling fine, and will undoubtedly be thrilling South Side fans for many a summer."[5]

The off-season also allowed Faber more time at home. That was not necessarily a pleasant prospect. His wife, Irene, was for years, as sportswriters of the day diplomatically phrased it, "in delicate health."[6] Faber relatives attributed it to chemical dependency — alcohol and painkillers. In any case, the situation strained the financial resources of a man who, even in his glory days, never earned more than $10,000 a year. *Baseball Magazine*'s F.C. Lane, in a profile on the veteran spitballer, noted, "There's never a month that the doctor's bill doesn't come through the mails just as regularly as the bill for the rent." Lane added, "But no one who has seen Faber upon the hurling mound, noted his coolness, perfect poise and mastery of the game would imagine that he had led other than a placid and untroubled career."[7] Decades later, a Faber niece was more blunt, stating that Urban was unhappy but he stayed married and "made the best of it."[8]

Meanwhile, Fonseca tried to make the best of strengthening the American League's worst team. After baseball's winter meetings, he lamented his inability to consummate a major trade. The rookie manager offered a conspiracy theory. "Trouble with the American League clubs, though, is that they refuse to make deals that would help the lower clubs. That's one reason why the races in the American have been so lopsided."[9] Another hindrance to deals was that the White Sox had little to offer in a trade. Even Luke Appling, a future Hall-of-Famer, was labeled a "bust" during the 1931 campaign.[10] Unlike his immediate predecessors, who made optimistic pre-season predictions for the White Sox, Fonseca departed for spring training without such a forecast. He only said, "We'll wait and see what happens when the season opens."[11]

Fonseca's conservative stance on his team's chances in 1932 was justified. The White Sox worked out for a few days in Mineral Wells, Texas, before moving on to San Antonio. Several players, including pitcher Hal McKain and catcher Frank Grube, showed up overweight. An infected toe sidelined Ted Lyons. Carey Selph had to be persuaded to leave behind his insurance business in Houston to report for camp. On the bright side, *The Sporting News* noted, old-timers Sam Jones (age 39) and Faber (43) were "bearing down like a couple of youths."[12] Fonseca's camp operated at a leisurely pace. "There has been some attempt to laugh off the Sox's miserable showing of last season with tales of this and that athlete having been overworked," wrote the *Tribune*'s Edward Burns, a sportswriter familiar with the flow of a training camp. "Where there are instances of overworking, the condition scarcely seems to warrant babying this year's artists indefinitely." He continued, "Understand, the players themselves are making no claims of invalidism. All this bathhouse splashing and tummy slapping has been accepted with thanks by the athletes, but few of them have insisted that they care to be coddled indefinitely."[13] A writer in *The Sporting News* dubbed it Fonseca's "arrested development" training camp.[14] Fonseca's optimism grew. He ventured a prediction of a first-division finish, and pointed to his pitchers as key.[15] He wasn't alone. Famed baseball writer Frederick G. Lieb said 1931's doormats could be the American League's most-improved team: "Lew Fonseca should have the best pitching shown by any White Sox team in years."[16]

The optimism about the pitching staff included Faber, about whom the conventional wisdom had changed. "Last year Faber's stuff was adjudged hotter than it had been for nine years," Burns wrote. "Red's improvement last year was said to have resulted from the fact that it was necessary for him to work oftener than had been his wont for several years. For many seasons the veteran had been pampered with rests much longer than he needed."[17]

Fonseca assigned Faber to again be a reliever and spot-starter. On a 40-degree Sunday afternoon in Detroit, the White Sox were poised to end a six-game losing streak. Chicago led 9–2 after seven innings and 9–6 after eight. The Tigers threatened again in the bottom of the ninth, loading the bases against reliever Ted Lyons. With nobody out, Fonseca summoned Faber. He induced Bill Lawrence to hit a shallow fly ball to Hal Anderson, who inexplicably held the ball and seemed surprised when Billy Rogell decided to dash home; that made it 9–7. Faber next fielded Roy Johnson's grounder and appeared to throw him out by a couple of steps. "However, umpire [Roy] Van Graflan apparently was surprised at Red's fielding agility and called Johnson safe, filling the bases," Burns wrote. "This caused loud yelps from the panicky Sox, but to no avail, of course." Harry Davis promptly tied the game

Faber poses with teammate Moe Berg and young Chuck Comiskey, probably after Berg suffered a knee injury in 1930. A scholar, linguist and U.S. spy, Berg was a career .243 hitter over 17 seasons. "He can speak seven languages," a teammate once said, "but he can't hit in any of them." Comiskey, grandson of The Old Roman, briefly held executive positions in the organization. (Courtesy of the Tri-County Historical Society, Cascade, Iowa.)

with a two-run single. The second out came on a liner to left, but Faber re-loaded by the bases when his pitch hit Charlie Gehringer. Billy Rhiel concluded the Tigers' fantastic comeback — eight runs in 1⅔ innings — with a game-winning single.[18] After losing in relief, Faber then lost his first start of 1932, departing in Cleveland after seven innings, trailing 6–5.[19]

Back in Chicago, thousands of White Sox fans listened to the bad news on the radio. In the eyes — and ears — of some people, the broadcasts were a poor substitute for being in the ballpark. "Even with the announcer trying to make popup flies, foul balls, and grounders with handles on them into something to get excited about, it was boring," fan John Ward told the *Tribune* in a letter. "But not quite as boring as watching a game and having women shriek when an outfielder catches a fly ball that the rankest amateur would catch barehanded."[20]

That annoyance was nothing compared to how fans felt about their team's performance. In a 13-game stretch from mid–April to early May, the Sox lost a dozen contests — several of the defeats coming after Faber and other pitchers failed to hold late leads. The worst collapse during that streak occurred May 2, when Sam Jones had Detroit down 3–0 with one out in the ninth but lost 5–3. By then, the White Sox had fallen to seventh place — where, aside from three or four straight days in June, they spent the entire season. Though he tried to remain positive, Fonseca admitted some irritation with players who groused about not being traded to contending teams. He felt inclined to invite them to try to make their own deals. "I believe two or three of our boys would settle down and be a little happier where they are if they knew how little they are wanted by other teams in the American League."[21] It is unlikely that Faber was among those hoping for a trade. Though he still competed at the major league level, he would be 44 by the end of this, his 19th season with the White Sox. He marked his 250th career victory on May 6 in Washington, where he relieved Pat Caraway and pitched shutout ball the final 3⅓ innings of a 5–3 contest.[22] Still, Faber's best work was a decade in the past.

A particular lowlight in their dismal season occurred on Memorial Day, when the White Sox dropped both ends of a doubleheader in Cleveland. The Indians rallied from an 11–5 deficit after seven innings to win it in the ninth 12–11. As if that weren't enough, umpire George Moriarty followed the Sox into the players tunnel and challenged them. Fonseca, coach Johnny Butler and several White Sox players accommodated Moriarty in a brawl. Pitcher Milt Gaston, who landed the blows, was suspended for 10 days and fined $500. Also fined were manager Fonseca and players Charlie Berry and Frank Grube. For his part, Moriarty — who was hospitalized with spike wounds, bruises and a broken hand — received a "severe reprimand" from the league president. "Moriarty was looking for a fight and it seems that he got it," Fonseca said. "Everyone in baseball knows many stories of Moriarty's brawling tendencies and his eagerness to start a fight at the slightest provocation.[23]

Friday, June 17, was an open date on the American League schedule, and many teams used it to play exhibitions against minor leaguers. The White Sox visited the Waterloo (Iowa) Hawks, an entry in the low-minor Mississippi Valley League. Faber sidetracked from the rest of the team to visit his native Cascade. Relatives then drove him to Waterloo, some 75 miles northwest, for the exhibition. Coach Butler, running the team in Fonseca's absence, used Faber just two innings — long enough to give the 2,300 fans jamming the ballpark a taste of big-league pitching. His reliever was a prospect named Nelson Potter, fresh out Mount Morris (Illinois) College. The 43-year-old

Faber and the 20-year-old Potter gave up just one single each in the 8–0 cake-walk.[24] After the game, Faber returned to the major leagues. Potter did not get there until 1938 — not counting his one inning pitched in 1936. Potter stayed in the majors through 1949.

Faber started only five games in 1932 — and lost all five. His record in relief was not much better — 2–6, with six saves. He pitched only 106 innings all year, allowing 123 hits. Still, his 3.74 earned-run average represented a slight improvement over his 1931 figure (3.82) and was more than a point below the team's total ERA (4.86). Further, several of his losses had less to do with his performance than that of his teammates. On July 12, for example, he was charged with the loss in a 13–12 contest in Washington, where the White Sox committed eight errors — three alone by Luke Appling, who continued to struggle when placed at shortstop.[25]

One of his two victories of 1932 came in the nation's capital May 6. A crowd of nearly 12,000 at Griffith Stadium — more than half of them Ladies Day guests — saw the White Sox take the field in new road uniforms. They eschewed their dark blue jerseys and pants for a "knobby gray and blue combination." Faber wore Number 19 after wearing 18 the previous season, when the team introduced uniform numbers.[26] (Three months later, the team's traditional white stockings acquired a single, horizontal red stripe.[27]) Spectators and players alike roared in laughter when Sox starter Pat Caraway delivered a pitch to batter Carl Reynolds to open the bottom of the second inning — only to realize that umpire Bill Dineen was absent. The arbiter was chatting with player Joe Judge near the Nationals' bench. The game remained tied 3–3 after 5½ innings — thanks to outstanding defense by Washington left fielder Heinie Manush (who three decades later entered the Hall of Fame with Faber). Then the Nationals threatened. With two out and a man on first, Caraway issued his second walk of the sixth inning and then delivered consecutive balls to Reynolds. Fonseca emerged from the White Sox dugout and, after a long discussion with Caraway and catcher Berry, summoned Faber to continue Reynolds' at-bat. Faber retired Reynolds on a fly ball, but it was not smooth sailing for the spitballer. The next two Nationals reached on questionable infield hits. The first came when Faber failed to reach first base in time to accept a throw. Then, a sacrifice bunt attempt skidded past the pitcher. Faber stiffened, and the Nationals did not score. Batting in the top of the ninth with a 4–3 lead, Faber botched a "safety" squeeze bunt and popped out to the pitcher. His teammate on third, rookie Elias "Liz" Funk, promptly covered for Faber's blunder by scoring on the front end of double-steal. Faber shut out Washington in the seventh, eighth and ninth innings to receive credit for the 5–3 victory.[28] It was the 250th win of his career.

Faber's other victory of 1932 came July 15 in Boston. The White Sox tied the Red Sox on Jack Hayes' blast over Fenway Park's "Green Monster" in the eighth inning. Chicago might have won it in the ninth if not for Faber's lack of running speed. The pitcher drew a two-out walk and advanced to second on Funk's bunt single. Hayes then stroked a single into left field — usually enough to score a teammate from second (especially with two out). However, Faber was not a usual baserunner; by the time he plodded to third, his coach gave him the stop sign. Unfortunately, Funk, forgetting Faber's footspeed deficiencies, passed second base and charged toward third. By the time he spied Faber — panting, his foot affixed to third base — it was too late for him to retreat safely. (In the inning, the White Sox recorded four hits but failed to score; Luke Appling also was caught stealing.) Faber was not too winded to pitch scoreless ninth and 10th innings to complete four innings of one-hit, shutout relief. In the 11th inning, Appling reached third, thanks to back-to-back errors, with nobody out. After Frank Grube struck out, Faber gave way to a pinch hitter, who also whiffed against Boston starter Larry Boerner. As he had in the ninth inning, Funk again reached on a two-out bunt; this time, Appling scored the go-ahead run. Hayes provided the insurance run with a triple that plated Funk. In the bottom of the 11th, Ted Lyons preserved Faber's victory by not allowing the ball to leave the infield.

Those were Faber's only victories of the year, and wins by the White Sox remained elusive. The team won only 49 times while losing 102, good (bad?) enough for seventh place in the American League. The previous season, they won seven more games while finishing last. The team was so bad that it celebrated rainouts. The White Sox, still in the lobby of their New York hotel, celebrated when Mother Nature wiped out their Friday the Thirteenth contest at Yankee Stadium. Burns of the *Tribune* watched Fonseca and Bill Cunningham lead the cheers:

> "Rickey rax! Rickey rex! Rain! Rain! Rain!
> "Rickey razz! Rickey rooze! When it sprinkles, we can't lose!"

Burns said the players then conducted a snake dance "with all the lads walking on their heels, a maneuver symbolic of their estate, and most impressive, too."[29]

While Faber completed his 19th season with the White Sox, one of his former teammates made a short-lived comeback bid. Playing for the Greenville (South Carolina) Spinners against the Columbia State Hospital team, he went 0-for-3 with a walk and left the game after the sixth inning. His name was Joe Jackson. Asked about his possible return to Organized Baseball, he responded, "If they want me, they can send for me. I'll never humble myself by asking to be reinstated." Banned for life in the Black Sox scandal, "Shoeless" Joe Jackson was 45 years old.[30]

Discussing the decade-long slump of the Sox became common among fans. *Chicago Tribune* sports editor Arch Ward opened one column, "Surprising as it may seem, the readers still are aware that Chicago has two teams in the major leagues. Among other things, they want to know why the White Sox cannot improve their system so that they can at least lift themselves from the second division." Ward continued, "To begin with, it is presumptuous, in view of results, to believe that the Sox have a system." He pointed out that the Sox scrimp on scouting and fail to replace aging veterans. (Faber, just days from his 44th birthday, was not mentioned by name.) "There is no evidence to support charges that the Sox refuse to play real money for players," Ward stated. "They have had no holdouts in recent years. That is pretty good testimony of the relations between the business office and the players." (It might have also been testimony to the impact of the Great Depression, where even many professional athletes felt fortunate to have jobs.[31]

Nonetheless, with the team mired in seventh place, Vice President Harry Grabiner — no doubt, he had new owner Lou Comiskey's blessing — detailed a five-step plan to remake the White Sox as contenders:

1. Make deals for one or two current American League stars.
2. Purchase a team in the high minors and place their "own man" in charge.
3. Hire two experienced scouts.
4. Sign one or two leading minor-league players and call up four or five others from the minors.
5. Spend money. "There will be no strings on the bank roll if any club in the league is willing to part with good players for cash instead of talent."

Unlike their previous dismal campaigns, the White Sox were denied a chance at redemption in the post-season City Series against the Cubs. It probably was just as well: the North Siders were National League champions. (Instead of contesting the City Series, the Cubs played the Yankees in the World Series. The historic series featured Babe Ruth's "called shot" and a New York sweep.) After the final home game of the regular season, in which Faber gave up six hits in six innings, White Sox officials excused eight players from the team's final road trip. Faber was among those sent home early.[32]

28

"A Stout-Hearted Old Warrior"

In early February 1933, Red Faber, signed his 20th contract with the Chicago White Sox. A major leaguer since in 1914, he was not the most experienced player in the majors — Jack Quinn (1909) and Rabbit Maranville (1912) had more seasons of service — but Faber was first among active players in years with the same club.[1] By the end of the season — he turned 45 in September — he was the oldest active player in the majors. Faber's contract for 1933 promised a salary of $7,500, a reduction from the $10,000 he earned in his prime.[2]

White Sox executives acted on at least one of their promises toward making the team a contender. During the 1932 World Series, as the Yankees swept the Cubs, the Sox grabbed some of the Chicago headlines with a blockbuster transaction. They paid the Philadelphia Athletics $150,000 for three stars — Al Simmons, Jimmie Dykes and George "Mule" Haas.[3] Within two seasons, Dykes would become player-manager of the White Sox and their winningest manager ever. The biggest catch was the outfielder Simmons. A former American League Most Valuable Player (1929) and batting champion (1930 and 1931), the Milwaukee native was midway through his Hall-of-Fame career. The acquisition must have been good news for Faber, who often described Simmons as the hitter he found most difficult to retire; the spitballer would no longer have Simmons as an opponent. However, Simmons' tenure with the White Sox got off to a slow start. Over the winter, he complained of numbness in his right thumb and traveled to Hot Springs, Arkansas, where he experimented with hot-bath treatments. Finally, X-rays taken during a team-ordered physical exam revealed his problem — five infected teeth. After the extraction and recovery, Simmons reported two weeks late to the White Sox's new training site, Pasadena, California.

Faber joined the team's official spring-training traveling party aboard the *Los Angeles Limited*. Dozens of loyal fans showed up at Chicago's Northwestern station the night of February 23, 1933, to see them off. A *Chicago Tribune* photograph shows a smiling Faber and others waving farewell from the train's rear platform. "The delegation was not large, only seven working members of the cast being on the list," the *Tribune* observed, "but in the two special cars there was an air of gaiety and enthusiasm which had been sadly lacking at the getaways of recent years."[4]

With so many new faces present, Fonseca and his staff made sure the players got acquainted at their headquarters, the Maryland Hotel, before heading to Brookside Park for the one-a-day workouts.[5] The team covered expenses, but the players endured their pre-season toil, including the exhibition contests, without compensation. Training camp was a time to get in condition for the regular season (and regular paychecks). In a light-hearted preview of Pasadena, Edward Burns of the *Tribune* detailed the players' ordeal trying to get into shape. "The fat men aren't the only ones who suffer," Burns said. "Some of the hardest cries we have heard in recent years have been the result of watching Red Faber struggle to the dining room after a brisk workout."[6]

In previewing the 1933 White Sox, prognosticators pointed to pitching as the team's greatest liability. Their top returnees were 32-year-old Ted Lyons and 40-year-old Sam Jones, both of whom were 10–15 in 1932. Though second among the regular performers in earned run average the previous season, Faber did not figure prominently in Fonseca's plans. Might he be released during camp? Sportswriter Irving Vaughan dismissed that notion, but said, "his starting days are about over. He may be handy to drop in here and there whenever a team gets too rough with one of the other workers."[7] For the 1933 season, Faber wore uniform Number 18, the number he wore in 1931. In 1932, he wore Number 19.[8]

Chicago was the scene of two major events in 1933 — a world's fair and the inaugural major league all-star game. The fair, pegged to Chicago's centennial, was called "A Century of Progress." It opened Saturday, May 27, with nearly 150,000 visitors.[9] Soldier Field was packed for the spectacular opening night ceremony in which the lights were turned on with energy from the rays of the star Arcturus. The rays, captured by photoelectric cells in a network of astronomical observatories, was transformed into electrical energy and transmitted to Chicago.[10] The exposition grounds, near the Lake Michigan shoreline, came within 1½ miles of Comiskey Park. However, Faber was not present for the opening: the White Sox found themselves in New York, where they were dropping three out of four to the Yankees. The one victory of the series came the afternoon before the Chicago fair opened, when Faber, fighting a two-out, ninth-inning Yankees rally, induced Babe Ruth to swing at a 3–0 pitch. The Bambino grounded weakly to player-manager Fonseca at first base to end the game and give Chicago an 8–6 win.[11]

Arch Ward, sports editor of the *Tribune*, initiated the major league all-star baseball game. (Like Faber, Ward formerly lived in Dubuque, Iowa.) Ward saw the game as a way to promote the Century of Progress and to boost baseball, which was suffering in the Great Depression. Proceeds went to the fledgling Association of Professional Baseball Players of America, which tried to help aged and disabled players and umpires.[12] Ward organized his counterparts at some 55 newspapers around the country to publish ballots upon which readers indicated their all-star favorites. John McGraw, summoned from retirement to manage the National Leaguers, and Connie Mack of the American League's Athletics picked the balance of their rosters. With his best seasons long behind him, Faber barely registered on fan ballots. Thus, July 6, 1933 — the day of the first All-Star Game, merely provided Faber a day off during the White Sox's eastern road trip. Meanwhile, with 49,200 fans filling Comiskey Park, the American League All-Stars, backed by Ruth's two-run homer, defeated the National Leaguers 4–2.

On Independence Day 1933, a former White Sox manager made headlines. James J. "Nixey" Callahan was observed using a cane to smash windows of his Kenwood Avenue home. Callahan kept police at bay for more than an hour, warning them that he had them "covered." Finally, police lobbed two tear gas canisters into the house and subdued Callahan, whose only weapon was the cane. According to the *Chicago Tribune*, the 59-year-old explained to authorities and his physician that his family was away and he had been "drinking too much."[13] (Callahan, who in 1902 became the first pitcher to throw a no-hitter in the American League, died 15 months later.)

Meanwhile, the corps of "grandfathered" spitballers dwindled. In mid–July, the Cincinnati Reds released Jack Quinn; his last major league appearance was July 7, 1933 — two days after his 50th birthday. Late that month, the Cubs released Burleigh Grimes, briefly leaving Faber as the only legal spitballer remaining in the major leagues; Faber's status was short-lived: "Old Stubblebeard" Grimes signed with the Cardinals the next day.

Faber's best effort of the regular season produced neither a win nor a loss. Summoned to relieve in the 12th inning of a tie game August 21 in Chicago, Faber held the world champion Yankees scoreless for seven innings. The teams matched runs in the ninth and 11th innings. After 18 innings and more than four hours and 11 minutes of play, umpire Harry Geisel announced it was too dark to continue and declared the battle a 3–3 draw.[14] *Tribune* sportswriter Ed Burns termed it "one of most remarkable games in the history of major league ball."[15] Other sportswriters noted that in his previous 13⅔ innings of shutout work — battling no less than the first-place Nationals and second-place Yankees — Faber allowed the 45 batters he faced just four singles.[16]

Throughout his career, Faber often lost games he "should" have won if not for teammates' defensive lapses or lack of offensive support. However, the record also shows that in the nightcap of a doubleheader August 27, 1933, the spitballer received credit for a victory although he did not pitch winning baseball. Rushed in to relieve a fading Whit Wyatt during a furious rally by the Athletics in the top of the ninth inning, Faber faltered. In just two-thirds of an inning, he gave up two run-scoring hits, uncorked a wild pitch and allowed the game-tying run. However, his teammates made a winner of Faber. With two out in the bottom of the ninth, Simmons, facing his former team, singled to right and scored Evar Swanson from second base.[17] No one knew it then, but the 9–8 victory was Faber's last in regular-season competition. However, more losses awaited.

Faber lost a tough game in Washington on September 9, three days after his 45th birthday. He retired the first two hitters in the 11th inning (his fourth inning of work) of a 2–2 contest. Suddenly, Luke Appling's error on a Goose

Urban Clarence "Red" Faber toward the end of his 20-year career. (Courtesy of the Tri-County Historical Society, Cascade, Iowa.)

Goslin grounder, a single and a walk filled the bases. Faber faced Fred Schulte with the game on the line. Umpire Geisel called the first two pitches balls; each decision unleashed a torrent of protest from the White Sox. Faber evened the count at 2–2. (Geisel was already unpopular with the White Sox that afternoon after his decision on a bizarre play in which third baseman and manager Jimmy Dykes failed to catch Joe Cronin as he raced toward an un-defended home plate.) Faber's next pitch was high and inside, bringing the 8,000 patrons in Griffith Park to the edge of their seats. *The Washington Post* described what happened next: "In the midst of a pitcher's nightmare, the score tied, the bases filled, and the three-and-two count on the batter, Urban (Red) Faber cocked his head back on his venerable right shoulder, drew his well-salivated glove up to his face, went through the motions of applying the slippery elm to his spitball, uncoiled the same wind-up that he has been using for 20 years with the

White Sox, and threw the ball game away." Faber's final pitch missed the strike zone. Goslin trotted in from third, touched home plate and made the Nationals' 3–2 win official.[18]

In his last regular-season appearance of 1933 — on September 20 in Yankee Stadium — Faber pitched well, allowing no earned runs in four innings. But his poor defense proved costly. His two errors contributed to three Yankees runs. In the third inning, Faber came off the mound to field a bunt, kicked it, recovered the ball and tossed it past first baseman Red Kress. In the next inning, Faber was slow covering first base on a grounder. He bobbled Kress' throw, and that allowed baserunner Ben Chapman to advance from first to third. Faber departed after four innings, trailing 3–0. The White Sox did not get onto the scoreboard until the seventh inning, and the Yankees held on for a 5–3 victory.[19] The game turned out to be Faber's last decision in a regular-season game.

After flirting with the first division for more than half the season — they were in fourth place in the eight-team American League as late July 22 — the White Sox faded in the final weeks. After reaching four games above .500 in May (29–25), the Sox went 38–58. Still, compared to 1932, the team gained 18 games in the win column and one place in the A.L. standings.

In the City Series against the Cubs, the White Sox won the opener 3–2 behind the pitching of 41-year-old "Sad Sam" Jones. Between the first two games of the series, Cubs president W.L. "Bill" Veeck died of leukemia. When he was a Chicago sportswriter using the pen name Bill Bailey, Veeck covered the 1913–14 World Tour and met an unproven rookie named Urban Faber. When Veeck was laid to rest, Faber was among the handful of current and former White Sox officials in attendance.[20] (Veeck's son and namesake later became a major league owner — twice, he owned the White Sox — and one of the game's greatest showmen.)

On a chilly October 4 in Wrigley Field, Fonseca wanted Ed Durham as his Game 2 starter. However, Durham was coming off an injury, so Fonseca had Faber join Durham during pre-game warm-ups — just in case. After only a few throws, Durham's arm was too weak.[21] (As it turned out, Durham never returned to major league service.) Though he started only twice during the regular season, 45-year-old Red Faber's name went onto the lineup card. Sox fans probably questioned Fonseca's selection when Cubs leadoff hitter Woody English rifled a Faber offering past second base for a single. However, English was erased in a double play, and Faber settled in. Registering his best performance in years — with the possible exception of his seven innings of scoreless relief against the Yankees a few weeks earlier — Faber shut out the Cubs on five hits 2–0. Al Simmons provided both runs batted in. (Simmons hit a sacrifice fly so deep in the eighth inning that even Faber, who had walked, could score from third base.) *Chicago American* sportswriter Jim Gallagher, calling Faber a "stout-hearted old warrior," reported that he won through "cunning and courage."[22] (The win pushed Faber's career record in City Series contests to 11–6. His mark would have been spectacular if not for a 1–6 stretch from 1925 through 1930.) The White Sox went on to sweep the favored Cubs and claim another city title.

Before the City Series, Faber accepted the invitation of his fellow Columbia College Alumni Association members to play in an exhibition to raise money for Depression-era relief. "Red Faber Day" would feature the pitching star with a team from his native Cascade against the Tri-State All-Stars, a hand-picked aggregation from the Dubuque area. "Students of the academy will be privileged to attend the Faber Day celebration," noted the student newspaper, "and every one should be on deck to root for a real *Columbian* who made good in the big show."[23] Virtually all the students had not even been born when Faber pitched for the college (then known as St. Joseph's). "Red Faber will be on the mound and he intends to stick until the last man has been retired in the ninth inning," promised "Scoop" Wilhelm, the sports editor in Dubuque.[24] Several preview articles recounting Faber's career did so with varying degrees of accuracy; none mentioned that when he pitched for the college nine, he was not enrolled as a student. Though organizers hoped to fill Dubuque's Municipal Ball Park, a downpour shortly before the mid-afternoon Sunday contest drastically cut into attendance. Though he struck out a dozen All-Stars, Faber also allowed nine hits and trailed 4–3 entering the bottom of the eighth. A two-run rally pushed Cascade into the lead, and Faber sealed the victory with a shutout ninth.

No one, especially Faber, knew that the exhibition was his last competition. It occurred in Dubuque, a former hometown and the city where he turned professional 24 years earlier. However, in mid–October 1933, Faber believed that he still had some major league baseball in him. For the right price.

29

Parting

With solid work in 1933 — his 3.45 earned run average was his best in 10 seasons — and his expressed desire to keep playing, there seemed little question that Faber would be in a White Sox uniform for his 21st major-league season. In early January, Ed Burns of the *Chicago Tribune* revealed that Faber reported that he had been training all winter. "His arm never has faded in the least," Burns wrote, "and for a decade his only trouble has been caused by his dogs and legs, especially his right knee." Faber told Burns that the knee, which underwent surgery in 1921, was feeling fine. The sportswriter shared Faber's optimism, and he noted an upturn in the spitballer's disposition despite season upon season of White Sox losses. "Several years ago it seemed that the south side patriarch was becoming a bit sour, but more recently the 45-year-old athlete has started to mellow. Today he is affable, and looking forward to a long career in baseball. And at times he is reminiscent about his career to date...." Burns noted that in his 20 seasons, Faber had seen nearly 800 players seek or hold positions on the White Sox. "He has toiled with some of the greatest players of all time ... and he has watched with kindly patience the awkward endeavors of some of the most ridiculous clowns that ever donned major league uniforms.... And if that right knee and those dogs will behave he'll play with other stars and maybe watch a few more clowns."[1]

With the post-season release of the National League's Burleigh Grimes, Faber was hailed as the last of the legal spitballers in the major leagues. He was poised to tie Walter Johnson's record of 21 consecutive seasons with the same major league club.

Then the postman arrived.

Faber and the team disputed the details, and press accounts were inconsistent. In any case, the White Sox offered Faber $5,000—a one-third cut from the previous year and half of what he earned in his prime — for his services in 1934. Faber was insulted. However, his options were limited; player agents and free agency were decades away. In winters past, Faber was consistently among the first players to return his contract, and 1934 was no exception. However, when Faber mailed back this contract, it was unsigned.

A few weeks later — on Friday, February 16, 1934 — Faber traveled the three miles from his residence in the Sutherland Hotel to Sox president Lou Comiskey's office at the ballpark. The men later presented conflicting accounts of the conversation. However, the next day, as Faber drove to Cascade, the Chicago White Sox announced that their senior player had retired voluntarily and on friendly terms. Sportswiters scrambled to reach him — a tough assignment with their primary source on the road. The *Tribune's* Irving Vaughan produced some Faber quotes, probably based on information fed to him by the team: "I'm sort of tired of it and there isn't much I can do any more, so I might as well take it easy." Vaughan continued: "It isn't the arm. That seems almost as strong as ever, but at 45 the legs don't hold up as well as they did at 25. They've been giving me trouble for a long time."[2] Those comments clearly were at variance his quotes of just a few weeks earlier. The *Tribune's* lead sports page paid tribute to Faber's long and noble service to the White Sox. However, the *Herald-Examiner's* report had a different tone. Sportswriter Ed Prell hit the jackpot when he reached a frustrated Irene Faber. She said that the team sent her husband just a "form letter," without a contract, inviting him to stop by the team office if a stated reduced salary amount was acceptable. She would not disclose the pay cut, but made it clear that her husband intended to catch on with another major league team. "He still wants to play baseball and is determined to do so," she told Prell. "He is not quitting the game by any means."[3] In the *Tribune*, perhaps updating his story from an earlier edition, Vaughan referred to an "outside source" who said that Faber's departure was financial, not physical; he followed it with Sox vice president Harry Grabiner's denial. By about 5 p.m. that Saturday, Faber arrived in Cascade, where his widowed mother still owned the Hotel Faber. Soon thereafter, telegrams and phone calls from Chicago started to arrive. He confirmed for sportswriters that money was the issue. "It seemed to me that the club wanted me to take too big a cut in my salary," Faber said. "I didn't hear anything from the club officials after I sent back, unsigned, the contract offered about a month ago, so I just walked in and quit."[4]

Their disagreement in the open, Lou Comiskey responded that before the parting he had invited Faber to make a counteroffer and that the contract included a possible $2,000 bonus if the team had a good financial year (a long shot while the Great Depression dragged on). Faber said the bonus was news to him. "If my salary had been the same as last year," he said, "I'd still be with the Sox." Faber said the termination came without rancor. "There was no argument between the club and myself. It was just an open and shut proposition, and I quit rather than take the cut. Mr. Comiskey said he would give me my release and I will be free to consider playing with some other club if a suitable contract is offered." Comiskey responded with his own statement, which opened, "I have the highest regard for Mr. Faber and always will have." Comiskey attributed the proposed salary cut to "general business conditions" but called attention to the bonus offer. The team president said that "some time after" receiving a contract offer, Faber came to his office and said he couldn't live with the terms. The Old Roman's son said his understanding was that Faber would return with a counteroffer. "Nothing further was heard from Mr. Faber until last week, when he called at Comiskey Park and advised me he was retiring from baseball. He left after wishing everyone a successful season. Naturally, I was greatly surprised upon further hearing of the matter."[5] At the time of their last face-to-face meeting, Vaughan reported, Comiskey told Faber that he could return to the team if he desired, "but in view of the subsequent unpleasantness, the Sox owner now is expected to give the old fellow his outright release."[6] That is what Comiskey did.

Faber received sympathy from many quarters. *The Sporting News* carried several letters of tribute from fans. However, the *Chicago Herald-Examiner* had a different view. "So Red Faber is tired of it all," wrote sports editor Warren Brown. "Or the White Sox haven't been doing right by him. Or something. Well, my private hunch, publicly expressed, is that the Sox haven't done badly by Red at all these last few seasons, and inasmuch as Red never has been done badly by the White Sox, I fail to see why there is so much gossip being tossed over the back fence."[7] (Three decades later, Brown would play a pivotal role in Faber's election to the Hall of Fame.)

A free agent for the first time in a quarter-century, Faber waited for offers. Almost immediately, Oakland of the Pacific Coast League expressed interest. The league already had signed two "grandfathered" spitballers, Clarence Mitchell and Jack Quinn, for 1934. Oakland officials asked White Sox manager Lew Fonseca, a native of the West Coast, to intercede for them in securing Faber's services.[8] However, nothing came of it. As spring training flowed into the regular season, Faber remained unsigned. Meanwhile, Quinn's stint in the Pacific Coast League was short-lived. By June 1934, he was pitching semi-pro ball in Chicago. A rival team reportedly tried to recruit Faber for a match-up between ancient hurlers, but the game did not come off.[9]

Still hoping to catch on someplace, Faber continued to work out. He regularly threw batting practice to the Cubs at Wrigley Field. "Red insists his arm is as good as ever," *The Sporting News* reported, "but complains about one of his dogs [legs] going back on him."[10] Two decades later, Faber told an interviewer that the Cubs were interested in signing him. "I'd have gone with them if I could have helped them," he said, but explained that he had enough.[11] However, based on an item in *The Sporting News*, it was not until the winter of 1935–36 — after two full seasons out of the majors — that Faber, by then 47 years old, fully accepted that his pitching career had ended.[12]

30

Odd Jobs

Early into his retirement, Faber bought a bowling alley in Grayslake, Illinois, about 50 miles north of Chicago.[1] Located on the southwest corner of Center Street and Seymour Avenue in the quiet community, Faber's enterprise consisted of just four lanes but, vital to the bottom line, also featured a bar. The enterprise employed teen-aged boys as pinsetters; they received a nickel a line. "Occasionally the job got dangerous for the pin boy," recalled one, Russell Ewing. "A good hit would send the solid maple pins flying and the pin boy could easily get hurt if one struck him, which happened more than I like to remember." Ewing recalled meeting the alley's new owner. "Red, as he wanted to be called, was kind of standoffish," Ewing wrote decades later. "He was probably that way as a result of his celebrity status. Strangers were constantly coming into the bowling alley to meet him."[2] Red and Irene moved into a house in nearby Fox Lake. The *Chicago Tribune* noted that the bowling alley was an "enterprise which has given him a great deal of time to devote to hunting, fishing, and reminiscing."[3] Some of that reminiscing took place in the bar of Fox Lake's Mineola Hotel, purportedly a former hangout of the incarcerated Al Capone. Faber, who liked to chase a shot of bourbon with a beer, and his cronies would "tear up the place."[4]

In 1936, when organized baseball presented Faber a gold lifetime pass, valid for admission to any professional game, *The Christian Science Monitor* noted that he was in the "oil business in Cascade."[5] That suggests that he was an investor in Al's "super service" gasoline station, which opened in May 1929.[6]

Faber maintained his ties to baseball through youth programs, amateur tournaments and nostalgic activities. A former big-leaguer's appearance was an exciting occasion. Tom Byrne recalled the Saturday morning 70 years earlier, when, as a 13-year-old member of the Dubuque American Legion team, he received Faber's instruction on the finer points of pitching.[7] In 1937, Faber

directed Illinois' semi-pro state tournament.[8] The next year, he donned his old
White Sox uniform and served as an
instructor at the Ray L. Doan Baseball
School in Hot Springs, Arkansas.[9] In
1944, he served as coach of a 500-youth
program in suburban Oak Park.[10] In
later years, when his own son entered
the program, he served as an assistant
coach of a neighborhood Little League
team. In Chicago or Milwaukee, rare
was the old-timers exhibition or Hot
Stove League banquet where Red Faber
was not on the guest list.

At home, however, Irene Faber's
health deteriorated. In addition to her
struggles with alcohol or other depend-
encies, in the late 1930s she started
receiving medical attention for meno-
pausal hypertension and secondary ane-
mia. Her condition worsened in the fall
of 1942. She was bedridden from Christmastime until early March 5, 1943,
when she underwent major surgery for
uterine tumors and ovarian cysts in St.
Therese Hospital, Waukegan, Illinois.
The procedure was termed a success, and
it appeared that she was improving.
However, at 6 a.m. March 11, Irene
Faber died at age 44. She was laid to rest
in her native Milwaukee. Thus ended

Faber, shown in 1936, always
enjoyed hunting and fishing. (Courtesy of the Tri-County Historical
Society, Cascade, Iowa.)

the 22 years of Urban and Irene Faber's troubled and childless marriage.

The Chicago White Sox's 1946, the first season after World War II, opened
with upheaval in the air. Longtime club executive Harry Grabiner quit in frustration with Charles Comiskey's heirs' meddling and bad decisions. During
the off-season many predicted — indeed, demanded — that manager Jimmie
Dykes be the next to go. Nonetheless, despite being sidelined by illness at the
start of the season, he returned to the helm. However, the team got off to a
10–20 start and in late May the Comiskeys made the change. They replaced
Dykes, the winningest manager in Sox history, with Ted Lyons, the franchise's
winningest pitcher. Lyons promptly hired as his pitching coach the Sox's
second-winningest hurler, his friend and former teammate Red Faber. The

The two winningest pitchers in Chicago White Sox history, Ted Lyons (left) and Red Faber, enjoy a light moment during a 1960s banquet in Chicago. They were teammates for 11 seasons. Lyons (260 wins) hired Faber (254) as his pitching coach for the 1946–48 campaigns. (Courtesy of the Tri-County Historical Society, Cascade, Iowa.)

former spitballer was available, having sold his bowling alley earlier that month.[11]

The team's equipment manager apparently was not ready for the leadership change. In his first day on the job, 6-foot-tall Faber squeezed into uniform No. 5, previously worn by the 5-foot-9 Dykes. (Meanwhile, the newly deposed manager showed up at Comiskey Park that day; he chatted in the clubhouse before game time and sat near the Chicago bullpen while the Sox swept a doubleheader from defending champion Detroit.) Neither the new manager nor pitching coach was terribly familiar with the squad. Faber had attended only four Sox games that season, and Lyons had just returned to the team in 1946 after four years in the military.[12] With a 1–4 record in his comeback season, Lyons immediately retired as a player to concentrate on his managerial duties. Under Lyons and Faber, the White Sox posted a 64–60 record over the balance of 1946.

The manager and coach enjoyed each other's company — especially during the rocky seasons that followed. In 1948, *Chicago Tribune* sports editor Arch Ward noted that Lyons remained "remarkably rational" during a nine-game losing streak. "He found it soothing to spend many hours off the field playing gin rummy with Coach Red Faber," Ward reported. "Red rarely says anything and generally loses, besides."[13] One of Faber's tasks was to turn in the White Sox lineup card at home plate before each game. "Some days, Red, probably the slowest moving man in baseball, barely makes it," Ward observed. Added Lyons, "Some day we are going to be rained out before Red completes the trip. Then won't he be surprised?"[14]

Faber's quiet side surely contributed to the surprise when, in April 1947, the 58-year-old coach married — and that his bride, stenographer Frances Susanna Knudtzon, was barely half his age. (The newspapers said she was 29, but she was actually a year older than that.) It was also the second marriage for the new Mrs. Faber. Her marriage to an alcoholic and abusive railroad executive had ended three years earlier. The couple met through mutual friends. Though she was seriously interested — and remained so for some time — he insisted that he was too old for her. Ultimately, Fran persuaded him, and they decided to tie the knot quickly — and quietly. The morning of the wedding, all the *Chicago Tribune* knew was the name of the groom. "A lot of people who should have known [about the wedding] hadn't even been informed," the *Tribune*

In 1947, the 58-year-old Faber married Frances Knudtzon, who was barely half his age. It was the second marriage for both. The couple had one son. (Courtesy of the Tri-County Historical Society, Cascade, Iowa.)

reported. Frances Knudtzon and Urban C. Faber tied the knot at 11:15 a.m.
April 12, 1947, in a civil ceremony in the Cook County Building in downtown Chicago. The newlyweds moved into her residence in the Webster
Hotel.[15] Years later, a sportswriter wrote that Fran Faber would win a "Sweetest Lady" contest hands-down. "Hers is the sweetness that comes from within;
not the exterior sugar-coating so many of the gals spray on themselves these
days along with their deodorant."[16] The groom probably appreciated Lyons
giving him the day off: In frigid conditions — the temperature hovered in the
mid–30s — the White Sox edged the Cubs in a pre-season game.[17] Fran Faber
became a regular at Comiskey Park. She attended nearly every home game
and arrived early enough to sit through pre-game warm-ups.[18] Most of the
baseball world knew him as "Red," but Fran Faber, like his close friends,
always called him "Fabe."

Among many of his Roman Catholic family, his marriage was unpopular. Fran was a divorcee, a Lutheran and woman half his age. When he visited Cascade for the first time after the wedding, his sister Mae walked him
across the room and had him look into a mirror. She demanded, "Do you
think that any young woman would marry a face like *that* for love?"[19] Still,
several in the family warmed up to Fran. Urban's goddaughter recalled Fran
as a "very nice person" who was justified seeking a divorce to escape an abusive situation. When Urban and Fran married, she said, "he started living
again."[20] Any family discord about the marriage did not involve his mother.
Margaret Faber died two months before the wedding; she was age 83.[21] (Many
years later, after Fran's ex-husband died, thus erasing her "divorcee" status in
the Catholic Church's eyes, she and Urban exchanged vows in a church ceremony.[22])

As the White Sox stumbled to the end of the 1947 campaign (70–84)
in St. Louis, Faber received permission to travel to New York City for an old-
timers game to benefit Babe Ruth's foundation. (The Yankees paid his expenses
and invited him to be their guest at the first two World Series games.) Other
former stars at Yankee Stadium included Ty Cobb, Tris Speaker and 80-year-
old Cy Young. Faber, 59 years old, pitched an inning in the exhibition, which
preceded the Yankees' regular-season finale. The Bambino himself was in
attendance, but was too ill to be in uniform.[23] Ruth died of throat cancer 11
months later at age 53.

Meanwhile, the Comiskey administration continued to scrimp and make
questionable personnel decisions. That put Lyons' temperament to the test,
and the results were evident. After leading the Sox above .500 in his first season and a .455 percentage in his second year, Lyons could barely win one out
of three contests in 1948, and the Sox finished in the American League cellar. He quit before he could be fired. New manager Jack Onslow kept two
members of Lyons' coaching staff — but not Faber.[24] Within a week of losing

his job, Faber became a first-time father — at age 60. Urban C. Faber II was born October 8, 1948. As a baby, he acquired the nickname "Pepper"; he started balking at the moniker as early as his eighth year.[25] (At a get-together after Pepper was christened, a young neighbor girl entertained with a little song and dance. In subsequent years, millions came to know her as Ann-Margret.[26])

Unemployed and a new father, Faber tried his hand in sales in Twin Lakes, Illinois, just south of the Wisconsin-Illinois border. He worked in the real estate office of his wife's brother, Elmer Knudtzon, who billed himself as the largest Realtor in Twin Lakes. (Knudtzon's claim might have been based on physique as much as sales volume. His "for sale" signs featured his caricature with an oversized belly.) Faber was not cut out for the real estate game. "He was too honest," his son explained. "He'd say, 'Oh, you don't want to buy this house; there's something wrong with it here or there.'"[27]

Eventually, Faber got out of real estate and tried his hand at selling cars for his friend and ex-major leaguer Tony Piet. The Pontiac dealership was on Chicago's South Side (6603 S. Western Ave.) — too far from the Faber home to accommodate a daily commute. He stayed in Chicago during the week and returned to Twin Lakes on weekends. He proved to be about as effective selling cars as he was selling houses.

Their employer-employee relationship eventually ended, but Faber and Piet remained friends throughout their lives. In 1950, they were among the founders of Baseball Anonymous, an organization created to help former ballplayers (and athletes from other sports) who were down on their luck. The need for such a group became evident when the American League had to step in to cover funeral expenses for a destitute former umpire, Bill Guthrie. Ray Schalk was elected the group's first president. Red Grange and George Halas represented pro football in the Windy City.[28] Growing to nearly 700 members (at $2 per year) in its first year, Baseball Anonymous performed many good deeds; most were handled quietly, but in 1958 the group arranged a Comiskey Park ceremony to honor former White Sox pitching great Ed Walsh, who was 77 years old and struggling physically and financially. Faber, as the group's general chairman, presented his former teammate with a check payable to the Ed Walsh Trust Fund.[29] The group also staged benefits for other former players who had fallen upon hard times, including Monty Stratton and Jackie Hayes.

After living exclusively in the Midwest, the Fabers tried a change of scenery. They loaded up their 1952 Ford station wagon and moved to Phoenix. The new location did not work out. Red and Pepper felt ill nearly all the time, and the family returned to the Chicago area after just six months in the Southwest.

In 1954, while most men his age were anticipating or enjoying retirement, 65-year-old Urban Faber was taking on a new job. The Cook County

When the White Sox moved their spring training camp to Southern California after World War II, Hollywood celebrities occasionally came calling. Coach Red Faber, who in his playing days regularly pitched to Babe Ruth, poses with William Bendix, who portrayed the Bambino in the 1948 movie *The Babe Ruth Story*. (Courtesy of the Tri-County Historical Society, Cascade, Iowa.)

(Illinois) Highway Department hired him as an inspector rodman and assigned him to a survey crew. Though his formal schooling was limited, the senior citizen showed his prowess at math. "They said, 'Why don't you take the engineer's test. You can get a promotion,'" his son said. "He said, no, he'd let the guys do that with the big family and stuff. That didn't really interest him. He wasn't really into money. We had enough to live on. We didn't live good, but we were never hungry or anything."[30] The Fabers rented a house on 65th Street between Hamlin and Lawndale. About 1955, they purchased a three-bedroom, red-brick bungalow at 10518 South Prospect Avenue. The house was in the Beverly neighborhood on Chicago's South Side, a quiet area with a suburban atmosphere.[31]

As was common among American boys in the 1950s, Pepper Faber played baseball. His team, the Rebels, might have been the only Little League squad in the nation to have *two* ex-major leaguers as assistant coaches — Pepper's father and Nick Etten, who played first base for the Yankees, Phillies and Athletics. Urban tossed batting practice and helped manager Ted Cushing wherever needed and without interfering. "If a first-base umpire is needed, Red takes the job and the opposing manager knows all decisions will be fair," columnist and neighbor Bill Gleason wrote.[32]

Though Faber did not throw spitballs to the Rebels, he did "pitch" the spitball to baseball officialdom. In the mid–1950s, Commissioner Ford Frick advocated lifting the ban against the spitball, and during an old-timers game in New York, he discussed the topic with Faber, who for years wanted the pitch reinstated.[33]

More than 15 years after Faber threw his last major league pitch, Chicago fans voted him onto the White Sox "all-time" team (1901–49). In between, he pitched an inning of an old-timers game at Wrigley Field, where he struck out Rogers Hornsby on three pitches. "Well, that's something," joked Lefty Gomez. "After 25 years they find out how to pitch to Hornsby!"[34] That same season, the Chicago Historical Society displayed one of Faber's uniforms in a baseball exhibition; he donated the uniform permanently in 1953.[35] In 1951, *The Des Moines Register* inducted the Iowa native into its Hall of Fame. For their 1954 home opener, the White Sox invited Faber and Ray Schalk, the star battery from the 1917 World Series, to handle first-pitch ceremonies.[36] Faber and Schalk were back in the spotlight five years later, tossing out the first pitch for Game 1 of the 1959 World Series. Watching the ceremony, Chicago manager Al Lopez quipped, "I wish they were in shape. I'd leave them in the whole game."[37] Those recognitions were appropriate and appreciated, but they were no substitute for the exclusive recognition Faber desired: a spot in the National Baseball Hall of Fame.

31

Cooperstown at Last

As professional baseball progressed into its seventh decade, fans and officials sought to preserve the history of the game and honor its early achievers. The result was the National Baseball Hall of Fame, established in the mythical cradle of the game, Cooperstown, New York. Among the five charter inductees in 1936 were three men against whom Faber competed — Babe Ruth, Ty Cobb and Walter Johnson. Also in the first class at Cooperstown were Christy Mathewson, whose withdrawal from the 1913–14 world tour gave Faber a chance to prove his major league mettle, and Honus Wagner.

Faber had an outstanding career. But was it worthy of the Hall of Fame? What qualifies someone for the Hall, and how those decisions are made, provides fertile fodder for baseball debates. The Hall's guidelines state, "Candidates shall be chosen on the basis of playing ability, integrity, sportsmanship, character, their contribution to the team on which they played and to baseball in general." To win election by sportswriters, candidates have to have been active players within 20 years, but not less than five years, of their election.[1]

Year after year, electors — 10-year members of the Baseball Writers' Association of America — denied Faber the game's highest honor. That he was stuck on also-ran teams in the prime of his career depressed Faber's win total, limited his time in the spotlight and hurt his prospects for Cooperstown. Many elections, *no one* appeared on the requisite 75 percent of the electors' ballots. During the period Faber was eligible, writers pitched a shutout, electing no one for long periods — from 1943 through 1946, from 1957 through 1961 and in 1963.[2] When the writers considered someone worthy of Cooperstown, they selected other stars, including Lou Gehrig (1939), Herb Pennock (1948) and Charlie Gehringer (1949).

Hall of Fame ballots bearing votes for Faber trickled in. One vote this year. Three votes that year. Several years, zero votes. His totals did not reach double-digits until 1954, and remained far short of winning election. In 1958,

Inductees into the National Baseball Hall of Fame on July 27, 1964. From left: Red Faber, Luke Appling, Henry Manush and Burleigh Grimes. Posthumously inducted were Tim Keefe, John Montgomery Ward and Miller Huggins. (National Baseball Hall of Fame Library, Cooperstown, N.Y.)

a couple of electors went to bat for him. Writing in *Newsweek*, John Lardner said the names of Max Carey and Faber topped his ballot. Carey's 25-year window of eligibility was running out — the writers did not elect him, but in 1961 the Veterans Committee did — but Lardner noted, "Faber has a few years of eligibility left, so the crisis is not so sharp for him."[3] New York columnist Red Smith also supported Faber, as well as another pitcher, Lefty Gomez.[4] When Gomez did win election in 1972, a reporter asked him to what he attributed his success. One of the game's quickest wits, Gomez replied, "Clean living and a fast outfield."[5] (Gomez is also credited with declaring, "I'd rather be lucky than good.")

Faber's totals jumped from nine votes (1953) to 68 (1958) to his high-water mark of 83 in 1960—just 31 percent, not even half the total required. After that, voters lost interest. In 1962, in his last at-bat with the writers, Faber finished 11th with just 30 votes (18.75 percent). Securing induction that year were Bob Feller and Jackie Robinson. That Robinson barely won election

(77½ percent) reflected the writers' high — critics said unreasonably so — standards. The clock ran out on Faber's eligibility with the baseball writers. His hopes were put in the hands of the Veterans Committee, which every other year considered players who had been retired at least two decades.

He did not have to wait long. On February 2, 1964, Urban "Red" Faber received the call. His wait was over: the Veterans Committee, headed by the *Chicago American*'s Warren Brown, selected him for induction into the National Baseball Hall of Fame. Within minutes, the Faber residence became a beehive, swarming with phone calls, visitors and Western Union messengers. One of the first to arrive at the Prospect Avenue bungalow was Ray Schalk, his friend, former batterymate and neighbor. Schalk, who entered Cooperstown in 1955, and Faber, attired in ties and sports coats, pulled out old mitts and baseballs for props in a photo session. Friends and well-wishers gathered at the Faber residence that night. New inductee Burleigh Grimes, the last active spitballer, also was present. Recalled Bill Gleason, a sportswriter and neighbor in attendance that night, "It was an emotional evening."[6] It is likely that, after that day of excitement, Faber the next morning was back in his work clothes for a full shift with the county highway crew.

Hall of Fame elections are the subject of debate — even decades later. Baseball statistical expert Bill James criticized Faber's selection in his 1995 book, *Whatever Happened to the Hall of Fame?* James considered Faber unworthy, saying he was "selected in all likelihood, for the same reason that Ray Schalk was — he was one of the Clean Sox of 1919, and Warren Brown was on the selection committee."[7] The Veterans Committee saw it differently, and Faber gladly accepted his invitation to Cooperstown.

In the half-year between election and induction, Faber was the subject of many sports columns and smaller honors. He returned to Iowa for the dedication of Faber Field at his

Red Faber delivers his acceptance speech in Cooperstown on July 27, 1964. (National Baseball Hall of Fame Library, Cooperstown, N.Y.)

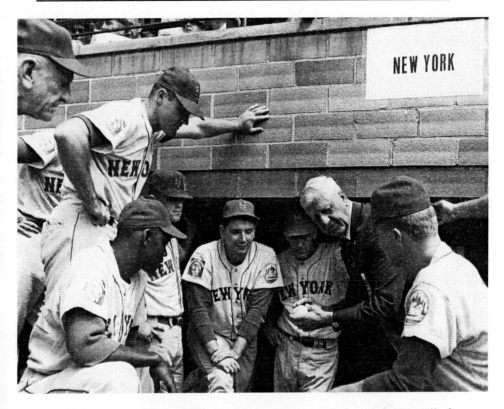

Red Faber discusses the spitball with the New York Mets before the 1964 Hall of Fame exhibition game in Cooperstown, New York. In the upper left corner is Mets manager Casey Stengel. (National Baseball Hall of Fame Library, Cooperstown, N.Y.)

alma mater, Loras College (previously St. Joseph's) in Dubuque. His St. Joe's manager of 55 years earlier, Joseph P. Flynn, was on hand to present him with a commemorative watch. Faber's status as a Hall of Fame inductee-elect gave him the platform to advocate for reinstatement of the spitball and to share his observations about contemporary baseball. "Instead of just loosening up their arm, they should practice throwing at a target," Faber said of 1960s pitchers. "I always threw a few pitches at the catcher's knees, then aimed belt-high and finally shoulder high. I wanted to know where I could put the ball before I got on the mound." He was critical of the trend toward "relief specialists," noting, "In earlier days, a manager wouldn't yank a pitcher for a pinch-hitter just for the sake of getting a few runs you didn't need."[8] However, Faber said he did not believe that pitchers of his era were superior. Concerning hitters, he said they would improve if they weren't "down on the end of the bat trying to knock the fences down." Finally, noting that many 1960s

players received signing bonuses rivaling his lifetime earnings, Faber claimed
the "exorbitant" salaries curbed the athletes' incentive.[9]

In making travel plans for Cooperstown, Fran Faber suggested that the
family take the train so that their son Urban II (nicknamed Pepper) could
experience "wonderful" and "elegant" railroad travel. However, once on their
way from Chicago, the Fabers discovered that riding the rails had lost their
luster. "It was such a disappointment," she recalled. "People were sitting there
in their bare feet, with their arms around each other. We couldn't get food
on the train. They stopped the train and we had to get off to get some food.
Only part of the station was open." The Fabers had to take a cab into town,
grab breakfast, and return to the depot. "That was such a disappointment,"
she said. "My son never got to see how beautiful the trains were."[10]

The White Sox had another inductee in the Class of 1964 — shortstop
Luke Appling, who squeaked in on the writers' ballot after edging Red Ruffing
in a runoff vote. The Veterans Committee selected the six other honorees.
On hand were Faber, fellow spitballer Grimes and outfielder Heinie Manush.
Inducted posthumously were 19th-century players Tim Keefe and John Montgomery Ward — they were friends and, briefly, brothers-in-law — and Yankees
manager Miller Huggins.

Though the railroad trip failed to meet the Fabers' expectations, the
accommodations in Cooperstown exceeded them. The Treadway Otesaga
Hotel featured a spacious lobby, majestic veranda and brass beds in every
room. Its most expensive room listed at $50 a night — breakfast and dinner

**Previous and new members of the National Baseball Hall of Fame acknowledge
fans at the Hall of Fame Game on July 27, 1964, in Cooperstown, New York.
From left: Elmer Flick, Joe McCarthy, Frank Frisch, Charlie Gehringer, Joe
Cronin, Bill McKechnie, Sam Rice, Ray Schalk, Henry Manush, Red Faber,
Burleigh Grimes and Luke Appling. (National Baseball Hall of Fame Library,
Cooperstown, N.Y.)**

included. A limousine was at their disposal throughout their four days in the village. Several Hall-of-Famers, including Faber's friends and ex-teammates Schalk and Ted Lyons, showed up for induction events. Also present were Frankie Frisch, Elmer Flick, Joe McCarthy, Charlie Gehringer, Joe Cronin, Bill McKechnie and Sam Rice.

The Hall of Fame's 25th anniversary induction ceremony took place Monday, July 27, 1964. Ford Frick presided. "It's always a happy occasion when the gentlemen who are honored have a chance to smell the roses, so to speak," the commissioner said, "and fortunately we have four men, great men, men who contributed much to baseball, who are here on the platform today to accept their induction into the Hall of Fame." Frick called forward the inductees in the order in which they entered professional baseball. It might have been the only time Faber ever batted leadoff.

> Mr. Commissioner, ladies and gentlemen. It's a great honor to me to be named to the Hall of Fame. It's very hard for me to even imagine that I would ever be elected to it. But now that I am, and about to join all those celebrities that I used to know and play against and with, why, I hardly know what to say. I know there are all baseball fans here. They must be or they wouldn't have come this far to see an event like this. And I'm happy to greet you all in our behalf. Thank you.[11]

Always a man of few words, Faber required only 100 for his acceptance speech.

After that ceremony, the Hall-of-Famers in attendance moved to Doubleday Field, where the Mets and Senators, two of the majors' worst teams, played an exhibition game. Beforehand, Faber chatted in the Mets dugout and demonstrated his spitball grip. (Taking it all in was the Mets manager, Casey Stengel, who two years later enjoyed a more prominent role in Cooperstown—as a Hall inductee.)

Fran Faber appreciated that her husband, nearly 76, could accept the accolades in person and that their son could attend. After all, Red had heart problems and Pepper was still recovering from a near-fatal swimming accident. "My contention is they should put you fellows in when you're younger so you can go back for a reunion every year," Fran Faber said in a letter to Harry Hooper, "not when you're too old to go out or travel anymore."[12] However, that soon was Red Faber's situation. He never returned to Cooperstown.

32

Twilight and Sunset

For Red and Fran Faber, the excitement of his election to the Hall of Fame followed months of worry about their son. Fourteen-year-old "Pepper" Faber nearly died in a swimming accident in late May 1963. He and friend Greg Kuhlman went to Rainbow Beach, on Lake Michigan at 75th Street. It was early in the season and there were no lifeguards on duty. Pepper sprinted into the shallow water, dove and struck his head on a concrete jetty. The blow left him paralyzed and floating facedown in the lake. Soon, Kuhlman spotted his friend's hair bobbing on the surface of the water and pulled him out. Pepper suffered a broken neck; it took a week in South Shore Hospital before he could wiggle one toe. After three weeks, his neck was back in place. However, during transfer to a rehabilitation facility, medical attendants accidentally re-injured him; his neck would never be the same. Months of rehab followed, and just days before Red's election into Cooperstown, doctors determined that Urban II could return to classes at Morgan Park High School. "Makes a man feel good," the elder Urban told a reporter, "Pepper getting better and me in the Hall of Fame."[1] Prayer might have been a contributor, too: Urban often read from a small book of prayers and made use of a beautiful silver rosary.[2]

During the general period of his Hall of Fame election, Red Faber experienced his own health problems. He suffered two heart attacks in a two-year span. Faber's preference for unfiltered Chesterfield cigarettes could not have helped. When he was in his early 70s, Faber, a smoker since age 8, attempted to follow his doctor's advice to quit. That lasted about a year. Faber was miserable, and he finally declared that he'd rather die than quit. Due to his health problems, he retired from the Cook County Highway Department in 1965. However, after a short time, he went back and even received a promotion. Faber retired for good in late 1967, when he was 79 years old.[3]

In September 1968, on the occasion of his 80th birthday, Faber's friends threw him a dinner party at the Swedish Club on Chicago's near North Side.

Greg Kuhlman (left) was credited with saving the life of Urban Faber II (right) after a swimming accident in May 1963. In the center of this 1964 photograph is Frances Faber. (Courtesy of the Tri-County Historical Society, Cascade, Iowa.)

In reference to the civil unrest that had just rocked the Windy City during the 1968 Democratic National Convention, sportswriter Bill Gleason (Faber's neighbor and friend) proposed a parade in the octogenarian's honor. "In a time of the non-hero who spits upon people," Gleason wrote, "it would be uplifting for the municipality to honor a hero who spat upon baseballs."[4] City officials were not swayed; the party would have to suffice. One of the celebration's attendees was the man who touted Faber's entry into professional baseball and managed the 1917 world champions: Clarence "Pants" Rowland, then 89 years old.[5]

Faber's health continued to deteriorate in his ninth decade. He lived with a heart aneurysm — doctors said he was too old to survive an operation — and pain in both legs from sciatica. "He had to rock back and forth three or four times just to get out of a chair," his son recalled. For weeks and months at a time, Red Faber never left his bungalow on Prospect Avenue. A barber came to the house every few weeks to take care of his tonsorial needs. Regularly watching baseball games on television, the Hall of Famer shook his head at the long-haired fashion of contemporary major leaguers. Meanwhile, a devoted Fran looked after her ailing husband. "Fabe hasn't been well for

Before and after his Hall of Fame induction, Faber was employed by the Cook County Highway Department, working on survey crews in the Chicago area. He kept the job until he was nearly 80 years old. (Courtesy of the Tri-County Historical Society, Cascade, Iowa.)

several years now," she wrote to Harry Hooper, a former teammate, in the summer of 1973. "It really isn't anything special now, just old age, I guess. He hasn't been out since Christmastime." Baseball fans and writers remembered the old spitballer, however, and they sent a steady stream of requests for interviews, information and autographs. He couldn't keep up with it all. "Don't tell anyone," Fran confided to Hooper, "but I do all the autographing, or it would never get done."[6] Decades later, their son downplayed that revelation, saying his late mother might have signed a few cards mailed in by some particularly insistent autograph sellers.[7]

Several of those who contacted Faber wanted to discuss the Black Sox. Over the years, Faber and most of the 1919 Sox ("Clean" and "Black" alike) rarely spoke of the scandal, and when they did they gave only brief answers. In pri-

Frances and Urban Faber in 1964, the year of his election to the National Baseball Hall of Fame. "If she were entered in a 'Sweetest Lady' contest," Chicago sportswriter Bill Gleason wrote, "Fran would win it going away." (Courtesy of the Tri-County Historical Society, Cascade, Iowa.)

vate moments, Faber occasionally discussed it with this son. "He said he didn't think Shoeless Joe Jackson was really in on it," Urban II recalled. "He said, to be honest, he didn't think he [Jackson] was smart enough to be in on it."[8] However, Jackson biographer David Fleitz cites accounts from Faber and Dickie Kerr that Jackson and fellow outfielder Happy Felsch repeatedly played out of position and allowed fly balls to fall for base hits. Jackson himself admitted receiving $5,000 for his role in the fix.[9] Though he is not credited in print, Faber is believed to have cooperated with Eliot Asinof, author of the 1963 book on the scandal, *Eight Men Out*. In the mid–1970s, writer Eugene Murdock interviewed Faber about the scandal. But, as Black Sox expert Gene Carney observed, Murdock was too late. "Red ... had not been out of his house in five years," Carney said, "and his memory was all but gone."[10]

In the early 1920s, Red Faber, the son of a small-town Iowa hotelier, was the best pitcher in the game. By the U.S. bicentennial year of 1976, he had outlived most of his peers and a great number of his fans. On September 25, 1976, Red Faber's heart gave out for the last time. He was 88 years old.

After a wake at Thompson Funeral Home in south suburban Oak Lawn and funeral Mass at St. Barnabas Catholic Church, he was laid to rest in Acacia Park Cemetery in Chicago. His grave marker is a small metal plaque atop a horizontal stone at ground level. The marker lists his name, indicates that he was a chief yeoman in the U.S. Navy during World War I and, on either side of a Christian cross, gives his dates of birth and death.

His marker does not mention baseball.

* * *

The Fabers lived comfortably but were not well-to-do. Urban never earned more than $10,000 a season as a player. Like millions of Americans, he lost money in the stock market crash of 1929.[11] His baseball pension was small — about $100 a month — and he kept working full-time jobs until he was 79 years old. Over the years, his widow and son sold most of his baseball memorabilia. His 1917 World Series championship ring was never sold; it was stolen during Red's playing days. Fran donated scrapbooks, photographs and a few souvenirs to the Tri-County Historical Society in his hometown, Cascade, Iowa. Many of those items are displayed in the organization's small museum.

After a below-average academic career at Morgan Park High School, Urban II completed automotive school, but back problems related to his neck injury forced a change in careers. He studied photography in Chicago before transferring to Brooks Institute of Photography in Santa Barbara, California. He returned to Chicago, where he worked in photo studios and a camera shop. Later, the Hall of Famer's son sold real estate and then insurance. Health problems have dogged him. As an adult, he survived kidney cancer and injuries from two motorcycle accidents; in one, he suffered yet another broken neck. As a cumulative result, by the early 21st century spinal and nerve problems prevented him from working. After being divorced about 20 years, he remarried in April 2001 and has two stepdaughters and a stepson.

Fran sold the house in Chicago and moved to Wheaton, the western suburb where Urban II resided. A diabetic, she developed a staph infection, which resulted in partial amputation of a leg in the mid–1980s. During her recovery, Urban II recalled, "I snuck in a couple of bottles and we had martinis in the hospital."[12] She died November 28, 1992, at age 76.

Back on Prospect Avenue in the Beverly neighborhood of Chicago, a subsequent owner of the Faber house climbed into the attic and found old baseball equipment. Obviously unaware of the house's connection to one of the game's greatest players ever, the owner pitched shoes, bats and baseballs into the trash.[13]

Appendix A: Statistics

Urban Clarence Faber
Chicago White Sox (AL)

Inducted into National Baseball Hall of Fame (1964)

Nickname: Red

Born: September 6, 1888. Cascade, Iowa   **Died:** September 25, 1976. Chicago, Illinois

Buried: Acacia Park Cemetery, Chicago, Illinois

First Major League Game: April 17, 1914.   **Final Game:** September 20, 1933.

Bat: Both. **Throw:** Right.

Height: 6–2.   **Weight:** 180.

Pitching

Year	G	GS	CG	SHO	IP	H	HR	R	ER	BB	K	HBP	W	L	ERA
1914	40	19	11	2	181.1	154	3	77	54	64	88	12	10	9	2.68
1915	50	32	21	2	299.2	264	3	118	85	99	182	11	24	14	2.55
1916	35	25	15	3	205.1	167	1	67	46	61	87	5	17	9	2.02
1917	41	29	16	3	248	224	1	92	53	85	84	10	16	13	1.92
1918	11	9	5	1	80.2	70	3	23	11	23	26	0	4	1	1.23
1919	25	20	9	0	162.1	185	7	92	69	45	45	8	11	9	3.83
1920	40	39	28	2	319	332	8	136	106	88	108	4	23	13	2.99
1921	43	39	32	4	330.2	293	10	107	91	87	124	7	25	15	2.48
1922	43	38	31	4	352	334	10	128	110	83	148	6	21	17	2.81

Year	G	GS	CG	SHO	IP	H	HR	R	ER	BB	SO	HBP	W	L	ERA
1923	32	31	15	2	232.1	233	6	114	88	62	91	6	14	11	3.41
1924	21	20	9	0	161.1	173	5	78	69	58	47	2	9	11	3.85
1925	34	32	16	1	238	266	8	117	100	59	71	2	12	11	3.78
1926	27	25	13	1	184.2	203	3	84	73	57	65	2	15	9	3.56
1927	18	15	6	0	110.2	131	2	64	56	41	39	5	4	7	4.55
1928	27	27	16	2	201.1	223	11	98	84	68	43	4	13	9	3.75
1929	31	31	15	1	234	241	10	119	101	61	68	9	13	13	3.88
1930	29	26	10	0	169	188	7	101	79	49	62	5	8	13	4.21
1931	44	19	5	1	184	210	11	96	78	57	49	3	10	14	3.82
1932	42	5	0	0	106	123	0	61	44	38	26	1	2	11	3.74
1933	36	2	0	0	86.1	92	2	41	33	28	18	1	3	4	3.44
Totals	669	483	273	29	4086.2	4106	111	1813	1430	1213	1471	103	254	213	3.15

Other career totals: Games finished 134, Hit Batsmen 103, Balks 2.

World Series

Year	G	GS	CG	SHO	IP	H	HR	R	ER	BB	SO	HBP	W	L	ERA
1917	4	3	2	0	27	21	1	7	7	3	9	2	3	1	2.33

Statistics obtained free of charge from Retrosheet, 20 Sunset Road, Newark, Delaware 19711.

Urban Clarence "Red" Faber
Chicago White Sox (AL)

Batting

Year	G	AB	R	H	2B	3B	HR	RBI	BB	K	HBP	SAC	SB	AVG	OBP	SLG
1914	40	55	3	8	1	0	0	1	10	16	0	2	0	.145	.277	.164
1915	50	84	11	11	1	2	0	6	20	33	2	12	4	.131	.311	.190
1916	35	63	4	6	0	0	0	2	5	34	1	4	0	.095	.174	.095
1917	41	69	1	4	1	0	0	2	10	38	0	8	0	.058	.177	.072
1918	11	24	1	1	0	0	0	0	3	11	0	2	0	.042	.148	.042
1919	25	54	8	10	0	0	0	4	6	20	0	3	0	.185	.267	.185
1920	40	104	10	11	1	0	0	1	19	39	0	6	1	.106	.244	.115
1921	43	108	8	16	0	0	0	4	17	35	1	8	1	.148	.270	.148
1922	43	125	8	25	2	0	0	5	7	42	1	10	0	.200	.248	.216
1923	33	69	7	15	3	0	1	5	10	28	0	8	1	.217	.316	.304
1924	21	54	6	8	0	0	0	1	7	15	0	2	0	.148	.246	.148
1925	34	77	3	8	1	0	0	4	10	24	2	6	0	.104	.225	.117
1926	27	60	7	9	2	0	0	10	8	21	0	6	0	.150	.250	.183
1927	18	37	2	10	3	0	0	4	2	8	0	5	0	.270	.308	.351
1928	27	70	3	8	2	0	1	10	4	31	0	4	0	.114	.162	.186

Year	G	AB	R	H	2B	3B	HR	RBI	BB	SO	HBP	SAC	SB	AVG	OBP	SLG
1929	31	78	8	10	2	0	1	5	8	24	0	4	0	.128	.209	.192
1930	29	49	4	2	0	0	0	2	9	21	0	5	0	.041	.190	.041
1931	44	53	4	4	1	0	0	3	6	26	1	4	0	.075	.183	.094
1932	42	18	0	4	1	0	0	1	8	7	0	4	0	.222	.462	.278
1933	36	18	0	0	0	0	0	0	0	6	0	1	0	.000	.000	.000
Total	**670**	**1269**	**98**	**170**	**21**	**2**	**3**	**70**	**169**	**479**	**8**	**104**	**7**	**.134**	**.240**	**.161**

World Series

Year	G	AB	R	H	2B	3B	HR	RBI	BB	SO	HBP	SAC	SB	AVG	OBP	SLG
1917	4	7	0	1	0	0	0	0	2	3	0	1	0	.143	.333	.143

Statistics obtained free of charge from Retrosheet, 20 Sunset Road, Newark, Delaware 19711.

Urban Clarence "Red" Faber
Chicago White Sox (AL)

Fielding

All games as a pitcher.

Year	G	PO	A	E	DP	AVG
1914	40	7	58	2	3	.970
1915	50	7	85	8	4	.920
1916	35	3	71	5	1	.937
1917	41	13	84	8	0	.924
1918	11	1	29	1	1	.968
1919	25	6	48	5	1	.915
1920	40	15	78	10	5	.903
1921	43	10	90	5	3	.952
1922	43	4	94	4	1	.961
1923	32	8	70	4	3	.951
1924	21	4	31	1	1	.972
1925	34	13	67	4	1	.952
1926	27	1	33	2	1	.944
1927	18	5	37	0	1	1.000
1928	27	11	52	1	2	.984
1929	31	7	61	2	1	.971
1930	29	3	47	1	2	.980
1931	44	6	33	3	0	.929
1932	42	3	21	1	1	.960
1933	36	3	19	4	1	.846
Total	**669**	**130**	**1108**	**71**	**33**	**.946**

World Series

Year	G	PO	A	E	DP	AVG
1917	4	2	18	0	4	1.000

Statistics obtained free of charge from Retrosheet, 20 Sunset Road, Newark, Delaware 19711.

Appendix B: Milestones

National Baseball Hall of Fame: Inducted July 27, 1964.

Pitching

First professional appearance: July 27, 1909, at Dubuque. (Three-I League) Dubuque 12, Springfield 1.

Final professional appearance: October 4, 1933, at Chicago's Wrigley Field. (Chicago City Series) White Sox 2, Cubs 0.

Major League Regular Season

First appearance and first start: April 17, 1914, at Chicago. (No decision.) White Sox 6, Cleveland Indians 5.

First victory: June 7, 1914, at Chicago. White Sox 4, New York Yankees 0.

100th victory: August 20, 1920, at Philadelphia (first game). White Sox 7, Philadelphia Athletics 4.

150th victory: September 16, 1922, at Chicago. White Sox 9, Boston Red Sox 2.

200th victory: September 13, 1926, at Chicago. White Sox 3, Philadelphia Athletics 2.

250th victory: May 6, 1932, at Chicago. (Relief) White Sox 5, Washington Senators 3.

Final victory: August 27, 1933, at Chicago. (Relief) White Sox 9, Philadelphia Athletics, 8. (254 wins)

Final start, appearance and loss: September 20, 1933, at New York. New York Yankees 5, White Sox 3. (483 starts, 669 appearances, 212 losses)

One-hitters

June 17, 1914, at Chicago. White Sox 5, Philadelphia Athletics 0.
September 15, 1915, at Boston. White Sox 3, Boston Red Sox 1.
May 26, 1929, at Chicago. White Sox 2, Detroit Tigers 0.

300-inning seasons

1920: 319.   1921: 330.2   1922: 353

20-win seasons

1915: 24–14   1920: 23–13   1921: 25–15   1922: 21–17

Miscellaneous

Most victories in single World Series: 3, vs. New York Giants, 1917 (Six-
   game series.)
Fewest pitches delivered in a complete game: 67, May 12, 1915, in Chicago.
   White Sox 4, Washington Senators 1.
Career shutouts: 29.
Career complete game 1–0 victories: 7.
Highest percentages of team's wins: 40.3 (25 of 62), 1921.
Most strikeouts (game): 13, May 17, 1922, at Philadelphia.

Offense

Home Runs

June 6, 1923: vs. Herb Pennock at Yankee Stadium, New York (bounce
   homer). Bases empty.
August 15, 1928: vs. Hank Johnson at Yankee Stadium, New York. Bases
   empty.
June 24, 1929: vs. Emil Yde at Tiger Stadium, Detroit. One runner on.

Miscellaneous

Stole second, third and home in same game: July 14, 1915, in Chicago vs.
   Philadelphia Athletics.
Stole home: July 14, 1915, in Chicago vs. Philadelphia Athletics; April 23,
   1923, at St. Louis vs. Browns.
Stolen bases (career): 7
Caught stealing (career): 2 (records for four seasons not available).
Highest batting average (season): .279 (10 H, 37 AB), 1927.
Lowest batting average (season): .000 (0 H, 18 AB), 1933.
Strikeout average (career): .328 (417 K, 1269 AB)

Chapter Notes

Chapter 1

1. *Cascade Pioneer*, October 18, 1917.
2. Urban Faber, as told to Hal Totten, "My Three Wins in '17 Series." *Baseball Digest*, February 1948.
3. Ibid.
4. *The New York Times*, October 16, 1917.

Chapter 2

1. *Cascade Pioneer*, August 26, 1909.
2. *Dubuque Times-Journal*, February 28, 1916. Reprinted from the *Chicago Tribune*.
3. *Cascade Pioneer*, September 7, 1888.
4. Ibid., October 10, 1890.
5. U.S. Census, 1860. Dubuque County, Iowa, Page 78.
6. *Cascade Pioneer*, October 10, 1890.
7. *Dubuque County Recorder*.
8. *Cascade Pioneer*, January 5, 1883, and February. 6, 1947.
9. Ibid., September 21, 1888.
10. Ibid., February 20, 1891.
11. Ibid., May 23, 1929.
12. Ibid., February 22, 1923.
13. Sanborn-Perris Map Co. Limited, July 1894; *Cascade Pioneer*, February 2, 1905.
14. Sanborn-Perris Map Co. Limited, July 1894.
15. Theater program for *Union Spy*, 1899.
16. *Cascade Pioneer*, March 23, 1905, and December 1, 1904.
17. Ibid., April 7, 1904, April 3, 1913, January 29, 1914, and May 23, 1929.
18. Mary Ione Theisen. Telephone interview, June 18, 2003.

19. *Dubuque Times-Journal*, February 28, 1916. Reprinted from *Chicago Tribune*.
20. *Cascade Pioneer*, April 28, 1904.
21. Oldt, *History of Dubuque County*.
22. Urban Faber, as told to Edward Burns, "How I Got My Start in Baseball," *Chicago Tribune*, April 6, 1932.
23. Urban C. Faber II. Interview with author, March 19, 2003.
24. *Baseball Magazine*, September 1915.
25. Archives, Center for Dubuque History, Loras College.
26. *Baseball Magazine*, September 1915.
27. *Cascade Pioneer*, March 30, 1905.
28. 1910 Census, U.S. Department of Commerce and Labor, and Dubuque city directories.
29. Dubuque County Auditor's Office.
30. Dubuque City Directory and *Cascade Pioneer*, May 23, 1929.
31. St. Joseph's College "Catalogue," 1905–06.
32. *Baseball Magazine*, September 1915, Page 64.
33. *Chicago Tribune*, April 6, 1932.
34. *Baseball Magazine*, September 1915, Page 64.
35. *Telegraph-Herald*, May 11, 1908.
36. Ibid., May 25, 1908.
37. Undated clipping from a Dubuque newspaper, 1908.
38. Ibid.
39. *Telegraph-Herald*, August 17, 1908.
40. *Chicago Tribune*, August 22, 1908.
41. *Baseball Magazine*, September 1915.
42. Loras College archives and Faber's handwritten responses to questionnaire of the National Baseball Hall of Fame, 1964.

43. Farrell, *My Baseball Diary.*
44. "Retrorsum," Columbia (now Loras) College, 1923.
45. *Telegraph-Herald*, May 9, 1909.
46. Ibid., January 17, 1932.
47. Ibid., July 11, 1909.
48. Ibid., July 13, 1909.
49. Ibid., August 6, 1909.

Chapter 3

1. *Dubuque Telegraph-Herald*, July 28, 1909.
2. *Dubuque Times-Journal*, August 9, 1909.
3. *Telegraph-Herald*, July 28, 1909.
4. *Times-Journal*, August 12, 1909.
5. *Telegraph-Herald*, April 7, 1911.
6. *Cascade Pioneer*, August 5, 1909.
7. *Telegraph-Herald*, August 10, 1909.
8. Ibid., June 2, 1911.
9. Ibid., July 16, 1911.
10. Ibid., September 16, 1909.
11. *Cascade Pioneer*, August 12, 1909.
12. *Telegraph-Herald*, September 13, 1909.
13. Ibid., October 4, 1909.
14. Ibid.
15. Ibid., September 27, 1909.
16. Ibid., February 1, 1910.
17. *Dubuque Telegraph-Herald*, July 31, 1910.
18. *Telegraph-Herald*, August 20, 1910.
19. Ibid., August 18, 1910.
20. Finch, Addington and Morgan, *The Story of Minor League Baseball.*
21. *Chicago Tribune, The New York Times, The Washington Post*, August 19, 1910.
22. *The Daily Times*, Dubuque, Iowa, August 19, 1910.
23. *Telegraph-Herald*, August 20, 1910.
24. Farrell, *My Baseball Diary.*
25. *Cascade Pioneer*, August 5, 1909.
26. *Telegraph-Herald*, September 2, 1910.
27. Ibid., September 19, 1910.

Chapter 4

1. *Dubuque Telegraph-Herald*, May 19, 1911.
2. Farrell, *My Baseball Diary.*
3. *The Washington Post*, April 6, 1911.
4. *Chicago Tribune*, December 26, 1954.
5. *Telegraph-Herald*, May 17, 1911.
6. *Chicago Tribune*, May 10, 1911.
7. *Telegraph-Herald*, May 17, 1911.

8. *The Sporting News*, May 25, 1911.
9. Thornley, *On to Nicollet.*
10. *Minneapolis Tribune*, May 29, 1911.
11. *Minneapolis Journal*, June 1, 1911.
12. *Telegraph-Herald*, June 1, 1911.
13. *Minneapolis Journal*, June 1, 1911.
14. Ibid.
15. *Minneapolis Tribune*, June 5, 1911.
16. *Telegraph-Herald*, June 14, 1911.
17. Ibid.
18. *Telegraph-Herald*, July 2, 1911.
19. *The Sporting News*, October 16, 1976.
20. *Minneapolis Journal*, June 1, 1911.
21. Lesch, "Denver and Pueblo," in *Road Trips*, Altherr, ed.
22. *Denver Times*, July 18, 1911.
23. *Telegraph-Herald*, October 2, 1911.
24. *Des Moines Register and Leader*, September 28, 1911.
25. *The Sporting News*, February 1, 1934.
26. *The Washington Post*, August 22, 1911.

Chapter 5

1. Clark Griffith, "Why the Spit Ball Should Be Abolished," *Baseball Magazine*, July 1917.
2. *Chicago Tribune*, February 17, 1929.
3. *Chicago Sun-Times*, August 3, 1966.
4. *Cascade Pioneer-Advertiser*, August 20, 1964.
5. *Baseball Magazine*, September 1922.
6. *Cascade Pioneer-Advertiser*, August 20, 1964.
7. *Chicago American*, July 26, 1965.
8. *The Sporting News*, February 3, 1921.
9. *Chicago Sun-Times*, August 3, 1966.
10. Waggoner, Moloney and Howard, *Spitters, Beanballs, and the Incredible Shrinking Strike Zone*, 248; *The Washington Post*, December 18, 1924.
11. Simon, *Deadball Stars of the National League.*
12. Smith, *Red Smith on Baseball*, 264. Column originally published June 8, 1961.

Chapter 6

1. Lesch, "Denver and Pueblo," in *Road Trips*, Altherr, ed.
2. Lindberg, *White Sox Encyclopedia.*
3. *Des Moines Register and Leader*, August 26, 1913.
4. Ibid., April 3, 1912.
5. Ibid., April 20, 1912.

6. Ibid., September 30, 1912.
7. *Chicago Tribune*, April 6, 1913.
8. *Register and Leader*, April 22, 1913.
9. Ibid., June 29, 1913.
10. Ibid., May 7, 1913.
11. Ibid., May 24, 1913.
12. Ibid., August 26, 1913.
13. *Chicago Tribune*, August 27, 1913.
14. *Dubuque Telegraph-Herald*, November 5, 1913.
15. *Cascade Pioneer-Advertiser*, October 9, 1913.

Chapter 7

1. James E. Elfers, *The Tour to End All Tours*.
2. SABR, *Baseball Research Journal*, No. 24.
3. *Chicago Tribune*, December 26, 1954.
4. Ibid., October 24, 1913.
5. Clarence Rowland, quoted in the *Chicago Tribune*, December 27, 1954.
6. *The Sporting News*, January 3, 1962.
7. Elfers, *Tour*.
8. *Dubuque Times-Journal*, October 27, 1913.
9. *Chicago Tribune*, November 2, 1913.
10. Ibid., November 8, 1913.
11. Elfers, *Tour*.
12. Ibid.
13. *Chicago American*, November 20, 1913.
14. Lee Allen, "Cooperstown Corner," *The Sporting News*, May 30, 1964.
15. *Dubuque Telegraph-Herald*, November 4, 1913.
16. Elfers, *Tour*.
17. *Times-Journal*, November 16, 1913.
18. *Chicago Tribune*, March 27, 1914.
19. *The Sporting News*, November, 5, 1914.
20. *Chicago Tribune*, December 27, 1913.
21. *Cascade Pioneer*, January 1, 1914.
22. Elfers, *Tour*.
23. Ibid.
24. *Cascade Pioneer*, January 1, 1914.
25. The *Baseball Magazine*, November 1914, Page 78.
26. Elfers, *Tour*.
27. *Telegraph-Herald*, March 11, 1914.
28. Elfers, *Tour*.
29. *Baseball Magazine*, November 1914.
30. Ibid., December 1914.
31. *Telegraph-Herald*, March 11, 1914.
32. *Chicago Record-Herald*, February 27, 1914.
33. Ibid.

34. *Telegraph-Herald*, February 27, 1914.
35. Obituary, *The New York Times*, November 8 1946.
36. *Chicago Record-Herald*, February 27, 1914.
37. *Times-Journal*, March 8, 1914.
38. *Telegraph-Herald*, March 11, 1914.
39. Bingham, Dennis, "A Fan's-Eye View of the 1906 World Series," in Jim Charlton, ed., *Road Trips: A Trunkload of Great Articles from Two Decades of Convention Journals* (Lincoln: University of Nebraska Press, 2005).
40. *Cascade Pioneer*, October 18, 1917.
41. *Telegraph-Herald*, March 11, 1914.
42. Ibid., March 11, 1914.
43. *Times-Journal*, March 11, 1914.
44. *Telegraph-Herald*, March 12, 1914.
45. Ibid., May 14, 1964.

Chapter 8

1. Paso Robles Inn Web site (www.pasoroblesinn.com)
2. *The Sporting News*, March 12, 1914.
3. R.W. Lardner, "In the Wake of the News," *Chicago Tribune*, May 12, 1914.
4. *The Sporting News*, May 7, 1914.
5. Ibid., March 26, 1914.
6. *Chicago Tribune*, April 18, 1914.
7. *The Sporting News*, May 7, 1914.
8. *Chicago Tribune*, May 12, 1914.
9. Ibid., June 2, 1914.
10. Dubuque *Telegraph-Herald*, June 8, 1914. Also in the *Chicago Record-Herald*.
11. *Chicago Tribune*, June 8, 1914.
12. *Telegraph-Herald*, June 19, 1914.
13. I.E. Sanborn, *Chicago Tribune*, June 18, 1914.
14. John P. Carmichael, *Chicago Daily News*, May 27, 1946.
15. *The Sporting News*, June 25, 1914.
16. *Chicago Tribune*, June 22, 1914.
17. *Telegraph-Herald*, June 18, 1914.
18. Ibid., June 24, 1914.
19. *Chicago Tribune*, June 30, 1914.
20. *Telegraph-Herald*, August 10, 1914.
21. *Cascade Pioneer*, August 27, 1914.
22. *The Sporting News*, September 10, 1914.
23. *Baseball Magazine*, August 1914.
24. *Cascade Pioneer*, January 29, 1914, and September 24, 1914.
25. Ibid., January 15, 1914, and June 29, 1914.
26. Ibid., May 14, 1914.
27. Ibid., October 22, 1914.
28. *Chicago Tribune*, February 27, 1916.

Chapter 9

1. *Cascade Pioneer*, January 28, 1915.
2. Ibid., February 14, 1915.
3. *Baseball Magazine*, February 1915.
4. Ibid., March 1915.
5. *Chicago Tribune*, December 26, 1954.
6. Ibid., May 1, 1915.
7. Ibid., June 5, 1915.
8. Ibid., July 5, 1915
9. Ibid., June 19 and June 23, 1915.
10. Al Kermisch, "Pitcher Faber Walked Seven Times in Row As Batter," in *Baseball Research Journal* No. 12, SABR.
11. *Chicago Tribune*, May 13, 1915.
12. *The Washington Post*, May 13, 1915.
13. *Chicago Tribune*, May 13, 1915.
14. *Dubuque Telegraph-Herald*, May 13, 1915.
15. *The Washington Post*, May 15, 1915.
16. *Chicago Tribune*, May 15, 1915.
17. *Telegraph-Herald*, May 16, 1915.
18. *Chicago Tribune*, May 15, 1915.
19. Ibid., July 9, 1915.
20. *Baseball Magazine*, August 1915.
21. Ibid., September 1915.
22. *Chicago Tribune*, May 22, 1915
23. Ibid., February 16, 1930.
24. Richard C. Lindberg, *White Sox Encyclopedia*.
25. *Chicago Tribune*, September 16, 1915.
26. Ibid., July 26, 1915.
27. *Cascade Pioneer*, October 7, 1915.

Chapter 10

1. *The Sporting News*, March 16, 1916; *Cascade Pioneer*, March 16, 1916.
2. *The Sporting News*, March 30, 1916.
3. *Chicago Tribune*, April 13, 1916.
4. *Dubuque Telegraph-Herald*, April 30, 1916.
5. *Dubuque Times-Journal*, May 3, 1916.
6. *Chicago American*, May 3, 1916.
7. *Times-Journal*, May 3, 1916.
8. *Chicago Tribune* (9–0); *Dubuque Telegraph-Herald* (8–0); *Dubuque Times-Journal* (8–0), May 4, 1916.
9. *Times-Journal*, May 4, 1916.
10. *Chicago American*, May 4, 1916.
11. *Chicago Tribune*, May 4, 1916.
12. *Telegraph-Herald*, June 7, 1916.
13. Ibid., May 4, 1916.
14. *Total Baseball*, Sixth Edition, Page 341.
15. *Chicago Tribune*, September 27, 1916.
16. Ibid., July 29, 1916.

17. *Chicago Tribune*, August 5, 1916.
18. *The Sporting News*, July 13, 1916.
19. Ibid., July 20, 1916.
20. Ibid., August 24, 1916.
21. *Chicago Tribune*, August 13, 1916.
22. *The Sporting News*, August 31, 1916.
23. *Chicago Tribune*, September 12, 1916.
24. Ibid., September 15, 1916.
25. Lindberg, *White Sox Encyclopedia*
26. *Cascade Pioneer*, October 12, 1916.
27. Ibid., November 16, 1916; December 21, 1916; January 4, 1917; January 11, 1917.

Chapter 11

1. *The Sporting News*, August 23, 1917.
2. Ibid., August 16, 1917.
3. The *Baseball Magazine*, September 1915.
4. *The Sporting News*, September 6, 1917.
5. Ibid., August 2, 1917.
6. *The New York Times*, May 6, 1917.
7. *Chicago Tribune*, May 7, 1917.
8. Ibid., June 18, 1917.
9. *The Sporting News*, June 21, 1917.
10. *Chicago Tribune*, January 5, 1927.
11. Thebaseballpage.com
12. *Chicago Tribune*, January 3 and January 8, 1927.
13. Affidavit of Arnold Gandil, published in the *Chicago Tribune*, January 7, 1927.
14. *Chicago Tribune*, May 12, 1922.
15. *The Sporting News*, September 27, 1917.
16. Lindberg, *White Sox Encyclopedia*.
17. Eliot Asinof, *Eight Men Out*, 21–22.
18. *Baseball Magazine*, July 1918.

Chapter 12

1. *Dubuque Times-Journal*, October 5, 1917.
2. *Cascade Pioneer*, October 18, 1917.
3. *The Sporting News*, October 11, 1917.
4. Farrell, *My Baseball Diary*.
5. "Tad's Ticker," *Chicago American*, October 9, 1917.
6. *The Sporting News*, October 11, 1917; *Chicago American*, October 9, 1917.
7. Urban Faber, "Where the Breaks Decide," *Baseball Magazine*, December 1917.
8. Urban Faber. Undated newspaper article.
9. *Cascade Pioneer*, October 11, 1917.
10. Lindberg, "*White Sox Encyclopedia.*"
11. *The Sporting News*, October 18, 1917.

12. *Chicago Daily Journal*, October 16, 1917.
13. *The New York Times*, October 12, 1917.
14. Urban Faber, as told to Hal Totten, "My Three Wins in '17 Series." *Baseball Digest*, February 1948.
15. Clarence Rowland, as told to Jack Ryan, "My Biggest Baseball Day." *Chicago Daily News*, February 12, 1945.
16. *The Sporting News*, October 18, 1917.
17. Lindberg, *White Sox Encyclopedia.*
18. Faber, as told to Totten.
19. *The Sporting News*, October 18, 1917.
20. Lindberg, *White Sox Encyclopedia.*
21. Faber, as told to Totten.
22. Rowland, as told to Ryan.
23. *Chicago Tribune*, December 27, 1954.
24. *Dubuque Telegraph-Herald*, October 17, 1917.
25. *Chicago Herald*, October 18, 1917.
26. *The New York Times*, "White Sox Take World Title In A Torrid Finish," October 16, 1917.
27. *The Sporting News*, October 18, 1917.
28. *Chicago Herald*, October 16, 1917.
29. Frank Graham, "McGraw of the Giants."
30. *The Sporting News*, October 11, 1917.
31. *Telegraph-Herald*, October 16, 1917.
32. *The Sporting News*, October 18, 1917.
33. *Baseball Magazine*, December 1917. Page 203.
34. *Chicago Herald*, October 16, 1917.
35. *Chicago Tribune*, October 16, 1917; *Cascade Pioneer*, October 18, 1917.
36. *The New York Times*, October 18, 1917; *Telegraph-Herald*, October 18, 1917; *Chicago Daily Journal*, October 16, 1917.
37. www.baseball-almanac.com. Accessed September 30, 2006.
38. *Telegraph-Herald*, October 17, 1917.

Chapter 13

1. *Cascade Pioneer*, quoting Dr. W.P. Slattery, October 18, 1917.
2. *Chicago Herald*, October 18, 1917.
3. *Dubuque Telegraph-Herald*, October 18, 1917.
4. *Cascade Pioneer*, December 13, 1917.
5. *Baseball Magazine*, April 1926.
6. *Cascade Pioneer*, December 20, 1917.
7. *Telegraph-Herald*, November 19, 1917.
8. *The Sporting News*, October 25, 1917.
9. Ibid., November 22, 1917.
10. *Cascade Pioneer*, December 5, 1918.

11. *The Christian Science Monitor*, May 23, 1918.
12. *The Washington Post*, June 22, 1918.
13. *The New York Times*, June 22, 1918.
14. *Cascade Pioneer*, June 13, 1918.
15. *The Washington Post*, June 16, 1918.
16. *The Sporting News*, November 21, 1918.
17. *Cascade Pioneer*, June 27, 1918.
18. Ibid., August 8, 1918.
19. *The Christian Science Monitor*, October 5, 1918.
20. *The Sporting News*, October 3, 1918.
21. *The Christian Science Monitor*, November 1, 1918.
22. *The Sporting News*, June 18, 1918.
23. U.S. General Accounting Office. Claim document N-279149-AR; *Cascade Pioneer*, January 9, 1919.

Chapter 14

1. Reprinted in the *Cascade Pioneer*, February 6, 1919.
2. *Chicago Tribune*, March 19, 1919.
3. Ibid., March 30, 1919
4. U.S. Department of Health and Human Services. Web site accessed November 24, 2004.
5. *Chicago Tribune*, February 21, 1920.
6. Farrell, *My Baseball Diary.*
7. *Chicago Tribune*, April 5, 1919.
8. Ibid.,April 20, 1919.
9. Ibid.,
10. *The New York Times*, June 9, 1919.
11. *The Washington Post*, July 10, 1919.
12. *Chicago Tribune*, September 25, 1919.
13. Asinof, *Eight Men Out.*
14. *Chicago Tribune*, July 20, 1919.
15. Ibid., July 24, 1919.
16. Ibid., July 27, 1919.
17. Ibid., September 16, 1919.
18. *The Sporting News*, September 18, 1919.
19. *Chicago Tribune*, September 25, 1919.
20. Ibid., September 25, 1959.
21. *The New York Times*, September 14, 1919.
22. Ibid., September 27, 1919.
23. *Cascade Pioneer*, October 2, 1919.
24. Farrell, *My Baseball Diary.*
25. Asinof, *Eight Men Out.*
26. Ibid.
27. Mary Ione Theisen, telephone interview with author, June 18, 2003.
28. Asinof, *Eight Men Out.*
29. The Associated Press. "University library says rare tabloid with stories about 1919 White Sox missing," December 6, 2005.

30. David L. Fleitz, "Shoeless: The Life and Times of Joe Jackson," citing the *New York Evening World*, December 15, 1919.
31. *Chicago Tribune*, December 16, 1919.
32. *The Wall Street Journal*, October 28, 2005.
33. *The Sporting News*, May 6, 1920.
34. *Cascade Pioneer*, October 23, 1919.

Chapter 15

1. *Chicago Tribune*, February 21, 1920.
2. Ibid.
3. *Cascade Pioneer*, March 25, 1920.
4. *Palimpsest*, Iowa Historical Society, Vol. 36, No. 4, 1955.
5. *The Sporting News*, February 3, 1921.
6. Ibid., November 21, 1940.
7. *Chicago Tribune*, April 4, 1920.
8. Ibid., April 23, 1920.
9. Ibid., April 28, 1920.
10. Asinof, *Eight Men Out*.
11. *Chicago Tribune*, May 6, 1920.
12. Ibid., May 9, 1920.
13. Ibid., May 16, 1920.
14. *The Washington Post*, May 21, 1920.
15. *The Sporting News*, May 27, 1920.
16. *The New York Times*, August 4, 1920.
17. *Chicago Tribune*, August 10, 1920.
18. Ibid., August 5, 1920.
19. *Cascade Pioneer*, June 10, 1920; *The Sporting News*, June 10 and June 17, 1920.
20. Lindberg, *White Sox Encyclopedia*.
21. *Chicago Tribune*, August 20, 1920.
22. Lindbergh *White Sox Encyclopedia*.
23. Ibid.
24. *The Sporting News*, October 14, 1920.
25. *Cascade Pioneer*, October 14, 1920.
26. *Dubuque Telegraph-Herald*, September 9, 1920.
27. Iowa Official Register, 1921–22.
28. *Cascade Pioneer*, October 14, 1920.
29. Ibid.
30. Ibid., October 21, 1920.
31. Ibid., November 11, 1920.
32. Ibid., November 10, 1920.
33. Mary Ione Theisen, telephone interview with author, June 18, 2003.

Chapter 16

1. Waggoner, Moloney and Howard, *Spitters, Beanballs and the Incredible Shrinking Strike Zone*.
2. *Chicago Tribune*, January 28, 1921.
3. Ibid., March 5, 1921.

4. Ibid., April 12, 1921.
5. Ibid., April 20, 1921.
6. *The Sporting News*, April 28, 1921.
7. *Chicago Tribune*, April 30, 1921.
8. Ibid., May 6, 1921.
9. Ibid., May 11, 1921.
10. *Chicago Tribune*, May 17, 1921.
11. *The New York Times*, May 20, 1921.
12. Ibid., May 19, 1921.
13. *Chicago Tribune*, May 28, 1921.
14. Ibid., June 4, 1921.
15. Ibid., June 9, 1921.
16. *The New York Times*, June 12, 1921.
17. *Chicago Tribune*, June 14, 1921.
18. Ibid.
19. Ibid., June 19, 1921
20. Ibid., June 26, 1921.
21. Ibid., June 30, 1921.
22. Ibid., July 4, 1921.
23. Ibid., July 6, 1921.
24. Ibid., July 7, 1921.
25. Ibid., July 11, 1921.
26. Asinof, *Eight Men Out*, 242–243.
27. *The New York Times*, July 12, 1921.
28. Asinof, 242–243.
29. *Chicago Tribune*, July 12, 1921.
30. Ibid., July 15, 1921.
31. Ibid., July 18, 1921.
32. Ibid., July 22, 1921.
33. Ibid., July 19, 1921.
34. *The Sporting News*, July 28, 1921.
35. *The Washington Post*, July 27, 1921.
36. *Chicago Evening Post*, July 28, 1921.
37. *Chicago Tribune*, July 30, 1921.
38. Ibid., July 29, 1921.
39. Ibid., July 31, 1921.
40. Ibid., August 4, 1921.
41. *The New York Times*, August 8, 1921.
42. *Chicago Tribune*, August 8, 1921.
43. Ibid., August 13, 1921
44. Ibid., August 19, 1921.
45. Ibid., August 24, 1921.
46. Ibid., August 28, 1921.
47. *Cascade Pioneer*, September 1, 1921.
48. *The Sporting News*, September 8, 1921.
49. *The New York Times*, September 15, 1921.
50. *Palimpsest*, The State Historical Society of Iowa, Vol. 36, No. 4 (1955).
51. *Chicago Tribune*, September 20, 1921.
52. *The Washington Post*, September 22, 1921.
53. *Chicago Tribune*, September 25, 1921.
54. Ibid., October 1, 1921.
55. *The Sporting News*, December 29, 1921.
56. *Chicago Tribune*, "In the Wake of the News," October 5, 1921.

57. *The Sporting News*, "Two Sad Incidents in Chicago Series," October 13, 1921.

58. *Chicago Tribune*, December 1, 1921.

59. *Cascade Pioneer*, October 13, 1921.

60. Ibid., November 3, 1921.

61. *The Sporting News*, December 8, 1921.

Chapter 17

1. *Chicago Tribune*, January 10, 1922.

2. Ibid.

3. Ibid., January 13, 1922.

4. Ibid., February 23, 1922.

5. Ibid., February 28, 1922.

6. Ibid., March 8, 1922.

7. Quoted by the *Chicago Tribune*, March 28, 1922.

8. *The Sporting News*, April 13, 1922.

9. Lindberg, *White Sox Encyclopedia*.

10. *Chicago Tribune*, April 5, 1922.

11. *The New York Times*, April 5, 1922.

12. *Chicago Tribune*, April 9, 1922.

13. *The Sporting News*, April 13, 1922.

14. Ibid., April 20, 1922.

15. *Chicago Tribune*, April 13, 1922.

16. Ibid., April 21, 1922.

17. Ibid., April 25, 1922.

18. Ibid., April 30, 1922.

19. "Home Run Log," Society of American Baseball Research, accessed December 29, 2004.

20. *Chicago Tribune*, May 8, 1922

21. Ibid., May 12, 1922

22. Ibid., June 19, 1922.

23. Ibid., June 21, 1922.

24. Ibid., July 21, 1922

25. Ibid., April 23, 1922.

26. Ibid., May 28, 1922.

27. Ibid., May 18, 1922.

28. Ibid., August 14, 1922.

29. Ibid., May 23, 1922.

30. Ibid., April 8, 1922

31. *The New York Times*, July 17, 1922.

32. *Chicago Tribune*, July 17, 1922.

33. *Chicago Herald-Examiner*, August 2, 1922.

34. *Chicago Tribune*, August 29, 1922.

35. *The Sporting News*, November 19, 1925.

36. *Chicago Tribune*, August 21, 1922.

37. Ibid., August 27, 1922.

38. *The Daily Times*, Davenport, Iowa, July 21, 1961.

39. *Chicago Tribune*, September 26–27, 29, 1922.

40. Ibid., September 30, 1922.

41. *The Sporting News*, August 10, 1922.

42. Baseball-Reference.com. 1922 Leaderboard. Accessed November 27, 2005.

43. *Chicago Tribune*, October 6, 1922.

Chapter 18

1. *Cascade Pioneer*, February 1, 1923.

2. Ibid., February 22, 1923.

3. Ibid., February 1, 1923.

4. Ibid., March 8, 1923.

5. *Chicago Tribune*, March 5, 1923.

6. Ibid., March 28, 1923.

7. Ibid., March 15, 1923.

8. *The New York Times*, March 25, 1923.

9. *Chicago Tribune*, April 2, 1923.

10. *The Washington Post*, March 27, 1923.

11. *Chicago Tribune*, April 19, 1923.

12. Ibid., April 21, 1923.

13. Ibid., April 24, 1923.

14. Ibid., April 26, 1923.

15. Ibid., April 27, 1923

16. *The Washington Post*, February 18, 1928.

17. *Chicago Tribune*, April 27, 1923.

18. Ibid., May 1, 1923.

19. Ibid., May 11, 1923.

20. Ibid., May 15 and 21, 1923.

21. *The Sporting News*, May 25, 1923.

22. *Chicago Tribune*, July 4, 1923.

23. Ibid., July 14, 1923.

24. *The New York Times*, June 7, 1923.

25. *Chicago Tribune*, June 7, 1923.

26. Ibid., June 13, 1923.

27. *The Washington Post*, June 17, 1923.

28. *Chicago Tribune*, June 21, 1923.

29. Ibid., July 16, 1923.

30. Ibid., July 3, 1923.

31. Ibid., August 11, 1923.

32. Ibid., July 27, 1923.

33. Ibid., September 2, 1923.

34. Ibid., September 10, 1923.

35. *The Sporting News*, October 4, 1923.

36. *Chicago Tribune*, October 8, 1923.

37. Ibid., October 9, 1923.

38. Ibid., October 12, 1923.

39. *The Sporting News*, October 25, 1923.

40. Faber's personal correspondence regarding income tax filing, dated February 26, 1924.

41. *The Washington Post*, February 16, 1926.

42. *Chicago Tribune*, October 17, 1923.

43. *Cascade Pioneer*, October 25, 1923.

Chapter 19

1. *Chicago Tribune*, February 9, 1924.
2. Ibid., March 4, 1924.
3. Ibid., March 19, 1924.
4. Urban Faber, correspondence dated February 26, 1924.
5. *Cascade Pioneer*, March 20, 1924.
6. *Chicago Tribune*, April 13, 1924.
7. *The Sporting News*, March 27, 1924.
8. Ibid., May 1, 1924.
9. *Chicago Tribune*, April 22, 1924.
10. *The Washington Post*, February 16, 1926.
11. Medicinenet.com, accessed January 2, 2005.
12. *The Sporting News*, May 15, 1924.
13. *Chicago Tribune*, June 19, 1924.
14. Ibid., June 24, 1924.
15. Ibid., July 1, 1924.
16. Ibid., July 14, 1924.
17. Ibid., July 15, 1924.
18. Ibid., July 29, 1924.
19. Ibid., August 2, 1924.
20. Ibid., August 27, 1924.
21. Ibid., September 2, 1924.
22. Ibid., September 27, 1924.
23. Ibid., October 2, 1924.
24. Ibid., October 4, 1924.
25. *Cascade Pioneer*, October 9, 1924.
26. *The Washington Post*, November 4, 1924.
27. *The New York Times*, December 3, 1924.

Chapter 20

1. *Cascade Pioneer*, January 1 and 15, 1925; *The Sporting News*, February 12, 1925.
2. *Cascade Pioneer*, February 5, 1925.
3. *The Sporting News*, February 12, 1925.
4. Ibid., March 12, 1925.
5. *Chicago Tribune*, March 6, 1925.
6. Lindberg, *White Sox Encyclopedia*.
7. *Chicago Tribune*, April 17, 1925.
8. *The Sporting News*, April 23, 1925.
9. *Chicago Tribune*, April 27, 1925.
10. Ibid., May 22, 1925.
11. Ibid., June 2, 1925.
12. Ibid., June 8, 1925.
13. Ibid., June 13, 1925.
14. Ibid., June 22, 1925.
15. *Cascade Pioneer*, June 18, 1925.
16. *The Sporting News*, June 11, 1925.
17. *Chicago Tribune*, June 27, 1925.
18. Ibid., July 27, 1925.

19. *The New York Times*, September 25, 1925.
20. *Chicago Tribune*, June 16, 1925.
21. Ibid., November 7, 1925.
22. Ibid., October 14, 1925.
23. Lindberg, *White Sox Encyclopedia*.

Chapter 21

1. *Cascade Pioneer*, December 10, 1925.
2. Ibid., February 11, 1926.
3. Westbrook Pegler, "Ball-Players by Marriage," *The American Magazine*, March 1934.
4. *Chicago Tribune*, March 27, 1926.
5. Ibid., April 17, 1926.
6. Ibid., April 22, 1926.
7. Ibid., April 26, 1926.
8. Ibid., May 2, 1926.
9. Ibid., May 11, 1926.
10. Ibid., May 12, 1926.
11. *The New York Times*, May 16, 1926.
12. *Chicago Tribune*, May 23, 1926.
13. Ibid., June 9, 1926.
14. *The Washington Post*, June 16, 1926.
15. *Chicago Tribune*, June 21, 1926.
16. *The New York Times*, June 21, 1926.
17. Ibid.
18. *Chicago Tribune*, June 26, 1926.
19. Ibid., July 5, 1926.
20. Ibid., July 7, 1926.
21. The Franklin Institute Online, Philadelphia Weather Data; and *Chicago Tribune*, July 11, 1926.
22. *Chicago Tribune*, July 11, 1926.
23. Ibid.
24. Ibid., July 12, 1926.
25. Ibid., July 15, 1926.
26. Ibid., July 21, 1926.
27. *The New York Times*, July 25, 1926.
28. *The Washington Post*, July 29, 1926.
29. *Chicago Tribune*, July 29, 1926.
30. *The New York Times*, August 3, 1926.
31. *Chicago Tribune*, August 3, 1926.
32. Ibid., August 8, 1926.
33. Ibid., August 13, 1926.
34. Ibid., August 17, 1926.
35. Ibid., August 19, 1926.
36. Ibid., August 21, 1926.
37. Ibid., August 22, 1926.
38. Ibid., August 27, 1926.
39. Ibid., August 31, 1926.
40. Ibid., September 7, 1926.
41. Ibid., September 14, 1926.
42. *The New York Times*, September 21, 1926.

43. *Chicago Tribune*, September 30, 1926.
44. Ibid., October 5, 1926.
45. Ibid., November 12, 1926.

Chapter 22

1. *Chicago Tribune*, February 10, 1927.
2. Ibid., January 5, 1927.
3. Ibid., January 6, 1927.
4. Ibid., January 8, 1927.
5. Hal Chase profile, BaseballLibrary.com
6. *Chicago Tribune*, January 7, 1927.
7. Asinof, *Eight Men Out*, 284–5.
8. *Chicago Tribune*, February 10, 1927.
9. Ibid., March 6, 1927.
10. Ibid., March 8, 1927.
11. Ibid., March 9, 1927.
12. *The Washington Post*, March 10, 1927.
13. *Chicago Tribune*, March 18, 1927.
14. *The Sporting News*, April 14, 1927.
15. Urban C. Faber II, telephone interview with author, November 22, 2004.
16. Eugene Converse Murdock, *Baseball Players and Their Times: Oral Histories of the Game, 1920–1940*. Page 85.
17. *Boston Globe*, January 27, 1951.
18. *Chicago Tribune*, March 15, 1927.
19. Ibid., March 18, 1927.
20. *The Sporting News*, April 14, 1927.
21. *Chicago Tribune*, April 9, 1927.
22. Ibid., April 19, 1927.
23. Ibid., April 20, 1927.
24. Ibid., April 20, 1927.
25. Ibid., April 3, 1927.
26. Ibid., April 26, 1927.
27. Ibid., May 4, 1927.
28. Ibid., May 10, 1927.
29. Ibid., May 23, 1927.
30. Ibid., May 27, 1927.
31. *The New York Times*, June 9, 1927.
32. *Chicago Tribune*, June 21, 1927.
33. *The Washington Post*, July 24, 1927.
34. *The Sporting News*, July 14, 1927.
35. *The Washington Post* (Associated Press report), September 4, 1927.
36. *The Washington Post*, September 12, 1927.
37. *Chicago Tribune*, September 23, 1927.
38. Ibid., September 20, 1927.

Chapter 23

1. *Chicago Tribune*, March 28, 1928.
2. *The Sporting News*, March 22, 1928.
3. *Chicago Tribune*, February 19, 1928.
4. Ibid., March 11, 1928.

5. Ibid., March 31, 1928.
6. Ibid., April 1, 1928.
7. Ibid., April 23, 1928.
8. Ibid., May 1, 1928.
9. Ibid., May 5, 1928.
10. Ibid., May 7, 1928.
11. Ibid., May 10, 1928.
12. Ibid., May 17, 1928.
13. Retrosheet.org. Game log of White Sox's 1928 season.
14. *Chicago Tribune*, May 26, 1928.
15. Ibid., May 31, 1928.
16. *The Sporting News*, May 31, 1928.
17. *Chicago Tribune*, June 5, 1928.
18. Ibid., June 11, 1928.
19. Ibid., June 15, 1928.
20. Ibid., June 24, 1928.
21. Ibid., July 5, 1928.
22. *The Washington Post*, July 7, 1928.
23. *The New York Times*, July 12, 1928.
24. Retrosheet.org. Game log of White Sox's 1928 season.
25. *The New York Times*, July 23, 1928.
26. Ibid.
27. *Chicago Tribune*, July 29, 1928.
28. Ibid., August 2, 1928.
29. *The New York Times*, August 7, 1928.
30. *Chicago Tribune*, August 16, 1928.
31. Ibid., August 21, 1928.
32. Ibid., September 21, 1928.
33. Ibid., September 11, 1928.
34. Ibid., September 15, 1928.
35. Ibid., September 21, 1928.
36. *The New York Times*, September 21, 1928.
37. *Chicago Tribune*, September 21, 1928.
38. *The Washington Post*, September 26, 1928.
39. *Chicago Tribune*, September 27, 1928.
40. Ibid., September 30, 1928.
41. *Chicago Tribune*, October 4, 1928.
42. *The Sporting News*, October 18, 1928.
43. *Chicago Tribune*, October 7, 1928.
44. Ibid., October 10, 1928.
45. *Dubuque Telegraph-Herald*, October 15, 1928.
46. *Cascade Pioneer*, October 18, 1928.

Chapter 24

1. *Chicago Tribune*, February 27, 1929.
2. Retrosheet.org. Falk transaction information.
3. Retrosheet.org. Barrett transaction listing.
4. *Chicago Tribune*, December 14, 1928.

5. Ibid., February 27, 1929.
6. Ibid., March 2, 1929.
7. *The Washington Post*, April 5, 1929.
8. *Chicago Tribune*, April 2, 1929.
9. Lindberg, *White Sox Encyclopedia*.
10. *Chicago Tribune*, March 16, 1929.
11. Ibid., April 10, 1929.
12. Ibid., April 9, 1929.
13. Ibid., March 29, 1929.
14. Ibid., February 28, 1929.
15. Ibid., April 20, 1929.
16. Ibid., April 27, 1929.
17. Society of American Baseball Research.
18. Baseball-almanac.com.
19. *Chicago Tribune*, May 9, 1929.
20. Ibid., May 13, 1929.
21. *The Washington Post*, May 13, 1929.
22. Mary Ione Theisen, telephone interview with the author, June 18, 2003.
23. *Dubuque Telegraph-Herald*, May 19, 1929.
24. *Chicago Tribune*, May 23, 1929.
25. Ibid., May 27, 1929.
26. Ibid., May 31, 1929.
27. *The New York Times*, June 6, 1929.
28. Ibid., June 5, 1929.
29. Red Smith conversation with the author, April 1976, in Columbia, Missouri.
30. *Chicago Tribune*, June 18, 1929.
31. Ibid., June 22, 1929.
32. Ibid., June 23, 1929
33. Ibid., June 25, 1929.
34. Ibid., July 19, 1929.
35. Ibid., July 30, 1929.
36. Waggoner, Moloney and Howard. *Spitters, Beanballs and the Incredible Shrinking Strike Zone*.
37. George Moriarty, article for the North American Newspaper Alliance, *Los Angeles Times*, July 14, 1929.
38. *Chicago Tribune*, July 30, 1929.
39. Ibid., August 3, 1929.
40. Pat Patten, published in *The Sporting News*, August 1, 1929.
41. *The Washington Post*, August 16, 1929.
42. *Chicago Tribune*, August 16, 1929.
43. *The New York Times*, August 21, 1929.
44. *Chicago Tribune*, August 18, 1929.
45. Dr. Alfred Faber, interview with author June 6, 2003.
46. *Chicago Tribune*, August 19, 1929
47. *Chicago Evening Post*, August 20, 1929.
48. *Chicago Daily News*, August 20, 1929.
49. *The Christian Science Monitor*, August 3, 1964.
50. *Chicago Tribune*, August 21, 1929.
51. Ibid., August 20, 1929.

52. *The Sporting News*, September 19, 1929.
53. *Chicago Tribune*, September 15, 1929.
54. Ibid., September 9, 1929.
55. Ibid., September 15, 1929.
56. Ibid.
57. Ibid., September 30, 1929.
58. Lindberg, *White Sox Encyclopedia*.

Chapter 25

1. Lindberg, *White Sox Encyclopedia*.
2. *Chicago Daily News*, February 7, 1930.
3. Ibid., February 4, 1930.
4. *Chicago Tribune*, February 14, 1930.
5. Ibid., February 17, 1930.
6. Ibid., February 18, 1930.
7. Ibid., February 21, 1930.
8. Ibid., March 7, 1930.
9. Ibid., March 14, 1930.
10. *The New York Times*, April 10, 1930.
11. *Chicago Tribune*, April 11, 1930.
12. Ibid., May 6, 1930.
13. Ibid., May 11, 1930.
14. Ibid., May 27, 1930.
15. Ibid., June 1, 1930.
16. Ibid., June 15, 1930.
17. Ibid., July 6, 1930.
18. Ibid., July 15, 1930.
19. Ibid., July 16, 1930.
20. *Chicago American*, August 2, 1930.
21. *Chicago Tribune*, August 3, 1930.
22. Ibid., August 2, 1930.
23. *Chicago American*, August 4, 1930.
24. Ritter, *The Glory of their Times*.
25. *Chicago American*, August 7, 1930.
26. *Chicago Tribune*, August 7, 1930.
27. Ibid., August 11, 1930.
28. Ibid., August 12, 1930.
29. Ibid., August 18, 1930.
30. *The New York Times*, August 18, 1930.
31. *Chicago Tribune*, August 25, 1930.
32. Ibid., October 4, 1930.

Chapter 26

1. Ballparks of Baseball.com
2. *The Sporting News*, February 12, 1931.
3. Ibid.
4. National Baseball Hall of Fame.
5. *Chicago Tribune*, March 5, 1931.
6. Ibid., October 26, 1931.
7. Ibid., February 28, 1931.
8. Ibid., April 10, 1931.
9. Ibid., April 14, 1931.
10. Ibid., May 16, 1931.

11. Ibid., May 27, 1931.
12. Ibid., June 6, 1931.
13. Ibid., August 2, 1931.
14. Ibid., July 24, 1931.
15. Ibid., July 27, 1931.
16. Ibid., August 8, 1931.
17. *St. Louis Star*, May 15, 1931.
18. *Chicago Tribune*, August 16, 1931.
19. *The Sporting News*, November 19, 1931.
20. Urban C. Faber II. Personal interview, August 4, 2003.
21. *Chicago Tribune*, September 10, 1931.
22. Ibid., October 2, 1931.
23. Ibid., October 7, 1931.
24. Ibid., October 10, 1931.

Chapter 27

1. *Chicago Tribune*, October 13, 1931.
2. *The Sporting News*, December 11, 1989.
3. *The New York Times*, October 28, 1931.
4. *Chicago Tribune*, October 31, 1932.
5. *Dubuque Telegraph-Herald*, January 17, 1932.
6. *Baseball Magazine*, July 1932.
7. *Baseball Magazine*, July 1932.
8. Interview with Mary Ione Theisen, June 18, 2003.
9. *Los Angeles Times*, January 8, 1932.
10. *The Sporting News*, March 10, 1932.
11. *Chicago Tribune*, February 25, 1932.
12. *The Sporting News*, March 10, 1932.
13. *Chicago Tribune*, March 7, 1932.
14. *The Sporting News*, April 7, 1932.
15. *Los Angeles Times*, March 21, 1932.
16. *The Sporting News*, March 17, 1932.
17. *Chicago Tribune*, March 23, 1932.
18. Ibid., April 25, 1932.
19. Ibid., April 30, 1932.
20. Ibid., May 2, 1932.
21. Ibid., May 14, 1932.
22. Ibid., May 7, 1932.
23. Ibid., May 31, 1932, and June 1, 1932.
24. *Waterloo Courier*, June 19, 1932.
25. *The New York Times*, July 13, 1932.
26. Baseball-Almanac.com.
27. *Chicago Tribune*, August 3, 1932.
28. *The Washington Post* and *Chicago Tribune*, May 7, 1932.
29. *Chicago Tribune*, May 14, 1932.
30. *The Sporting News*, August 11, 1932.
31. *Chicago Tribune*, August 22, 1932.
32. Ibid., September 20, 1932.

Chapter 28

1. *The Sporting News*, February 2, 1933.
2. *Chicago Tribune*, February 19, 1934.
3. Lindberg, *White Sox Encyclopedia.*
4. *Chicago Tribune*, February 24, 1933.
5. *Los Angeles Times*, February 27, 1933.
6. *Chicago Tribune*, February 5, 1933.
7. *The Sporting News*, March 23, 1933.
8. National Baseball Hall of Fame.
9. *Chicago Tribune*, May 28, 1933.
10. Chicago Timeline, Chicago Public Library Web site: www.chipublib.org.
11. *Chicago Tribune*, May 27, 1933.
12. Ibid., July 6, 1933.
13. Ibid., July 5, 1933.
14. *The New York Times*, August 22, 1933.
15. *Chicago Tribune*, August 22, 1933.
16. Ibid.
17. *Chicago Tribune*, August 28, 1933.
18. Ibid., September 10, 1933.
19. Ibid., September 21, 1933.
20. *The New York Times*, October 8, 1933.
21. *Chicago Tribune*, October 6, 1933.
22. *Chicago American*, October 5, 1933.
23. *The Cee Ay*, student newspaper of Columbia Academy, October 13, 1933.
24. *Dubuque Telegraph-Herald*, October 15, 1933.

Chapter 29

1. *Chicago Tribune*, January 7, 1934.
2. Ibid., February 18, 1934.
3. *Chicago Herald-Examiner*, February 18, 1934.
4. *Cascade Pioneer*, February 22, 1934.
5. *Chicago Tribune*, February 19, 1934.
6. Ibid., February 20, 1934.
7. *The Sporting News*, March 1, 1934.
8. *The Washington Post*, February 21, 1934.
9. *The Sporting News*, July 5, 1934.
10. Ibid., May 17, 1934.
11. Farrell, *My Baseball Diary.*
12. *The Sporting News*, February 20, 1936.

Chapter 30

1. Frances Faber. Interview with Bill Thompson, 1992.
2. Russell Ewing. Essay courtesy of Grayslake (Illinois) Municipal Historical Museum.

3. *Chicago Tribune*, May 26, 1946.
4. Urban C. Faber II. Personal interview, March 19, 2003.
5. *The Christian Science Monitor*, August 19, 1936.
6. *Cascade Pioneer*, May 23, 1929.
7. Tom Byrne, correspondence, July 21, 2005.
8. *Daily Herald*, Arlington Heights, Illinois. February 1937.
9. *Look Magazine*, May 10, 1938.
10. *Chicago Tribune*, June 18, 1944.
11. Ibid., June 6, 1946.
12. *Chicago Daily News*, May 27, 1946.
13. *Chicago Tribune*, May 20, 1948.
14. Ibid., August 6, 1947.
15. Ibid., April 12, 1947.
16. Bill Gleason, *Chicago American*, December 21, 1963.
17. *Chicago Tribune*, April 13, 1947.
18. Frances Faber, interview with Bill Thompson, 1992.
19. C.M. Less, May 1953.
20. Mary Ione Theisen. Interview with the author, June 18, 2003.
21. *Dubuque Telegraph-Herald*, February 3, 1947.
22. Urban C. Faber II. Interview with the author, March 19, 2003.
23. *The New York Times*, September 29, 1947.
24. *Chicago Tribune*, October 5, 1948.
25. *Chicago American*. 1955.
26. Urban C. Faber II. Interview with the author, March 19, 2003.
27. Ibid., October 20, 2005, and August 4, 2003.
28. *The Sporting News*, April 5, 1950.
29. Ibid., July 2, 1958.
30. Urban C. Faber II. Interview with the author, August 4, 2003.
31. Diane Dunn. Telephone interview with the author, December 2003.
32. *Chicago American*, June 13, 1958.
33. National Baseball Hall of Fame archives.
34. *Chicago Tribune*, July 18, 1949.
35. Ibid., May 22, 1949, and August 28, 1953.
36. Ibid., April 14, 1954.
37. Ibid., October 2, 1959.

Chapter 31

1. National Baseball Hall of Fame.
2. Ibid.
3. *Newsweek*, February 3, 1958.
4. *Chicago Sun-Times*, January 19, 1958.
5. Bill James, *The New Bill James Historical Baseball Abstract*. Page 891.
6. Bill Gleason. Telephone interview with the author, August 10, 2004.
7. Bill James, *Whatever Happened to the Hall of Fame?*
8. *Dubuque Telegraph-Herald*, May 14, 1964.
9. *Cascade Pioneer*, August 20, 1964.
10. Frances Faber. Interview with Bill Thompson, 1992.
11. National Baseball Hall of Fame audiotape in collection of Tri-County Historical Society, Cascade, Iowa.
12. Frances Faber. Correspondence to Harry Hooper dated July 13, 1973.

Chapter 32

1. *Chicago Sun-Times*, February 4, 1964.
2. Urban C. Faber II. Personal interview with the author, August 4, 2003.
3. Cook County Highway Department Newsletter, December 1967.
4. *Chicago Sun-Times*, September 1, 1968.
5. *Chicago Tribune*, September 6, 1968.
6. Frances Faber. Letter to Harry Hooper dated July 13, 1973.
7. Urban C. Faber II. Telephone interview with the author, November 8, 2005.
8. Ibid. Personal interview with the author, August 4, 2003.
9. David Fleitz Web site accessed November 30, 2005. Fleitz is the author of *Shoeless: The Life and Times of Joe Jackson* (Jefferson, NC: McFarland, 2001.)
10. Gene Carney. Web site.
11. Urban C. Faber II. Telephone interview with the author, November 8, 2005.
12. Ibid.
13. Diane Dunn. Telephone interview with the author, December 2003.

Bibliography

Books

Appel, Martin, and Burt Goldblatt. *Baseball's Best: The Hall of Fame Gallery.* New York: McGraw-Hill, 1977.

Asinof, Eliot. *Eight Men Out.* New York: Holt, Rinehart and Winston, 1963.

Axelson, G.W. *Commy.* Jefferson, NC: McFarland, 2003. Originally published: Chicago: Reilly & Lee, 1919.

Benson, Michael. *Ballparks of North America.* Jefferson, NC: McFarland, 1989.

Bingham, Dennis. "A Fan's-Eye View of the 1906 World Series." In Jim Charlton, ed., *Road Trips: A Trunkload of Great Articles from Two Decades of Convention Journals.* Lincoln: University of Nebraska Press, 2005.

Charlton, Jim, ed. *Road Trips: A Trunkload of Great Articles from Two Decades of Convention Journals.* Lincoln: University of Nebraska Press, 2005.

Clark, Jerry E. *Anson to Zuber: Iowa Boys in the Major Leagues.* Omaha: Making History, 1992.

Farrell, James T. *My Baseball Diary.* New York: A.S. Barnes / Copp Clark, 1957.

Finch, Robert L., L.H. Addington, and Ben M. Morgan, eds. *The Story of Minor League Baseball.* Columbus, OH: Stoneman Press, 1952.

Fleitz, David. *Shoeless: The Life and Times of Joe Jackson.* Jefferson, NC: McFarland, 2001.

Frommer, Harvey. *Shoeless Joe and Ragtime Baseball.* Dallas: Taylor, 1992.

Graham, Frank. *McGraw of the Giants.* New York: G.P. Putnam's Sons, 1944.

James, Bill. *The Bill James Historical Baseball Abstract.* New York: Villard Books, 1986.

_____. *The New Bill James Historical Baseball Abstract.* New York: The Free Press, 2001.

_____. *Whatever Happened to the Hall of Fame? Baseball, Cooperstown, and the Politics of Glory.* New York: Fireside, 1995.

Kaufman, Louis, Barbara Fitzgerald, and Tom Sewell. *Moe Berg: Athlete, Scholar, Spy.* Boston: Little, Brown, 1974.

Kogan, Herman, and Rick Kogan. *Yesterday's Chicago.* Miami: Seemann, 1976.

Kuenster, John, ed. *From Cobb to Catfish.* New York: Rand McNally, 1975.

Lesch, R.J. "Denver and Pueblo." In *Above the Fruited Plain: Baseball in the Rocky Mountains,* edited by T.L. Altherr. Cleveland, OH: Society for American Baseball Research, 2003.

Lindberg, Richard C. *The White Sox Encyclopedia.* Philadelphia: Temple University Press, 1997.

Murdock, Eugene Converse. *Baseball Players and Their Times: Oral Histories of the Game, 1920–1940*. Westport, CT: Meckler, 1991.

Nemec, David, ed. *The Baseball Chronicle*. Lincolnwood, IL: Publications International, 2003.

Oldt, Franklin T., ed. *History of Dubuque County*. Chicago: Goodspeed Historical Association, circa 1911.

Reichler, Joseph L., ed. *The Baseball Encyclopedia*. 7th ed. New York: Macmillan, 1988.

Ritter, Lawrence S. *The Glory of their Times*. New York: Macmillan, 1966.

Seymour, Harold. *Baseball: The Golden Age*. New York: Oxford University Press, 1971.

Simon, Tom, ed. *Deadball Stars of the National League*. Dulles, VA: Brassey's, 2004.

Smith, Red. *Red Smith on Baseball*. Chicago: Dee, 2000.

Spinney, Robert G. *City of Big Shoulders*. DeKalb: Northern Illinois University Press, 2000.

Thompson, S.C. *All-Time Rosters of Major League Baseball Clubs*. Cranbury, N.J.: A.S. Barnes, 1967.

Thorn, John, and Pete Palmer, eds. *Total Baseball*. New York: Warner Books, 1989.

Thornley, Stew. *On to Nicollet: The Glory and Fame of the Minneapolis Millers*. Minneapolis: Nodin Press, 1988.

Waggoner, Glen, Kathleen Moloney, and Hugh Howard. *Spitters, Beanballs, and the Incredible Shrinking Strike Zone*. Chicago: Triumph Books, 2000.

Wilbert, Warren N., and William C. Hageman. *The 1917 White Sox: Their World Championship Season*. Jefferson, NC: McFarland, 2000.

Periodicals

Arlington Heights (Illinois) *Daily Herald*, 1937.

The American Magazine. March 1934.

Baseball Magazine.

Baseball Research Journal, No. 24. Cooperstown, NY: Society for American Baseball Research, 1995.

Cascade Pioneer. (Also known as *Cascade Pioneer and Advertiser*.) Cascade, Iowa.

Cee Ay, The. Student newspaper of Columbia Academy, Dubuque, Iowa. October 13, 1933.

*Chicago American (*and *Chicago's American).*

Chicago Daily Journal and Daily Commercial Chronicle.

Chicago Daily News.

Chicago Evening Post.

Chicago Herald-Examiner.

Chicago Sun-Times.

Chicago Tribune.

Des Moines (Iowa) *Register (and Leader)*.

Dubuque (Iowa) *Telegraph-Herald* (later, *Telegraph Herald*).

Dubuque (Iowa) *Times-Journal*.

Kermisch, Al. "Pitcher Faber Walked Seven Times In Row As Batter." In *Baseball Research Journal*, No. 12. Cooperstown, NY: Society for American Baseball Research, 1983.

Lardner, John. "Against the Clock." *Newsweek*. February 3, 1958.

Los Angeles Times.

Minneapolis Journal.

Minneapolis Tribune.

The New York Times.

Palimpsest, The State Historical Society of Iowa. Des Moines, Iowa. Vol. 17, 1936; Vol. 36, No. 4 (1955); Vol. 64. September-October 1983.

"Pitcher Faber Talks of Hitting." *The Christian Science Monitor*. August 3, 1964.

"Shaming Youth." *Collier's.* July 4, 1931. Page 22.
Sports Digest.
St. Louis Star, May 15, 1931.
"The Names of Chicago Baseball Teams." *Chicago History* 8, No. 11 (Spring 1969).
The Sporting News.
The Wall Street Journal, October 28, 2005.
The Washington Post.
"This School Teaches Young America How to Play Baseball." *Look.* May 10, 1938.
Waterloo (Iowa) *Courier.*

Other Sources

Baseball-Almanac.com
Ballparks of Baseball.com.
BaseballLibrary.com.
Carney, Gene, Web site: www.baseball.com/carney/
Less, C.M. Loras College thesis. On file Carnegie-Stout Public Library, Dubuque, Iowa.
Retrosheet.org. Some information in this book was obtained free of charge from, and is copyrighted by, Retrosheet, 20 Sunset Road, Newark, Delaware.
Sanborn-Perris Map Co. Ltd., New York, N.Y. Map of Cascade, July 1894.
Sanborn Map Co., New York, N.Y. Map of Cascade, May 1914.
The Franklin Institute Online, Philadelphia. www.fi.edu. Philadelphia weather data.

Index